ALSO BY ERIC LIU

The Accidental Asian

*Next: Young American Writers on
the New Generation* (editor)

Guiding Lights

Guiding Lights

THE PEOPLE WHO LEAD US TOWARD OUR PURPOSE IN LIFE

ERIC LIU

RANDOM HOUSE NEW YORK

Published in the United States by Random House, an imprint of The Random House
Publishing Group, a division of Random House, Inc., New York.

RANDOM HOUSE and colophon are registered trademarks of Random House, Inc.

Library of Congress Cataloging-in-Publication Data
Liu, Eric.
Guiding lights: the people who lead us toward our purpose in life / Eric Liu.
p.   cm.
ISBN 0-375-50863-5
1. Mentoring. I. Title.

BF637.M45L58 2005
158—dc22   2004046815

Printed in the United States of America on acid-free paper

Random House website address: www.atrandom.com

246897531

First Edition

Book design by Ellen M. Cipriano

For my teachers

CONTENTS

OVERTURE

1

Let me tell you a story.

It's a story of a young man. His life was as stable and steady as a continent. But beneath, the plates were shifting; the drift had begun. Between what he was and what he wanted to be, a gap opened. He felt it: his possible self was starting to slip away, as a dream escapes our consciousness when we wake. He didn't know much, but he knew he wanted someone to guide him across. He needed a teacher. He searched for thousands of miles and dozens of months. He traversed arid canyons and icy cities and wooded hills. He met fools and sages, children and elders, each striving to resemble the other. He listened and watched and asked questions of everyone he encountered. He slept beneath unfamiliar roofs and was visited by unfamiliar visions. *Teach me,* he said. They saw him. They touched him. No one saved him. When he came home, he did not think he had found his teacher. He sat down to record his travels, and that is when the teacher appeared.

This is a true story. It is my story, in part. But listen closely. It is, on some wavelength, your story too.

2

One day I was speaking with a group of doctors who teach in medical residency programs. I asked them who their most significant influences were. Their answers were wonderful: *My mom. My grandfather. My first boss. My husband. My swim coach. Franz Kafka. My residency director. My freshman econ professor. Bach. A family friend. My hometown physician. Virginia Woolf. My piano teacher. My eighty-seven-year-old neighbor who taught me how to live.*

If you were named not only for your ancestors but for your teachers, what would your full name be? If you were to give your name not only to your children but to all those you have taught and influenced, who do you think you would find in this extended extended family?

This book is animated by a simple and powerful idea: We are all teachers. Every day, in every setting and social role we play, we are teaching. Teaching is at the core of our humanity. Teaching is to behavior what sex is to genes. It literally is what life is all about: *passing it on.* As parents or leaders, managers or mentors, coaches or instructors or neighbors, we are constantly teaching—sometimes intentionally, sometimes skillfully, sometimes neither. We teach to transmit a culture. We teach to impart facts and skills. We teach to instill a conscience. We teach to articulate for ourselves what on earth matters. We teach to be sure that we have not lived in vain. We teach to learn.

Coupled with the idea that we are all teachers is an equally powerful faith: We can all become *better* teachers. And it matters that we do. Understanding how we teach is a crucial way of enhancing the way we live and grow—as individuals and as a society. By listening and watching, by entering the lives of the guiding lights all around us, we become more effective in how we reach and shape others. We change the nature of our relationships. We change people's lives. We change our own lives.

I know this because I lived it. I came to this book at a time when I was deeply uncertain about what kind of life to make. I had recently become a father. I became newly aware of the absence of my own father, who had been gone nearly a decade. I was writing, teaching, managing people. But what I was really doing was wandering. I was searching for a calling. For purpose. I was hungry for someone to show me the way, not only in parenthood or career but in life. No one showed up. No one descended from a mountaintop. So I decided to go to the mountain. I decided to write this book, and to make it a quest. I set out to gather up as many examples as I could—of *what*, exactly, I wasn't even sure. I knew I wanted to meet people who, regardless of circumstance, were pure and powerful teachers. Beyond that, the journey was inductive, intuitive: the gathering, I trusted, would reveal the *what*.

It did. The journey transformed me. The people I encountered expanded my capacity for empathy. They gave me the courage to see myself more clearly. They made plain the nature of our obligations. They made me realize how I'd let down the people I had managed and taught in my life up till now. They gave me models for being a better father, husband, son, leader, follower, and learner. They gave me a good way to plumb the heart of any other human, which is to ask this question: *Who influenced you?* And together, though they didn't know it or mean to do it, they became, in composite, the mentor I had been seeking.

3

To write this book, I spent more than two years finding interesting teachers, coaches, mentors, and guides from every walk of life and every corner of the country. I interviewed hundreds of people and spent time at work and at play with several dozen of them. Some were well known—world-class educators and artists and CEOs and athletes and directors and scientists. Some were not. I got to know them all, and their students as well. They came from schools and homes poor and rich; from hushed high-rise offices and union job sites; from playfields and studios; from the officer corps and the clergy. You name it. I started out thirsty for stories. The challenge, I found, wasn't finding water; it was drinking from a fire hose. Everyone I talked to had an idea that I should see this guru or that program or this school. At the urging of my wise editor, I focused. I looked not simply for gifted teachers but for relationships between gifted teachers and their learners. Relationships in which the question might be: who changed whom? I looked for stories of how one or both confronted a challenge and got past it—or didn't.

You are about to encounter some remarkable people. The ones you will get to know best are a Hollywood acting coach, a major league pitching coach, an inner-city teacher of entrepreneurship, a deprogrammer of Juilliard musicians, a corporate executive, a senator and college president, a master clown, a jazz legend, a painter of public murals, a homeboy priest, an unorthodox rabbi, a fabled chef, a Marine drill instructor, a champion high school debate coach, an orchestra conductor and leadership guru, a flight instructor. You will also get to know many of the people they have touched and taught. But as remarkable and unique as they are, what is most important about them is the universality of their stories. The songline that runs through each story is this: Their lives are yours. Their lessons are yours.

It took me a while to hear that songline, but I did. So can you. What it requires is the willingness to take an idea from one place to another. In these pages are numerous stories set in workplaces of many kinds. These stories will speak to you directly if you are interested, as a leader or manager, in developing the human capital of your organization. There are stories about persuasion and influence that will speak directly to you if care about marketing an idea or product to the public. There are stories in these pages set in schools and on campuses. These will speak to you directly if you too are in a classroom. Finally, there are stories here about parents and children. These will speak to you directly if you are interested in creating more mindful and humane family relationships.

At work, at school, at home: you'll find something here that speaks directly to you. But let me be straight. If you're going to filter the experience to take in only those stories that speak *directly* to you, you'll be missing the point of this book. The idea of this book is to see apples and oranges not as the idiom would have us see them—each foreign to the other—but as a toddler would see them: as objects deeply related, surface differences aside. The boardroom can teach you about the classroom, the classroom about the playroom, the playroom about the locker room, the locker room about the rehearsal room, and so on. If you can imagine changing places, with anyone or anything, then learning can truly begin.

4

I'm of the Socratic view that we already know most of what we need to know; we simply don't know we know. It's a teacher's job to draw out the knowledge—to spark and spur the act of recollection. If some of the things you learn in this book seem familiar, I think that will be a good sign. It will mean the pathways of intuition are becoming visible. It will mean you are opening your mind and finding out what's inside.

Early in my travels, I went to the renowned Bob Bondurant School of High Performance Driving, outside Phoenix. I wanted to see how the instructors there taught not only the mechanical act of car racing but also the *feel* of it. I wanted to experience it for myself, so I signed up for the Grand Prix course. They strapped me into a bright orange, racetrack-ready Mustang GT. One of the first exercises they had me do was a slalom run through ten orange traffic cones. This would be easy, I thought. I've always been a good driver, always loved speed. Roaring the engine, I awaited the signal. Then off I went, reaching 50 mph on the short straightaway. I got past the first cone cleanly. I knocked down five of the remaining nine. I could feel the *thump* each time, and in the rearview mirror I could see those cones bouncing out of the lane like bowling pins.

I finished the run and pulled up sheepishly to the instructor, a young Formula One driver. He leaned into my open window. "Well, your feet are fast," he said. "It's your eyes that suck." It was obvious, he explained, that my gaze had been fixed on the cones as I weaved past them. Which, at that speed, left no time to react. By the time I saw one cone it was time to avoid the next. The thing I had to do was to imagine a line snaking its way between the cones and drive along that line. "Don't stare at the cones," he said. "Follow the line."

It was a great lesson. A life lesson. But I realized, as he said it, that it was not a new lesson. When my father was teaching me how to drive, in our stick-shift Mazda station wagon, he taught me something quite similar. He had learned to drive a jeep when he was just thirteen, in wartime China. To this day I can feel the rocking motion of his aggressive gear-shifting. To this day I emulate it. I was with him on a Sunday morning. I'd already gotten the basics down and now we were ready to venture out of his office parking lot. The counsel he gave, as I took us onto a road with long, slow curves, was this: *Don't focus too much on what's right in front of you. Keep your eye on the next curve and the next curve. That way, you won't overthink each moment's steering.*

I'd forgotten all about this long-ago conversation until I showed up at the Bondurant School. Then I remembered it. Remembering it prompted me to search out what else I might already know. And by degrees, that has illuminated a line that now weaves its way through hills and valleys, curves and obstacles, from my life and many others. A simple question guided me as I traveled: What do life-changing mentors and teachers do that makes them so transformative?

At first I paid close attention to method. I put together a taxonomy of methods that people and organizations use to teach: Story. Drill. Immersion. Example. Ritual. Indirection. Each of these tools is indispensable if you're trying to guide someone to greater knowledge. But it became clear very quickly that great teachers don't confine themselves to any one of these tools, any more than a great plumber or carpenter confines himself to the drill or the screwdriver or the wrench. Mastery resides in knowing when to use what.

What I looked for then were the larger patterns. And over time, five such patterns emerged, five durable strategies that recurred across diverse domains. First of all, these life-changing teachers *receive before they transmit.* That is, they are more than simply powerful communicators. They tune in to a learner's unique frequency of motivation and makeup, and only then do they send out the signals of their lesson. Second, they *unblock and unlock* their students, helping them move aside the inner obstacles—fear, doubt, shame, pride—that impede learning. Third, they *zoom in and zoom out,* which is to say, they break down the subject to its basic elements and then use analogy and metaphor to connect the elements to something else the learners already know. Fourth, they know when to avoid direct instruction and to allow the *invisible hands* of a well-conceived, well-designed culture to do the teaching for them. And fifth, they know when to *switch shoes,* putting the learner in the role of the teacher. For often the best way for an apprentice to master something is to have to teach it to someone else.

These five strategies are what emerged from all my encounters and travels, and they provide a framework for the stories in this book. The strategies are neither scientific nor sacrosanct, though they do form a circle of sorts. They are useful mainly because they give us a way to make sense of the relationships, the yearning, the method, and the mystery of mentorship. In the end, they give us a vocabulary to express some of the wonder we feel when we realize how our own paths have been shaped by a guide, and when we in turn guide others.

5

A lost child, someone you'll meet later in the book, tells of a dream. In the dream, he is stuck in a pitch-dark room, helpless and confused, awkwardly feeling his way around. His mentor is there too in the dream, and knows just where the light switch is. But instead of turning it on, the mentor waits, then aims the beam of a flashlight at the switch. It's up to the child to do the rest. When he does, if he does, both his life and his mentor's will be changed beyond reckoning. The true dimensions of each one's purpose will be illuminated.

This is what guiding lights do. We show the way. And in so doing, we find the way. But to begin, we must first wake up. See the world and its web of obligation with new and mindful eyes. It's time to move to a state of consciousness. It's time now to search out the stories.

PART I

Receive Before You Transmit

THE QUEST

1

She saw right through me. Right through my careful presentation of self, my reportorial pose, into the inner chambers. We'd known each other for fifteen minutes. I was there to interview her. Had my leather-bound notebook, my questions all lined up. We chatted. I told her about this book. In passing, in response to I don't even remember what, maybe something she'd said about her family, I mentioned that my father was deceased.

An hour and a half later, after answering my queries about how she had become an acting coach, about her challenging students, her general philosophy of teaching—after all the preliminaries—Ivana decided to show rather than tell. We did a little exercise. She asked me to pretend I was drunk. I hadn't expected this, but here we were, and I felt more awkward about *not* playing along than about playing. So I gave it a shot. At first I stumbled about her living room, mimicking the weave and wobble of someone who's had one too many drinks. But my imbalance was too studied, and my eyes were too alertly scanning her face for reactions. She asked me to remove my glasses. Without them my vision descends to 20/400: the world dissolves into bleeding pools of color.

It worked. I was utterly disoriented. I couldn't see, but more important I couldn't tell where I was going next. I was genuinely in less control of myself than I'd been only a few minutes ago. Pretty soon I was doing quite the drunk act in her house, and she chuckled with approval, paced around me in the high-ceilinged, echoey room, giving loose direction, telling me to pick up this glass or that book, to talk to her, to slur my words more when speaking.

Then, out of the blue, she asked me to think about my father. Just when I thought we were playing one game, she revealed another. As my father's face flashed across my mind, my own face slackened involuntarily. My mouth fell open. I exhaled, then again, like a last gasp. It was over in a second. I wasn't able to play a drunk anymore. But neither was I in the state I'd been in prior to our little scene. "Do you feel the difference?" she asked. I nodded, swallowing. Maybe now, her arched brow suggested, I would be ready to learn.

2

Ivana Chubbuck is one of Hollywood's most successful and sought-after acting coaches. And she'll tell you that. She'll tell you that she's transformed Halle Berry and Elisabeth Shue, that Beyoncé Knowles and Jim Carrey and Charlize Theron have sought her touch, that studios and television networks turn to her for emergency house calls, to rescue leading men and women who aren't quite cutting it. She seems to have a raw need to prove her potency, to advertise it, and there is something both compelling and distasteful about her naked hunger for recognition. She is a curious specimen: the sensitive listener and the obsessive winner.

She is fifty-one and has the way of a savvy and world-weary lioness. It's her voice more than anything that reveals her. *Eye-VAAAH-nah.* A husky, smoky rumble that reveals a past of drugs, beatings, failed relationships. She yells and shouts in class but in private she slows to an energy-conserving deadpan. She often punctuates her own witticisms with a slow, almost menacing "A-heh-heh-heh" laugh, pushed out through bared teeth. Her cheekbones are high, and she has a mane of dark brown hair. She doesn't try to hide her wrinkles but she has curves still, and in the classes she teaches at night, you can spy some of the young male actors slumped in the seats before her, their eyes drawn to the red sweater wrapping her torso. She knows this.

Ivana has a gift, an uncanny ability to take a jumble of unintended signals—a darting look, a tiny flinch, a catch in the voice—and to convert them into a whole story about what moves and makes a person. *What do you need to be pushed? Do you freeze when you are attacked or do you fight?* In this, she reminds me of politicians I've known, or of cops I've been on the beat with. She knows even before she knows why she knows. What was it about me that had told her an act of drunkenness was called for, that inhibitions and self-control were the first things? What did I do in mentioning my father that told her to circle back to him? What did I give away? "I guess it's just intuition," she offers.

Of course. But Ivana's intuition is not just a current that carries her along blithely. Ivana has seized this intuition of hers, this sixth sense, and wrought it with the force of her formidable will into a powerful and re-fined instrument. Her hyperperceptive listening, her ability to be an actor whisperer, is not simply a "gift." It is the result of a deeper process that has unfolded over many years, making her the teacher and the woman she is. A cauldron of life history roars inside her unseen, burning without rest, reducing to liquid all that it encounters.

3

"Eva will have a hard time remembering what she used to be like," Ivana once said to me. "When you change and grow it's hard to remember what you used to be. Halle doesn't remember what she was like before she be-came a strong woman." But Eva does remember. She remembers the first classes, the way she felt. Ivana was her first coach, her only one so far. Whatever Eva is about to become is because Ivana has helped her be-come it.

When Eva Mendes arrived, she wasn't quite sure how she'd gotten there. Eva stumbled into acting. A typical Hollywood story, except that it's really the opposite of typical. It's the story of one in ten thousand, or a million. She was twenty-three, an on-and-off marketing student at Cal State Northridge, hanging out with friends and not sure what was next, when an agent saw a picture of her in the portfolio of her neighbor, a photographer. That's all it took. A marketable Latina, sultry and smart, alluringly distant. The agent found Eva, hounded her. In fairly short order, this daughter of Cuban immigrants found herself in studio auditions and screen tests. She appeared in music videos, a commercial or two, and then was cast in the 1998 teen horror flick *Children of the Corn 5*.

At first it was like a freak accident, not a sign that her calling had come calling. She thought, "Cool, I was in a movie." The work helped pay the bills. Not that anyone watched *Children of the Corn 5* for the acting, but she did seem comfortable. In truth, she was miserable during that experience—precisely because she wasn't a natural. She'd never acted, and had no preparation going into that role. "I didn't realize how hard it would be. When I wanted to express something," she says, "I had no idea how to do it. It was always so frustrating." She got a few other roles like these, which got her more exposure, but also reflected the limits of her ability. Eva knew this. And as she looked around, thinking about her accidental career, she discovered she had something in her, a catalytic mixture of pride and humility, that spurred her to seek out a teacher. She wanted a path to an identity still undefined. She quit school and committed herself to acting. She started auditing classes all over town. The first six teachers she met left her cold. "They were nuts. I just didn't see how acting like a tree was connected to anything I was doing," she recalls.

The last teacher she audited was Ivana Chubbuck. "Within five minutes, I knew," Eva remembers. As she watched class unfold, she responded to Ivana's directness, critiques that were tough but never abusive. It was also Ivana's searing rationality she responded to. Ivana has a system. She drills her system into her students. And here was a girl, Eva, who literally by chance was becoming a movie star, and who wanted to know—needed to know—that there was a structure to this work that she might know and master, so that what had come so easily and quickly would not just as easily evaporate. She began in the basic classes that Ivana's former students teach, and soon advanced into Ivana's own class. "She can deconstruct me," Eva now says of Ivana, "and peel all the layers back. She can give a reason for everything."

A reason for everything. I've come to know Eva at an interesting moment. It's late 2003 and she is not a household name yet but she's on the
brink of—well, either becoming one or not. Her next film, *2 Fast 2 Furious,* was essentially a feature-length music video with a sexy multicultural
cast, including the rapper Ludacris, and souped-up cars in noisy drag
races. But it was a hit. Fame has begun to arrive—the kind of early fame
that puts her on the cover of lifestyle magazines, nets her a presenter role
at the Golden Globes, and rates her a mention in *The New Yorker* as
someone whose career has prospered while other starlets in her cohort,
the "Almost-It Girls" like Jaime Pressley, have begun to plateau. Eva's life
at this moment in late 2003 is one of ever more admiring reviews, high-
profile supporting roles with the likes of Denzel Washington, a big role
in *Stuck on You,* a broad comedy by the Farrelly brothers, and much more
work already booked for the coming year, including a role opposite Will
Smith. The neon halo of celebrity has flickered on, at first tentatively but
now more brightly, and soon, perhaps, it may seem to everyone that she
was always this way: born a star.

4

The Ivana Chubbuck Studio is a crowded windowless room on the second floor of a building on the corner of Melrose and Formosa. Forty or
fifty theater-style seats. A futon, a desk, a few chairs, a table, a coatrack,
and a scattered assortment of props on the kitchen-sized stage. And that's
it. The central air conditioner is so noisy it drowns out the actors' voices,
so whoever's sitting closest to the switch turns it off during scene work
and back on during critiques, creating a thermal echo wave of stuffiness
and chilliness all night long.

Before class, the French doors into the studio are locked, so the students hang out on an unlit veranda that overlooks the side street. They
smoke and sit around talking in the soft nighttime Los Angeles air. A few
carry on cell phone conversations, but mainly they're hanging out, as if
it were a little cocktail party, or a hip vodka commercial. As we stand

around, waiting for Ivana's assistant to arrive and open the studio, I'm suddenly cognizant of the fact that I've never been in the midst of so many gorgeous young people before. The men, the women, are truly the L.A. cliché—*Send me your prom queens, your handsome boys with scruffy hair and sensitive eyes, send me the lithe lean beauties who once stunned your towns in the Kansas prairie and the Florida wetlands and the Idaho mountains with their floral splendor, and we will make them our waiters, our valets, our personal assistants' assistants: our acting students.*

As the doors open the students file in quickly, some finding seats and others scurrying about the stage to move around the furniture and props for the first scene on today's list. These are professionals. None is famous but a few have appeared in commercials and sitcoms, a couple even in films. Many others don't have acting work lined up right now. There is no prelude, no pep talk from Ivana. After everything is set up, the first pair of actors stands onstage, waits a moment for conversation to subside, and then one says, "Ready." They begin. On this night's class, which will run from seven till past eleven, students in twos and threes play six or seven scenes. The scenes are drawn from plays and films of all kinds. A whiteboard on the wall lists them all: something from *Speed the Plough,* then *Beyond Therapy,* then *The Hours.*

Ivana has selected and assigned these scenes with a keen sense of intention. Isaac is a nebbishy, anxious stand-up comic who's used to performing solo; Jack is into "fine" theater, more focused on the meter and timbre of the spoken word than on the inner terrain of character. She'd paired these two last week and given them a scene in which a criminal is trying to get a priest to absolve him but the priest is too self-absorbed to listen. Ivana didn't choose this scene to make them look good. Isaac and Jack overact, struggle to connect, revert to their worst habits, and pretty much fall flat. Ivana sits in the front row, just a few feet away (the stage isn't raised), and remains silent through even the most excruciatingly awkward moments. When they're done, they look deflated, and a little surprised that Ivana let the scene go on so long. She observes, finally, that the two actors seemed to be feeling a great deal of pain. "Actors like to feel the pain," she says. "But that's bullshit. Real people try to *overcome* the pain." And she proceeds to prod them on what their *characters* would do to get out of the emotional cul-de-sac that the *actors* put them in.

This idea recurs in everything she says and does—that achieving an emotional state is not the point of acting; that meaningful acting, like meaningful living, involves a desire to get somewhere. To get something. To *win.* She conveys it with sarcasm, taunting, profanity. "It's ineffectual just to play the problem; you have to play the solution," she'll say. Or: "I'm getting a pretty half-assed effort to win here." Or: "Why don't you act like you have a dick? Show me you have one. Swing it around." Another evening, she's working with two men, a black guy and a white guy, in a scene from *Knockout.* They're boxers, the white guy coaching his cocky pupil at the gym. The actors play the scene like it's a buddy movie, a playful, physical interaction. They're pretty good, and their cross-racial camaraderie makes everyone in the room feel good about themselves.

Ivana tears the work apart. She asks the white guy what his character's objective is and he says something about mentoring his buddy. "Stop. Right there. Your goal is not to *empower* anyone," she sneers, "it's to prove you've still got it, that you're still superior to this guy." It's a brilliant interpretation: the coach's obligation to teach is not his objective; it's his *obstacle.* Likewise, the protégé's objective is not to be validated. It is to beat the coach. "We have to make this more than just a friendship thing," Ivana says, and she directs them to play it again. This time there's more testosterone and electricity, maybe even too much, but that's okay. "You have to have the possibility, always, that you're going to take it too far," she says. She smiles with satisfaction. They were dancing before. Now they're sparring. As the coach bobs and weaves, telling the pupil with a taunting, competitive smile that "You're getting better," Ivana shouts to the coach: "Point to *yourself* when you say that." She thumps her own chest for emphasis, fist balled like a boxing glove. "Point to yourself!"

5

From *Script Analysis,* by Ivana Chubbuck:

#4. SUBSTITUTION: TO ENDOW THE OTHER ACTOR IN THE SCENE WITH A PERSON FROM YOUR REAL LIFE

THAT YOU NEED YOUR OBJECTIVE FROM. . . . By using SUB-
STITUTION you can endow the actor playing, for instance, your
mother, with the involved history you have with your real mother.
The needs, the covered pain, the love, the uncertainty of her love
for you, the disappointments—all the nuances of a relationship that
is in every element, every speech, every glance, of how you would
relate to your own mother.

Around the time she was twelve Ivana learned that she had a 172 IQ.
It was not long afterward that she and her parents stopped having meaningful communication. It wasn't the IQ test that did it; the number, the
"genius" designation, only quantified what had created so many problems for her at home.

Long before she became an actor, long before she found that she was
a better student of acting than many of her fellow actors, long before she
discovered that she was a better teacher of acting than most of her directors, Ivana was a smart girl growing up in a stifling household in the De-
troit suburbs. She was the second of seven siblings but the most forceful
and kinetic one and, in effect, she was the caretaker for the entire household. She raised her siblings because her mother, a housewife, was mired
in unhappiness and beset with all manner of ailments, and because her
father worked all the time. "I never asked for help from my dad," she says,
"with my homework or anything else."

Ivana's father, a lawyer in private practice, was gentle and thoughtful.
He was a scholar at heart. At one point, when she was entering adoles-
cence, he stopped practicing law and went back to college to get a degree
in psychology. Ivana thought this was wonderful. One afternoon she went
to the bookcase carved into the head of her parents' bed and took out the
psychology textbook her father was studying. "At first I thought I had
every psychological disease known to man," she says. "I didn't realize yet
that we all have every element of every disease in us, just usually not to
the extremes." She put her father on a pedestal, she freely admits, and
when she was a girl they would have these interesting conversations,
about the world, about the news, whatever. He had these deep conversations with Ivana because she was precocious enough to hold her own. He
had them with Ivana also because he did not respect her mother enough,
intellectually, to have them with her. The competition was on.

As Ivana blossomed into a beauty, the competition became more vicious, and violent. Her mother would berate her, put her down, undermine her. Soon her mother hit her too, Ivana said, breaking her nose on one occasion and several fingers on another. When Ivana was in sixth grade, her mother told her father that Ivana was having sex and taking drugs—which she wasn't. But her mother persisted in saying it, persisted in punishing her. Her father was silent. By the time she was fifteen or sixteen, she decided that "if I'm doing the time I might as well do the crime." At school she began to float from clique to clique. "Girls can be evil," she remembers, and she didn't want to align with any single crowd. Instead she tried to be all things to all people, to listen intently to each crowd's way of talking and being, and because she was smart and pretty and a little bad, because she was an adaptive shape-shifter, she cobbled together a kind of popularity.

Her father saw what was unfolding around him at home. Maybe that's why he began to work later and later, often not returning from the office until midnight. Even at that hour, Ivana would stay awake so she could see him, so she could press her grievances and tell him about how her mother—his wife—was treating her. Unable, unwilling to confront or comprehend, he could muster only one response that Ivana remembers: he giggled. That's the word she uses; not "he laughed it off." He giggled. And after downplaying it, he went up to bed.

From that time on, true conversation between Ivana and her father stopped. They still talked, and perhaps there was sometimes a hopeful note in his voice when he spoke, an implied asking for forgiveness, but what they talked about was the weather. She has no idea to this day whether he got that degree in psychology. Her father now is dead. Her mother is not. She speaks to her only occasionally. Along the way Ivana learned of her mother's own history of violent abuse. This helped explain some things. But locating the headwaters of this river of pain and resentment didn't change things fundamentally.

One day I ask Ivana whether either of her parents comes to mind when she needs someone for a substitution. "My father," she says without hesitation. His passivity—his day-in, day-out crumbling; his cosmic and willful failure to set anything right; his creeping unspoken impotence—has shaped her far more than the inciting act of her mother's abuse. "He should've done something," she says, "and he never did. He never did anything. That upsets me much more." Her eyes water, and for the first and only time in my presence she looks vulnerable. She looks her age. "That's why I have this instinct," she says—and it seems she is with her father now—"this primal instinct to get my power back."

6

Her extraordinary ability to see people—truly see them—is worth seeing again, as research. But it's the promise that she can reveal what is transparent in *me* that keeps bringing me back to her. And so here we are one afternoon in a private class, a one-on-one session like she'd provide for Eva or another of her stars. The week we arranged this, she'd assigned me a scene from Neil Simon's comedy *Chapter Two* in which a recently widowed man returns with his brother to the apartment he had shared with his wife. We sit across from each other, and I smile nervously. "Let's read it through," she says. As I go through the scene, Ivana plays the brother. She reads in a flat voice, not playing the part but keeping the dialogue moving so I can read in tempo. Unlike her, I'm supposed to put some feeling into my lines. I'm tight at first, self-conscious, but her approach of simply being a neutral foil relaxes me. There's no pressure to *Act*.

After one read-through, she asks me to go over one part of the scene again, in which the widower reads aloud a letter of condolence awaiting him at his apartment. "This time," she says, "I want you to read the letter to yourself, silently, and imagine it's your father that the letter is about." I do. She studies me for a moment. "Now read it to yourself again," she says, "and imagine that it's your daughter." I do. And now, to my surprise, my throat gets dry and constricted—not from nervousness but from the impulse, the unbelievable impulse, to cry. I've been reading silently, not even looking at her. "Now read it aloud," she says. I do, and the improvement over my first attempt is palpable.

Ivana, as Eva Mendes notes, is "a rare combination of the intuitive and the rational." For every moment that Ivana is seemingly capable of extrasensory perception she is equally capable of treating acting like mathematics. Method acting, Ivana says, was about finding emotional truth; her approach is about what to *do* with truth. For the rest of the hour we break down the scene using the Stanislavskian vocabulary she has expanded and adapted and christened the "Chubbuck Method": objectives, obstacles, substitutions, beats and actions, moments before, inner monologues. Ivana self-published a short monograph called *Script Analysis,* which led to a book deal with a major publisher to write her magnum opus, *The Power of the Actor.* Both works have as their spine a religion of potency, this banishment of victimhood and an absolute insistence on winning.

But the whole time we are working through the mechanics of the scene, and talking about how and why my character would be saying what he's saying, I am wondering to myself: what is it she has seen that's brought us to this point? Finally I ask her. Well, she says, she knew from our last (and only prior) visit, when we'd done the drunk scene, that I process things on an intellectual level first. She remembered that I have a preschool-age daughter, something else I'd mentioned in passing. So her plan on this day was to move me to a more emotional space, to pierce the veil of abstraction around my head. My first read-through felt to her detached, buffered. As expected. When she pushed the first button, mentioning my father, the effect of emotional surprise was now reduced because she'd gone there the last time. To mention my wife would be too predictable in this scene. Which is why she tried my daughter. This was a thought I had never contemplated, and it produced the response.

In a different setting, such manipulation would've made me mistrustful; here it made me open up. Why? Because I knew this was not a parlor trick. This is how she connects to her students. Manipulation, in the literal sense, is moving things around to get a desired result. When motivated by selfishness or spite, it's contemptible. When it springs from an authentic desire to teach, it can be truly admirable. Ivana's first genius is not for acting but for seeing angles of entry into someone's psyche. "When you apply varnish," she observes, "the varnish grabs on to the wood better if the wood isn't smooth. I have to find the nicks and gashes and imperfections in you. That's where I have to start."

There is more at work than her ability to manipulate. There is also my desire to be manipulated. I was drawn to Ivana for the very reason I was moved to begin this book: I am searching always for someone who can know me, someone who can guide me. Ivana's spooky intuition is strangely magnetic but so is her ambition. Her ambition is so feral, so unapologetically fierce and needy. She has to win every scene. She has to teach every student to win every scene, to conceive of scenes and of life as something you either win or lose. "If you want to be a dynamic and powerful actor you must duplicate the true behavior of dynamic, powerful people," she writes in her handbook of acting. "And those people are always, in one form or another, goal oriented."

When I conceived this book, I had spent a decade on a fast track of career achievement, collecting one shiny merit badge after another. Youngest this. First that. But slowly and insidiously, the badges, rather than the way they were earned, became the point—and once that happened, the joy of doing was replaced by the imperative of achieving. My hunger for the next great résumé line—and my anxiety that the wave would evaporate beneath me—was warping my sense of what mattered. I could see that. And I sensed that this book, and the journeys it would require, would re-center me. I had no idea how but I had an instinct that it was time to search. Of course, as this search has unfolded, I've been hounded by the fear that inner peace, if it arrives, will neuter me and drain me of ambition. The more I listened to Ivana, the more I understood that she mesmerized me because her unadulterated obsession with winning, her starkly Darwinian view of life, was a reminder of the self I was trying to tame—but not kill. She writes in her acting guide: "We human beings love to watch the quest, the fight. We are drawn to the person who gives every ounce of his being to win." That is precisely why I am drawn to her. My confusion, though, is whether to be drawn in as a spectator or as a fellow participant—an *actor*.

All this, I assumed, was my own neurotic interior monologue, perceptible only to those to whom I chose to reveal it. I should have known better. I asked Ivana one day what in her nearly three decades of teaching has helped her ward off laziness—or worse yet, contentedness. She laughed. No matter how stable and balanced she may become, Ivana said, "I'm in a business that creates drama and trauma whether or not I want it, and that helps me keep up my edge." She reflected on a sister who had made different choices, and who in Ivana's view gradually surrendered that edge. She lives a normal, perfectly admirable existence today, in leafy suburbs, with minivans, kids in sports leagues. We moved on to other topics, talked for another hour. As I left her that afternoon, she stopped in the doorway and said: "You know, you have to keep stretching." Was she recapping her life's rule or suggesting one for me? I responded with an ambiguous, "Mm-hmm." She paused, and as I walked through the door she looked hard at me and said, "Don't settle for a nice little life."

7

From her baseline of zero acting experience, Eva worked her way up to the ability to cry when tears were called for, to wail and scream when anger or desperation were needed. And that was progress. "I thought that if I could cry," she recalls, "I could act." Her voice is soft, cool, unaccented. She has a broad brown face with a signature mole above the lip, and though it is a face that can be many things—sunny, shrewd, vulnerable, fierce—the eyes are almost never unguarded. "I remember my first class with Ivana I did a scene from *Havana* and I cried all the way through it. That was *hard*. And after I'm done Ivana says to everyone, 'I saw real tears. But who felt something for this person?' It wasn't to make me feel bad. I saw what she was saying. She told me I wasn't going after anything in the scene, and she was right." Ivana remembers that first class exactly the same way. "I told Eva that the point wasn't to get to an emotional state. It's not just looking for movement. Paint drying is 'movement.' *Interesting* movement is something else. It's getting to a goal."

For nearly two years of class, Eva heard the words but the message did not sink in enough to truly change her approach to life. And then, it just did. There was no moment of epiphany. "I was auditioning a lot and working. I was really, really busy. And then I realized it was clicking. I noticed that things had changed. Now it was easy. Everything was clear. From then on, if I was doing a scene, I would do anything possible to get my objective in that scene." Temperamentally, Eva was perfectly suited to absorb Ivana's goal-oriented philosophy, as well as her blunt and methodical style of analysis: Eva could look clinically at her own shortcomings, see them as problems to fix, and take Ivana's critiques as part of the solution. Her feelings wouldn't be hurt. "I'm not one to wallow," she says.

At the outset, Ivana saw in Eva a responsible and loving child, youngest daughter of tradition-minded immigrants. The more time they spent together, the more Ivana sensed that this submissive stance—"this nice Catholic girl thing"—was a pose. And that Eva didn't even know it. Ivana divined a current of dynamism, of ferocious womanhood, inside. But Eva's clinical practicality, her unwillingness to wallow, made her reluctant to explore her full self, let alone express it. "She didn't know she could be funny. She didn't know she could be sexy," recalls Ivana. "Eva was afraid just to be sitting onstage and moving her body." Three months into their work, she gave Eva a scene from *The Seven Year Itch*. The idea was to get her to respond to a man. The idea was to get Eva to let go. For the first time she was being given permission—was being *told*—to combine playfulness and allure to make power.

With some students, Ivana offers stories about her own bouts with addiction, her own dysfunctional relationships, her own darkest secrets. In return, she gets "the stuff that people won't even tell their therapists," as she puts it—the stories, from one famous star after another, about family members whose existence they have never acknowledged, about their self-destructive hidden obsessions, about the shame they feel about their parents. She and Eva began to know each other this way. "I learned that anything Ivana asks of me," Eva says, "she will give to me first. She personalized our relationship, and she would teach me using examples from her life and mine. The woman knows my issues." Or as Ivana says, "I put my stuff on the table so we both would have something on each other." The aim, in part, was to build trust. But it was also to map and mine what Ivana described as "the illogic that leads to true logic."

When Eva started getting lots of work, she would complain sometimes that she needed a vacation. She was lazy, or at least nostalgic, reluctant to part so sharply with the life of easy drift. Ivana, seeing this, would push her hard, relentlessly, to work, to stop letting other actors drive the scenes, to keep fighting for something, to experiment more in auditions. Eva's breakout role came in *Training Day*, the film in which Denzel Washington plays a corrupt cop. The film won Washington the Best Actor

Oscar in 2001. Eva's part lasted all of ten minutes, but it was what she did with those minutes that made Hollywood take note of her. She was fearless and indelibly raw as Denzel's discarded lover. She did a scene nude. "That was a brave role for me," Eva says. "I was so naked, emotionally and physically." That role made possible the next project with Washington, the 2003 thriller *Out of Time,* which got fair reviews overall but high marks for Eva. She became increasingly interesting to casting directors. The spiral of opportunity began its twisting upward turn.

She thinks of herself as a risk-taker now. She is what Ivana calls "a viable person." She has goals now. And chief among them is to evolve into an actor of greater dimension. "I see things with more insight," she says. "Now I want to add more layers." From Ivana's perspective, Eva at twenty-eight has much more to discover—about relationships, about her subconscious, about motherhood, about "just being a full person and using that in her work." But there is no ceiling, she says, to Eva's potential as an actor. She doesn't say that lightly. In fact, she can't think of another actor she says this of. "Take Matthew Perry," ponders Ivana, referring to the *Friends* star. "He's great, but his ceiling is comedy. He goes to comedy when he's upset. He doesn't want to play the darkness. Eva can do high comedy or dark drama. She can do anything—unless she creates the barriers for herself"—and she lets out an exaggerated whine—"like *it's too hard* or *it's too tiring.*" Ivana names some other actresses who got lazy, stopped studying after they became hot, and who, sure enough, cooled off. "If you stop learning," she declares, "your life stops."

Today Eva's life is constant work—going to film festivals and premieres and press junkets to publicize the latest movie, then going on location to shoot the next one, then resetting the cycle. Sometimes she calls Ivana from the set for encouragement or advice, on whether to seek out a role, or on how to handle a scene. But she is in L.A. less and less and there is little time for face-to-face talk, almost none for anything like a formal class. Now it is up to Eva to carry what lessons she's acquired and to make something of them. "I know that if I'm trying to chicken out I will hear her voice," she says of her teacher, "and it's like, 'Get out of my head, woman!' " She laughs. "I hear her telling me, 'Don't be a victim.' "

8

A final night for me in the Ivana Chubbuck Studio. Only this time she's not teaching. She's out of town, on an emergency "house call" in Toronto, and Eriq LaSalle, one of the stars of *ER* and now a film director, is filling in. Eriq was Ivana's student more than twelve years ago, and whenever he's gearing up to direct, he'll come back and teach a class to keep his chops up, to sharpen his eye as he prepares to audition actors. He has a totally different presence from Ivana, a different kind of energy. For starters, he's a he—a big man dressed in jeans, a T-shirt, a tan beret and work boots. He's African American, and like the surgeon he plays on *ER*, a little prickly. He is precise in his explanations and in his questions, his eyes ever alert. He modulates his tone and timbre and tempo less than Ivana does. He's never as viscerally vulgar as she is; even when he's swearing, there is an inhibited formality to it. He moves around and talks more than she does. Where Ivana has a sinuous whiplike way of withholding and then unleashing comment, Eriq has a more straight-ahead rat-a-tat-tat intensity.

Whatever the stylistic differences, it becomes apparent as the evening goes on that this man was truly molded by Ivana. He tells one student she should do her scene believing, *If I don't get this I will die.* To a woman who is playing an unhappy lover: "Nobody wants a loser; you want to be a fighter. Even when we are weak we are trying to present a winner. We don't call up and say, 'Hi, I'm needy.' " He drills into every student in every scene the importance of having an objective that can be "a buoy that navigates you." There's nothing artificial about that, he reminds them: "That's where you are in real life. You're having lunch with an agent, and the whole time you're thinking, *Did he laugh? How long did he laugh? How'm I doing?*" Chuckles of recognition. When he asks the students for their feedback after another scene, and there's silence, he jumps in with a call to authority. "I'm going 'old school' Ivana. She didn't ever let us sit there. Let's start analyzing! Let's learn how to dissect a scene!"

When Eriq started studying with Ivana he was already a working actor with some major film credits under his belt. Class with her was graduate-level training, honing his sense of how to define objectives and seek out the telling details and gestures to give texture to his characters. "Ivana knows my instrument now," he says. It's impressive how seamlessly he's picked up this class, considering he walked in not knowing any of the students. But then it dawns on me: the fact that he was filling in on short notice, and couldn't tune in to the students, couldn't know their previous work, reveals what is in fact the key to Ivana's power. Eriq is a skilled teacher, arresting and philosophically faithful to the master. *But he doesn't know any of their instruments.* As a result, the instructions he gives are detailed in nuance, but generic in application. They mimic the form of instructions from Ivana but lack the animating knowledge of each student's needs and fears and weaknesses: the knowledge of each student's *purpose.*

It's easy, because of Ivana's force of personality and fierce worldview, to mistake what she is saying for what she is teaching. She is so vocal a transmitter that it's easy to overlook her power as a receiver. I think Ivana herself, in her obsession with winning, with conquering passivity in all its forms, sometimes blinds herself to what makes her as great as she says she is. When she's barreling over people at an industry cocktail party, talking up the movie she's producing with Halle Berry or the latest role a student has landed, her ambition blots everything else out. After my very first meeting with her, Ivana handed me a list of stars she had coached in her career. What is ultimately so interesting to me about her is that she appears not to realize that the measure of her success is not her list. That list is perishable, and Ivana must on some level realize this. Already some of the names on it seem dated, answers to a "Whatever happened to?" trivia game. Here's the reality: Eva Mendes may or may not turn out to be an "It" girl of lasting It-ness. She may or may not make the leap from a flavor of the month to a fixture in the firmament. She could become a megawatt superstar. She could become a regularly employed, nothing-to-be-ashamed-of working movie actress. Or she could fade into absolute oblivion.

The more durable measure of Ivana's success will be if Eriq LaSalle learns to direct like she teaches; if the students in her classes, the great majority of whom will fail as actors, attain her capacity for seeing themselves and others clearly, and develop that capacity for the rest of their lives; if Eva Mendes one day raises her children with Ivana's intuitive sensibility of inner wants and needs—if even I, an outsider, a student of an altogether different kind, can inherit something of her spirit and can touch and teach others with her in mind.

One day Ivana will be old. It happens even in Hollywood. Her energy will be spent. Or she'll be dead. Her famous students will have slid down the slope of celebrity and her studio will be dark and empty. When humans fight to survive—to win—it is ultimately not for the animal satisfaction and elemental thrill of the moment. It is so that their genes can worm their way into another generation. Ivana wants to be remembered as a winner. If she is remembered as what she is centrally—a listener of extraordinary power, a one-of-a-kind reader of human motivation—then the DNA of her teaching will have survived, in generations of learners after her. Then Ivana Chubbuck will have truly won.

PITCHERS AND CATCHERS

An Education in Nine Innings

1

It rained last night in Peoria, a torrential downpour that sent flash floods running into every cracked ravine across the southern Arizona desert, and this morning the groundskeepers are still working on the fields, their push brooms nudging shallow sheets of water into the drains beneath the grass. The sun hasn't burned through the clouds yet and so Bryan Price, pitching coach of the Seattle Mariners, has his men working under a covered bullpen. Actually, only the pitchers and catchers are covered, by two parallel carport-style roofs. The balls, once released, travel the sixty and a half feet from one hand to another through open, unsheltered air.

There's no joy like the joy of that week in February when pitchers and catchers report to camp. Spring training hasn't officially started and most position players have yet to arrive, but the air is charged. It's almost better that not everyone is here. It feels like dawn, before the noise. It feels like senior year of college when I got to campus a week early: amidst the empty halls and open quadrangles, everything everywhere is still possible, the place not as crowded with foibles and fears and the untidiness of human choices as it will soon enough become.

Norm Charlton, Arthur Rhodes, and Jamie Moyer, southpaws, are at work alongside righties Jeff Nelson, Freddy Garcia, and Kazuhiro Sasaki. They're lined up like gunslingers, six arms on six mounds facing six catchers. I hover behind them, observing, along with Bryan and a couple of the other coaches from the minor league system. First-year manager Bob Melvin stands a nervous watch nearby, lanky arms folded in what fans will learn is his late-game posture, wanting to intervene but keeping himself from stepping in too close. Pat Gillick, the general manager with colorful Hawaiian shirts and cool shrewd eyes, spies me from afar and whispers to a young assistant, who walks over and is about to ask who the heck I am and why I am at the mounds, when Bryan, radar on, intercepts him and says it's okay, I'm with him.

This close, you realize how large and strong these men are. They are like another species, at least from my five-foot-three vantage point. As I stand next to the six-eight Nelson, I wonder: how much white fabric did it take to create just one of his pant legs? This close, you can hear the seams of the ball slicing up the soft air. The pop-pop-poppops of the pitches as they arrive in the gloves are surprisingly loud. Already there is violence in the pitchers' faces as they let fly. These six will throw from the stretch position, throw from a windup, and then throw pitchouts for exactly ten minutes—Bryan has a stopwatch in hand—before another six will rotate in. Bryan paces from hurler to hurler. He notices a tiny hesitation in Charlton, who's coming off elbow surgery, and asks the catcher to move up a few feet in front of the plate, so Norm doesn't have to strain yet. He heads over to Nelson for a moment, notes with approval that Nelson's keeping his head still during his herky-jerky delivery. Then to Garcia, the incoming ace of the staff, to ask whether his front foot feels comfortable where it's landing. There are no pauses: Bryan speaks a word, the pitchers nod, adjust, throw again.

There's a seriousness in the air, a quiet mindfulness of every motion and minute. This is the season the Mariners, who've been contenders for several years now, are expected to really come on, to put it all together. Nobody knows yet that within a year, several of these pitchers won't be Mariners anymore, some will be written off, one won't even be pitching pro ball anymore. They don't know that Pat Gillick won't be running things in a year's time, resigning in the off-season before the calls for his head got louder, musing with rue that he's had four shots at a ring, ought to let someone else try now. They have no idea that they're about to enter a season in which great promise, after a long summer's stretch, curdles into futility and sour frustration: a season of lessons, intended and not. On this day—and this is the beauty of February in Arizona—they know only about great promise. Arms that have been idle for months are loosening, muscles recovering their memories. Everything is possible.

After the pitchers and catchers finish their session they head to the indoor gym for fielding drills, pulling dark blue Windbreakers over their mesh jerseys, spikes clicking on the concrete walk. There's an easy camaraderie among the veterans, while the rookies, invited for the first time to camp and assigned grimly high roster numbers like 74 and 81, are clenched and brave-faced. Uniforms obscure the gross differences among men, like age and size and color, but they cast the finer differences into higher relief. If you convert a set of fractions to a common denominator, what will you attend to but the numerators that remain? When you look at a photo of a team in uniform, you scan the eyes first.

As Bryan watches his troop, his eye is trained on those finer differences, of body and mind, and he weighs which of them can be harmonized, equalized, and which cannot. *All other things being equal* is an analytical tool every teacher uses to isolate a student's strengths and weaknesses, and yet is completely irrelevant in the practice of competitive sport. All other things are never equal on the field. Won-lost records, which is all that will remain when memories of the 2003 season are dust, don't even pretend to capture distinctions and subtleties like "strong arm, but weak heart" or "middling stuff, crafty mind" or "great command, terrible luck." Wins and losses don't necessarily convey the arc of someone's personal growth—or deepening lack. Bryan glances over at the groundskeepers before stepping inside. The grass on that spring field will be dry before long, but underneath, streams of runoff pulse through hidden channels.

2

I'm a righty, he bats left. Here's how I pitch Bryan Price:

Pitch 1: Fastball away.

As I often do, I come on a little strong, a little intense. This is the first time we've met. We were introduced by a friend I used to work in business with who quit to join the Mariners' scouting operation (he'd been a minor league outfielder). "BP said he'd be glad to talk to you," my friend reported. "BP." It's an unstated rule: everyone in the majors has to have a casual, not-too-creative nickname, usually achieved by adding "-ie" or "-y": Bret Boone is Boonie; Mike Cameron, Cammy; Shigetoshi Hasegawa, Shiggy. (I guess "Pricey" would not be an optimal nickname.) What happened to the evocative monikers of the past, "Goose" and "Oil Can" and "The Bird"?

Anyway, the Mariners' locker room is a surprisingly quiet, plush space, almost corporate. Not a place for Oil Cans. It's a few hours before game time and about half the players are in there, some in uniform, some half dressed and doing crosswords. Bryan and I meet in a small office down the hall from the lockers. Everything about this environment—its understated jockiness, its hushed professionalism—has me seeing myself through his eyes, as a geeky word guy. He's young, a former pitcher, only a few years older than some on his staff and, I suddenly realize, only a few years older than I am. The fact that Bryan has a very cool temper only accentuates the nervous rush I feel to impress him. I start telling him about my bona fides and why I set out to write this book and how long I have followed baseball and my impressions of how baseball is taught and I talk for a full five minutes before I wind my way to a question.

The whole time, he's eyeing me intensely, peering through studious wire-frame glasses that he'll trade for contacts at game time. Bryan has the large frame and self-possessed carriage of a big-league athlete, a broad boyish face, conservatively shorn brown hair and quick, observant eyes.

He's a graduate of UC Berkeley ("Cal," he calls it, evoking Pac-10 standings rather than SAT scores). He's expressionless, though his eyes scan me with an astuteness he seems to want to conceal. When it's finally his turn to talk, his answer is a fraction as long as my question, and then he's silent. I take a deep breath and wind up again. *Ball, high and outside.*

Pitch 2: Changeup.

The next time I see Bryan is at spring training. He's working with Jamey Wright, a tall right-hander who comes to camp with nasty stuff but poor command. Bryan knows that Wright has bounced from team to team, coach to coach, all of them getting on his case about his tendency to nibble and his high pitch counts. By now, Wright has heard enough about his weaknesses. Bryan works on his balance. Session after session, he's been getting Wright to think about keeping his weight back, freezing Wright in mid-delivery to get him to feel what his right leg, his push-off leg, is doing, asking him to exaggerate the extent to which his left leg crosses the vertical plane of his right leg during the windup. It's gotten to where Wright is having dreams at night about weight transfer. If you're not keeping your weight back, you lean forward too soon, you lose momentum as your throwing arm comes over the top, and you release the pitch with reduced force and command. But Bryan doesn't mention any of this. He doesn't talk about throwing strikes, or keeping pitch counts low. He asks Wright to focus on his weight, on his back leg. As more of Wright's attention is sopped up by that leg, the overthinking stops, the voices quiet.

After I watch this little session, Bryan and I break it down. Talking about work, actual work with a specific pitcher, is a whole lot easier than talking about teaching in the abstract. Seems to me, I say to Bryan, that your focus on balance was a diversionary tactic: addition by distraction. Bryan's eyes widen just a touch. Why yes, there was a little bit of that going on, he says. Wright has a reputation for overthinking, and so this session was about throwing a head fake. Of course, there was a legitimate mechanical issue to work out, but Bryan was aware of the residual benefits of giving Wright one thing and one thing only to worry about. He seems pleased that I noticed. *Strike, looking, on the outside corner.*

Pitch 3: Slider, tailing inside.

Bryan and I are sitting around with Carl Hamilton. Carl, a compact ex-Marine with a crew cut, is a little-recognized genius. He's the team's video coordinator, and is better than just about anyone at seeing baseball. The three of us are talking about how players today use video to break down an at bat or to review a pitch. Carl starts talking about the Marines, and what they do to drill motions into muscle memory. Which leads me to talk about a Marine drill instructor I've met. Carl says video is only as good as what you remember about it. Bryan mentions he used to keep notebooks of what he thought was working and how he felt when he was throwing well. That, in turn, reminds me of a tennis coach I've watched who preaches a "Zen tennis" philosophy of separating the playing self from the judging self. The more we start talking about other domains and stories from my travels, the more Bryan's ears prick up, the more animated he becomes. Pretty soon he starts asking me questions. I realize now that he doesn't get to do this much, talk about learning and teaching, especially about how folks outside baseball do it. *Pulled hard down the line, just foul, strike two.*

Pitch 4: Fastball inside.

Now the season's started. Bryan and I are keeping in touch, so I can ask him follow-up questions and because, well, we're finding it interesting to keep in touch. He's signing his e-mails "BP." *Ball two.*

Pitch 5: Curve.

After one of our chats late in the season, a bit out of the blue, Bryan says how lucky I am to be doing this project. And I'm thinking, you don't have to tell me—I'm getting to hang out with the Mariners' pitching coach! But what I say is, this project has given me a chance to reflect on how I've been taught all my life. I'm a self-made learner. There's no one person who's shaped me in his image, who's brought me along. I sensed this about myself going in, I tell him, and I'm writing this book so that I can put together a mosaic of teachers for other people like me, people who've never been blessed with a singular savior-mentor figure. As I say this, I see in him a look of recognition: he's one of those people too. I see the hunger, the foraging intelligence: he wants to connect. *The swing starts, the ball begins to break, his hands and eyes tracking it, and he begins to adjust. . . .*

3

When I was in third grade, when my love of baseball came into full blossom, I made my dad drive me on a cold dimming autumn evening to the field at the Sheafe Road Elementary School to play catch. Or rather, to catch me. He was wearing a winter jacket already, and wool dress pants. I made him crouch behind the plate and use my new catcher's mitt—the one I'd made him buy me from Sears that summer, the one I'd made him drive on top of, over and over, with his little yellow Volkswagen Beetle to break it in real nice. I stood on the mound, such as it was on this ill-kept patchy field, and made him catch my pitches. But it wasn't going well. My pitches weren't true, sometimes launching too far and sending shivers down the chain-link backstop, sometimes sputtering short and kicking up dirt. Even when the ball came right to Dad he kept dropping it in that stiff overpadded glove. The season was over now and I had been playing out the World Series in my head again and again, envisioning one perfect baseball moment after another, and here we were ready to reenact them, my father and I, and the magic was simply not materializing.

The previous fall my neighbor from across the street, John Garrity, had introduced me to the game. That was 1976, the year the Yankees fell in four games to the Cincinnati Reds in the Series. We had moved into the neighborhood only two months earlier, and I was glad to have this reason for a friendship. I played catch with John anytime it was not too wet or too dark, and when it became too wet or too dark, I read anything I could about baseball. I remember the entry "Baseball," in the 1977 *World Book Encyclopedia*. It had watercolor illustrations simulating frame-by-frame photographs of a perfect swing, as well as the grips (right-handed) of the four major pitches. I was so confused reading about Willie Keeler's gnomic explanation for his hitting success: "I hit 'em where they ain't." Where *what* ain't? How on earth could you hit something where it isn't? What was the meaning of this?

There was no one at home who I thought could explain what the saying meant, and since the matter-of-fact tone of the encyclopedia entry implied it was just perfectly obvious what the line meant, I was reluctant to ask John or a teacher or anyone outside. So I kept quiet until about . . . oh, until about fifteen years later, when, in a burst of Zen enlightenment, I finally understood that *'em* was the pitches and *they* were the fielders. But until then, how was I to decode this idiom?

My father and I watched a lot of games on TV during the 1977 season, my first full season as a Yankees fan. All throughout that tumultuous year, when Reggie Jackson and Billy Martin were ever at each other's throats, when Reggie and Thurman Munson glowered at each other and kept columnists in print about who was "the straw that stirred the drink," when the Bronx Zoo spirit inside the Stadium locker room reflected exactly the regenerative rot and life-bearing decay of the blacked-out, bankrupt rioting city outside, my devotion to this team and to baseball itself became deeper and more visceral. That summer I got glasses for the first time and I chose gold wire frames—just like Reggie. I swung an imaginary bat before the mirror, trying to mimic the way the torque of Jackson's mighty swing brought his rear shin parallel to and only inches off the ground.

That blessed night when Reggie hit three home runs on three pitches off three different Los Angeles Dodgers in the World Series, my father was upstairs tethered to the kidney dialysis machine he'd started using at home that year, the recliner tilting him back in repose. After each of those home runs, I would scream and run from the family room upstairs, scrambling around the corner, feet sliding under me like a dog's on ice, and arrive out of breath to describe the feat, a feat that with each swing went from prodigious to astounding to historic. I didn't stay long enough to note whether he was wishing he could watch with me, or wishing he could drift back to sleep. I was already gone, back to the game.

At one point that season—in July, I think—when I realized I was more passionate about the Yankees than about anything else in the world, when I was looking for Yankees flags and posters to put on my wall, I asked my father which team was *his* favorite team. He smiled, bemused at my fervor and by my assumption that everyone shared it, and he put down his Chinese newspaper and thought. I guess it would be the White Sox, he said. Really? I asked. Why? The White Sox, with their weird uniforms that had colorful horizontal stripes and the word "SOX" in a futuristic font, a team buried in the standings—what a loser choice. He explained that, well, he'd gone to the University of Illinois in Champaign-Urbana when he came to America and Chicago was the nearest city with a team. So had he been a White Sox fan since his youthful days in Illinois? Well, no. He'd decided just now that the Sox were his team.

From then on, I'd dutifully report to him how Chicago was doing, and he'd thank me for the report. But it was a little disconcerting, how cavalier he was about inventing an attachment. It reminded me of the unfixed, floating nature of his birthday: by the lunar calendar, it was one thing; when translated to a Western calendar, it was July 31 one year, August 17 another year, something else the next. My mother must have faced the same problem, but early on she fixed February 27 as hers. My father never really set his, and we as a family didn't either, celebrating it haphazardly on maybe a week's notice every year, until it came time to write a date certain in the obituary form mailed to us by the *Poughkeepsie Journal* shortly after July 8, 1991. I have no idea what date my mother and I wrote on that form.

I realize only now that on that chill autumn evening at Sheafe Road my father probably could've counted on one hand the number of times he'd ever actually played baseball. He knew he was supposed to be teaching me, but try as he might, he simply couldn't keep the ball in that fat catcher's mitt I'd assigned to him. Perhaps I sensed then that he was not going to be the one to show me the way. Maybe I was just such a control freak that I got upset when we could not get into a rhythm like other dads and sons I'd seen play catch. I'd had a vision of pitching perfectly, and it was getting dark and we were running out of time. So I became petulant and started scolding him. I started yelling that this was a waste, that he didn't know how to play, that I didn't want to play with him. I started blaming my bad throws on him.

My father was silent. And now I am not sure if he was exercising a wise and patient self-control, letting me vent, or if he was feeling some kind of shame or cutting disappointment. Even at the time I knew— I could feel in my gut—that I was being a brat. His silence taught me a lesson, but it is a lesson I interpret in different ways on different days. More than once, I have imagined what it'd be like to see him and say, "Dad, sorry I was such a jerk that time." Would he look at me wondering what on earth I was talking about, and laugh at me for carrying this guilt? Would he, instead, smile soulfully, reminded of the wound of inadequacy I'd worked, and forgive me? Or would he just nod, ever the teacher, and ask what I thought I'd learned from the experience?

4

Bryan Price is one of the most esteemed pitching coaches in major league baseball, and one of the youngest. Both facts come into play when you watch him work with a staff that ranges from Jamie Moyer, a seventeen-year veteran, to Joel Piñeiro, in only his third full season. They are as different as two pitchers can be, Jamie a trim and wiry left-hander, Joel a broad, powerful righty. Jamie tosses games of soft attrition, befuddling batters with fastballs that barely reach 85 mph but seem much faster after a steady diet of 65 mph curveballs and 72 mph changeups. Joel (*joe-EL*) can change speeds too, but his default is the hard, 93-plus fastball. Passive-aggressive and aggressive-aggressive. Moyer, at forty-one, is actually several months older than Bryan. Piñeiro, at twenty-five, is nearly the age Bryan was when his pitching career sputtered to an end.

Bryan entered the California Angels' farm system in 1984. Five years and two shoulder surgeries later, without a single day in the majors, he was done. Bryan, who'd grown up in the Bay Area, son of a prominent banker, was a Cal alum with options besides baseball. He didn't consider them. In his last year playing, he was pitching in the Seattle organization, bouncing between Double-A and Triple-A, and one of his managers saw that Bryan had a knack for explaining things, and for handling diverse personalities. He got an offer to be a coach on the Mariners' team in the Arizona Fall League for rookies. Then he got an offer to coach in the Carolina League, the Single-A league that includes the storied Durham Bulls. His coaching career moved at the pace his pitching career was supposed to have: He coached in the Carolina League for a few more years, then up to Double-A for two years, then became pitching coordinator for all the Mariner farm teams, then got the call from the big league club. In 2002, he was named Major League Pitching Coach of the Year by *Baseball Weekly*.

Today's pitchers are the latest in a long line of men who've taken the mound as professionals, and most every motion they make is inherited, the accreted sum of many generations of mechanical tinkering. When you see someone come along like Orlando "El Duque" Hernandez, the Cuban defector and Yankee whose knee-to-nose leg kick strained the groins of people *watching* him, you realize how conservative an institution pitching usually is. Exceptions like El Duque confirm the rule. At the same time, everything about today's pitchers marks them as pitchers of a particular era. In the 1970s, it was common for pitchers winding up to swing their arms back and raise both hands high above the head; today the windup is typically more compact, hands barely coming over the cap. Add to such signs of generational change the quirky indicia of personal style: the way Anaheim's Ben Weber double-pumps his hands violently as he starts up; the way Boston's Pedro Martinez pivots his hip and hands away from the batter as he unleashes a pitch, accentuating the sideways menace of his stare; the way former Yankee David Cone would pause slightly in mid-delivery, when his hands were about to break and his front leg was in midair, freezing his pose for a microsecond like a skater on ice. Pitching is a changeless art at the core yet ever-changing at the margins.

The limitations of the form are exactly what makes it fascinating. Like calligraphy or figure skating, pitching demands adherence to a rigorous and finite set of motions but it also rewards signature variations that flow from the accident of how each individual's bones and sinews fit together. Actually, how bones and sinews and *brain* fit together. Like calligraphy or figure skating, pitching is only the physical conclusion of a process that unfolds for a very long time inside one's head. And so a teacher of pitching is ever operating on two levels, a surface curriculum about how to pitch and a subterranean curriculum about how to *be*. To study a pitcher's mechanics and mentality is to realize how little things ever change—and how little things can change everything.

Moyer is obsessed with the little things, and his grinding obsessions have paid off. At twenty-five, his record with the Cubs was 12-15 with a 5.10 earned run average. At thirty-five, in his second year as a Mariner, he was 17-5 and 3.86. Last year, at forty-one, at the outer edge of most players' career spans, he went 21-7 and 3.27. Repetition and regimen are any pitcher's lifeblood, and Moyer's to an extreme. When he was a Cub he'd ask his coach Dick Pole a litany of questions about pitching mechanics, just to hear him repeat the same reassuring answers.

His orderly locker in the Mariner clubhouse is a shrine to self-coaching. On the top shelf is a fist-sized rock. That rock, which Pole once placed under Moyer's back foot during a workout, creating roughly the effect that high heels have on body alignment, reminds him to get on top of his curveball. On that shelf too are three laminated cards he studies with Talmudic intensity on game day: reminders in his hand about having a plan; a note about dealing with mistakes; and a tiny grid of randomly assorted numbers whose order he has traced over and again, wearing a groove in his mind. In the dugout, even if he's not pitching that day, he is keeping detailed notes on every batter, compiling a log of tendencies and vulnerabilities that he will exploit the next chance he gets.

Early on, after Bryan was promoted to pitching coach for the Mariners, Moyer could have said, Look, you haven't ever been here, you haven't pitched an inning in the big leagues, and I've done it in three different decades, so please buzz off. He never said that, or even signaled it. At the same time, he's never treated Bryan like an all-knowing guru. Moyer—wry, laconic, and assured—defers to few. He negotiates his own contracts, and on the field he is nearly as self-reliant. Initially Bryan came at him straight ahead with suggestions for ways to adjust his pitching style and Jamie, out of respect, tried them out. But they never felt exactly right and over time the two settled into a different relationship. Bryan pulled back, realizing that Jamie's anal-retentive attention to detail meant that eventually, he'd want another pair of eyes to verify what he was feeling, to troubleshoot. Bryan became that provider of second sight, and he and Jamie are more like peers now; they dissect and discuss an at bat or a session and disagree about what went wrong without fear of upsetting the balance of authority. If Jamie is feeling achy or sluggish late in the season, Bryan can also rib him about how a guy with a new multimillion-dollar contract can surely rouse himself to get off his ass and pitch a game.

With Joel, Bryan has had more leeway to form and shape. Piñeiro, a native of Río Padres, Puerto Rico, and a star junior college pitcher in Florida, is proud and intense. But he's not too proud to seek out and soak up lessons, and has been absorbing them from Bryan since 1997, when Bryan was his coach in Double-A. They came up to the big leagues together in 1998, teacher and pupil, and they work together today with an implicit trust that is earned with time—and, of course, with success, which Joel has now tasted. Joel went 14-7 in 2002, his first full season in the majors, and followed that with a 16-11 campaign. He mixes a live fastball with a devastating overhand curve and a changeup. Like Moyer, he has had long stretches of struggle. In 1999, Joel got lit up all season long in Double-A. He came back strong the next year.

In many ways, Joel is an ideal student: passionate but capable of detachment. Sometimes, Joel says, he'll seek out Moyer for some counsel. Jamie is silently fanatical about preparation and execution, and Joel, you can see, wants to be like that. What Bryan has been working on with Joel is harnessing his aggressiveness, ensuring that the young pitcher's emotions and pride don't derail him, during games or during his career. Between starts he gives Joel exercises to focus his attention and to set simple, short goals. They aren't goals like "let's get nine-plus strikeouts or fewer than three walks today"—goals that can be obliterated not only by bad pitching but just by a bad bounce in the infield or a bad call by the umpire. They are nonnumerical goals, like "let's have a plan of attack with this batter and execute it." Or "let's put our fastballs exactly where we want them." Or "let's not second-guess our pitch selection when we get hit." Success is achieving these goals, whatever the actual hits, runs, and errors recorded. Bryan's mantra is that "you can pitch winning baseball even if you lose the game," and Joel uttered it to me almost word for word.

A deceptively simple mantra. And a radical thing to say in pro sports. Accepting defeat comes dangerously close to excusing defeat. But the difference, though subtle, is stark: like the difference between pitching to win and pitching not to lose. Bryan's task is to steer his guys to the first mindset, and to do that he has to sense what drives each of them. Moyer is at the point where he knows that the mantra's corollary—that you win games consistently *only* if you are pitching winning baseball—is not tautological, as it may sound, but is a truth of the deepest order. Bryan may have to light a fire under him occasionally, motivate him to climb another foot, run another length. But for Jamie, this season will be focused, relentless, maybe a touch bittersweet: he's old enough now to be a master of self-improvement but too old to apply this knowledge for many more years on the diamond. For Joel, whose experience is still shallow, the trouble will be to know the mantra as more than words. His longer-term challenge will be to stay grounded as bigger expectations come his way.

At one point during the season Bryan paid both pitchers his ultimate compliment: "These guys," he said to me, "are accountable people." They attack, they are not afraid to lose, they eat their mistakes and digest them, and they take ownership of whatever happens in the game. He said this with pride—identification—and it was clear why he'd suggested I talk with these men. The two of them illustrate a story that Bryan wants to tell, about good pitching and, in a sense, about himself. Each one pitches winning baseball. Each wins games. And each, it turns out, is like a holograph of a Bryan Price that almost was but never will be—the young gun reaching his potential, the old hand deploying his accumulated cleverness.

5

They used to call him "The Chief." It wasn't clear whether this was because of the Mayan features of his broad flat face, because of his silent and brooding way, or because he was becoming the ace of the staff. Freddy Garcia as late as 2001 was seen as the untouchable, the guy around whom a rotation could be built. He'd come to the Mariners from Houston in 1999, an unknown youngster dealt in the trade that sent the

"Big Unit," Randy Johnson, to the Astros. Garcia was a big right-hander who knew how to pitch, not just throw hard, and was durable and strong. Quickly he'd established himself as someone with great upside, shutting down the Yankees in the 2000 playoffs and winning eighteen games in 2001.

But here we were in 2003, and The Chief had become The Enigma. In midsummer, while the Mariner offense sputtered, the pitching staff was keeping the team atop the AL West. The bull pen was airtight. Jamie was solid and consistent. Joel was showing front-of-the-rotation stuff and presence. Both seemed capable of being the ace. And alas, the job was now sort of open because Freddy, the putative ace, had inexplicably descended into a funk of deepening seriousness. A sloppy April (2-3, 4.21, seven home runs and sixteen walks in six games)—chalk it up to early-season slows—was followed by a horrendous May (2-3, 7.22), and the grumblings grew louder. Then, to everyone's relief, Freddy found his way. June, he was lights-out: five wins, no losses, a 2.05 ERA, twice as many strikeouts as in May.

Bryan saw this transformation, and of course was pleased, but was as much puzzled. He hadn't figured out what had caused the bad months, and couldn't figure out what was causing the good one. Garcia, an intensely private twenty-seven-year-old from Caracas, Venezuela, didn't care much for heart-to-hearts and personal talk. He'd told Bryan the facts of his life history once, but not the emotional content of it. Fine. That wasn't his style. And maybe chitchat in English still wasn't Freddy's forte. But he didn't respond appropriately to just-the-work work sessions either. The advice seemed to register in the moment, but during games, Freddy kept reverting to his own preferences instead of the pitch selection and strategy he'd discussed with Bryan earlier. Bryan couldn't make a connection, and this was galling: if there's one thing he knows how to do, it's make a connection. There emerged in his work with Freddy a sense of blindness, which made the success of June seem uneasy, even unreal.

Then as the July Fourth weekend approached, the Freddy of June dematerialized completely. It was as if he'd been spirited into a freakish parallel universe: his record in July was 0-5; his ERA that month was a dismal 9.45, which is to say he gave up more than a run an inning *for a month*. Opposing batters hit a softball-league .357 off him. Bryan's approach was not to motivate through quotes in the paper. He is very judicious about what he says to the press, and if he has nothing good to say he usually won't say much at all. So I knew Freddy was in trouble when, at the All-Star break in late July, Bryan was quoted in the Seattle papers saying that he didn't know what was happening with Freddy, and that at this point it was a matter of personal choice for Freddy to turn things around. The trading deadline was approaching, and incredibly, the name of the Mariners' preseason ace, a guy whose likeness fills a two-story banner outside the ticket window at Safeco Field, was now being floated in multiple trade rumors.

Bryan's quote about "personal choice" might have gone over the heads of some fans, but to me it was as forceful a statement of his code as one could ask for. When you think about it, it seems a pretty harsh and unforgiving thing to say, that someone's meltdown-level pitching performance is a result of "personal choice." It implies a masochistic love of suffering. Few pitchers would ever *choose* to be so bad for so long. But what Bryan was saying was simply a variation on his theme of pitching "winning baseball." Accountability. Responsibility. Carrying yourself with the right body language. Showing resiliency. What he asked from his pitchers, whether or not they were getting the statistical results they wanted, was that they take responsibility for their own education. *That* was a matter of personal choice, and the implication was that Freddy, who was drifting out of orbit in a tiny capsule of mistrust and misapprehension, had chosen not to engage.

Yet it was an interesting, and ambiguous, take on who ultimately is responsible for the success of a learning relationship. Was Bryan commenting about the limits of teaching, or about the limits of this teacher? Was his frustrated remark an assertion that a man can lead a horse to water but can't make it drink? Or was it rueful acknowledgment that while a teacher's duty is to search relentlessly for ways to unlock the student, sometimes he just can't locate the keyhole, let alone the key?

Late in the season, I was talking with Bryan in the locker room a few hours before game time when Freddy walked by. He was the starting pitcher tonight, and was immersed in pregame ritual, pacing the clubhouse and dugout with MP3 player in hand and tiny headphones tucked into his ears, his head bobbing faintly to some other frequency. "Hey, Freddy," Bryan said as they passed, the two words betraying more coolness, loss, and regret than a full-length soliloquy could have expressed. Freddy nodded, eyes wary and a bit wounded, and walked on.

6

I love to pitch. I dream of it. I daydream of it. The image of an unfolding pitch is literally the most constant background image in my mind, my mental screen saver. In meetings or conversations, I'll sometimes get up and do a tai-chi version of a pitcher's windup, slow and easy, to help sort out my thoughts. When I was writing my last book, a collection of personal essays about Asian Americans, race, and culture, the apartment we lived in had an unobstructed lane of about twenty-five feet from the sliding patio doors to the kitchen cabinets. When I got stuck in the writing, whenever I felt I was drifting away from what I had set out to express, I fashioned a crude ball out of a crumpled piece of my manuscript and a lot of Scotch tape and rubber bands, and down that lane I pitched simulated games against imagined lineups, trying to drop a curveball into a bucket or fire a fastball at a specific square inch on the corner of the cabinet. I threw hundreds of pitches a week, thousands in the course of the writing.

The funny thing is, I taught myself everything I know about pitching. For one year in Little League I was a pitcher for the New Hamburg (N.Y.) Chiefs, but the coach, big Joe Manginelli, didn't have a thing to tell me about pitching except to throw strikes. Which I only intermittently could do. Besides that, I have never thrown a pitch in a live, regulation game. Through high school and college and the first years after college, I might play catch occasionally and keep track of the standings, but my interest in playing and watching baseball receded.

I think it's no accident that around the time I began writing my last book, when I began to open the Pandora's box of my own identity, and of identity generally, pitching returned to my life after so many years of absence. It was a security blanket. The repetitive motions soothed, quieted the mind, carried me back to clarity. I began to study pitching obsessively, buying official MLB videos on how to pitch like a major leaguer, scanning websites about the physics of curveballs, gobbling up any reference in the sports pages that might offer insight. The obsession persisted well after the book was done. Once I saw an ESPN segment in which a left-hander demonstrated the grip for a changeup and a cut fastball and a splitter—advanced pitches, beyond the *World Book*—and I watched intently, grabbed a ball, and hurried to transpose the grips and seam alignments to my right hand. Any chance I got, I'd enlist my wife, my father-in-law, any houseguest, to catch me, to receive my experiments.

Writing honestly about race, about affinities chosen and inherited, was tricky enough. But around this time, the questions of identity I was wrestling with were not just about ethnicity. My wife and I were about to make the leap into parenthood. I was excited but scared. Throughout Carroll's pregnancy, which also marked the last nine months of a pleasantly meandering five-year law school education, a creeping sense of finality set in. I was leaving the "bright young kid" phase of my life and entering I wasn't sure what. I began to play not to lose. I got very numerical in my goals. I got pathological about who was returning my calls, whether the things I was doing were getting enough buzz, whether the plates I was spinning were still spinning. I started to do projects just so I could say I was doing them. I was losing my way. And the whole time, I was pitching. Frantically. It gave such an illusion of control. I paced the shrinking confines of my apartment, day after day, throwing those taped balls harder and harder until they unraveled and required repair, knowing that I was regressing but believing that regression, at least, was movement toward something I knew.

7

The dog days. By late August, the drought of the Mariner offense had extended to crisis proportions. But worse, the pitching, which had held up for so long, began to crumble. Whatever had ailed Freddy apparently faded—his August was a not-terrible 2-2, 4.28 ERA—but also apparently infected others in the staff. Joel flipped from a 5-0, 1.44 July to an 0-5, 8.31 August. The bull pen, which had been solid all year, was no longer. When the trading deadline passed and Seattle had added no stars to help down the stretch, the reliever Jeff Nelson sounded off to the media about the need for reinforcements and his frustration with GM Pat Gillick and the owners. Nelson was promptly traded, to the Yankees, of all places. Though it was arguable—as Gillick did argue—that the trade for Armando Benitez was strictly a baseball move, after it was done, any grousing stayed inside the clubhouse.

Not to say that the wrenching anxiety abated. If anything, the implicit gag rule laid down by Nelson's sudden departure made things tighter, because everyone could see what was happening but no one wanted to name it. The Oakland Athletics, who in recent years had developed a pattern of first-half indolence followed by second-half intensity that carried them to the postseason, were surging again. Seattle's first-place lead dwindled each day, and its slide in the standings began to take on a slow-motion sense of inevitability, an awful sapping of will, as if blood from unfound wounds were leaking out, congealing into pools of thick and ferric caramel. Fans in Seattle were alternately anguished, stunned, and scared that they too might catch this strain of paralyzing loseritis. By mid-August, the A's had taken first place from the Mariners, and talk now turned to whether Seattle could manage to get the wild card.

This was where the season stood when Bryan and I got together at the end of August for an early lunch at a downtown steak house. We'd had all these baseball chats, we figured, and this was to get to know each other a little more. The get-together had been his suggestion, obliquely—he'd mentioned that with his wife and daughter living in Arizona, he usually had some free time before games when the team was in town—and of course I'd jumped at the notion of an unhurried conversation with him. We talked. He told me about his upbringing, and his parents, how their parenting style has influenced his own. I told him about my family, my work in politics, about how one goes about writing a book, and he asked sincerely inquisitive questions.

The whole time I could see the tightness in his face. We knew each other well enough now so that I could broach this, the subject of the season's failure-in-progress, and he seemed almost relieved when I did. Bryan talked about how much the last month had been weighing on him, how he'd been up late every night trying to figure out ways to tweak the arms and minds of his pitchers, how he'd then started worrying about *over*correcting. "Control" and "command" are central to pitching; they are just as central, it turns out, to the coaching of pitching—and sometimes just as elusive. He was taking the struggles of the staff personally, and was reaching the boundaries of his knowledge. Never had he coached a group, been part of a professional team, where the psychology had become so contagiously oppressive. He could not place his own pitches—his directions and suggestions—where he wanted to. It seemed his command, his mastery, of his teaching repertoire was deserting him. The very thing he was asking of his pitchers he was forgetting—to focus only on what you can control.

Did he have anyone on the team who could help him? Bryan paused, and took pains to say that Bob Melvin, the rookie manager, had been a good sounding board, and that the two of them had been trying to puzzle their way through this together. But precisely because Bob was a first-year manager, Bryan felt a responsibility not to overtax him. I had a thought, hesitated, then went ahead. Bob must be under unbelievable pressure, I said. Maybe what he could use at a time like this is to feel like a teacher, to feel he can dispel this helplessness by helping somebody else. Bryan held his spoon in midair. Maybe you can help Bob by asking him to help you, I said. Give him a chance to coach you on your coaching. I offered it up casually, but I think he saw why I was framing this as something for Bob's benefit. He sat there processing, nodded, and dug into his dessert.

I was there to listen. That's why he had suggested we get together, so I might be for him what he is for Jamie Moyer, another pair of eyes and ears. By listening, by reading him and reading back what I picked up, I might reveal something for him to consider, even change. I'm not sure he knew his motive on a conscious level, but the intuition that moved him was right: he got a bracing glimpse into a mirror. For all his success as a coach, all his knowledge of the game and of human psyches, he is still in formation, mapping his own instincts and searching out routes from instinct to action. As we paid up and left, and I thanked him for getting together, Bryan stretched out his big hand. "This has helped more than you know," he said. I smiled the whole way home.

8

In September the pitching stabilized. Jamie Moyer was better than ever, going 4-1 with a tiny 1.70 ERA. Joel Piñeiro rebounded from his bad August, as Bryan had seemed confident he would, with a 3-1, 3.78 month. And Freddy Garcia finished strong as well, recording only one win against two losses in the month but achieving a 1.97 ERA. It was all too late, though. The offense remained anemic. Seattle kept on losing close, low-scoring games, and the team went under .500 for the month, as it had in August. The M's finished the season three behind the A's. They missed the wild card by two. On the year, Moyer went 21-7, 3.27; Piñeiro, 16-11, 3.78; and Garcia, 12-14, 4.51. Respectable stats for the front three of any rotation. But once again, the Mariners had achieved below their talent. A team that had won 393 games in four seasons, once again, was unable to win when it mattered. As the players packed up their lockers, the question in the air was whether the franchise's stated goal— to field a perennially competitive team—was now becoming its prison; whether the goal ought to be to have a championship-winning team.

I let a few weeks pass before I tried reaching Bryan. When I did, he was back home in Arizona, spending time biking, sharing meals with his wife, taking his teenage daughter to her basketball games. The playoffs were in their operatic second round, the ill-fated Red Sox and Cubs pushing their Sisyphean stones ever higher. The regular season was now far enough away to review. But over the course of several long phone calls, Bryan and I talked hardly at all about the past season. Our talk drifted instead to a pitcher he'd once coached in the Carolina League, someone who kept coming back to mind.

Rich Lodding was a classic overthrower, a kid who thought he could win by blowing pitches past everyone—and who, till then, probably *had* blown pitches past everyone. "The thing with Rich," Bryan said, "is that I wasn't prepared for him." The obvious problem Lodding faced, as an aggressive fireballer, was lack of command and poor pitch placement. Bryan treated this as a mechanical issue. He tried to steady Rich's delivery. He didn't try to steady his mind, to find out what was driving him to muscle through everything. It was only Bryan's third season of coaching. He was twenty-six, guiding pitchers who were twenty-two or -three. "Before then," he recalled, "I'd mainly been working on things like discipline and repetition. I never had to confront a guy on the mental game." They worked relentlessly on physical adjustments: arm angles, release points, breaking of the hands, weight transfer. Bryan, on a mission, even got consent from the head of the Mariners' farm system to take Rich out of the rotation for three weeks just to rebuild his delivery and improve his location. This was an extraordinary effort. It didn't work. Rich kept on throwing hard and kept on getting hit hard. When the next season arrived, he was released.

Who knows whether Rich Lodding could have been a great pitcher? Odds are, he wouldn't have been. But the end of Rich's pro career still haunts Bryan. "After he was released, it was very personal to me," he said. "I'd failed him. I hadn't given him a chance to succeed at the next level." I asked what kind of learner Rich was, how open he'd been to change. "He was soft-spoken, a good guy. He could've been a perfect student if I'd known what the hell I was teaching," Bryan replied. "He never lacked for physical effort. What he lacked was the trust that he could succeed using *less* physical effort. As a pitcher, if you're trying not to fail, you are sure to fail. He didn't have the confidence to be willing to fail." Bryan sighed. "If I could've said to him what I just said to you . . ."

But Bryan's regret is not just that he failed to say the right thing to Rich, as if it were merely a matter of pulling out the wrong tool. His remorse runs deeper. Bryan started telling me about another young pitcher he knew who, like Rich, never addressed the mental game; who thought that a 100 percent physical effort level was all that was needed; who was too focused on himself, his own power, his might, rather than on the end result he was seeking in a game; who didn't buy it when he was told that there was very little *physical* difference between pitchers in rookie ball and in the big leagues. That other young pitcher, of course, was Bryan Price. When his own career ended, he blamed it on injuries and bad luck. "The reality is, I just wasn't good enough to win—good enough in terms of having a mental plan and concept." When Bryan first became a coach, his playing days still so fresh, he wasn't willing to face his failures as a pitcher—which kept him from teaching Rich how to prevent his. Bryan sensed what Rich needed; sensed it all too well. A pitcher who "just wasn't good enough"—and who hadn't been taught to change his approach—was still too scary a thing to face.

Today Rich is a high school baseball and football coach in Southern California, and Bryan occasionally bumps into him at games in Anaheim. You can tell, the way he speaks of him, that seeing Rich standing among the fans still stirs in him some guilt. You can tell too that when he finally pieced together what had gone wrong with Rich, he was determined to learn from it. But here's the thing about teaching: you are never finished falling short. Equipped as he was by his reflections on Rich, Bryan still hadn't solved Freddy. "My greatest disappointment," he said, "is with myself, for not getting him to trust me to do anything I asked. When I threw Freddy a life ring he thought it was made of lead." Now Bryan realized he should've made Freddy come up with game plans for himself, plans that he would own. He should've perceived that Freddy's nonchalance "was really just his difficulty showing vulnerability."

Of course, another way to say you're never finished falling short is to say you're never finished learning—about your pupils and yourself. In the 2004 season, a dismal one for the Mariners, Freddy would pull it together in the first half—so well, in fact, that as Seattle fell deep into the cellar, the White Sox acquired Freddy in a trade and signed him to a three-year deal. It'll be interesting to see in the seasons ahead what Freddy will have taught Bryan about how to teach, and what alchemy Bryan can muster to turn lead to something lighter. This is where baseball and life can diverge, cruelly. In baseball, a long but finite off-season allows the husks of crushed, dried-out dreams to lie on the forest floor and become the nutrients that help a new set of dreams sprout. Bryan, in the winter, gathers up all the important notes he's kept during the season, scribbled on the cardboard backs of the pads that charted workaday issues. He absorbs what he's collected, and comes to spring training bearing new knowledge.

In real life, the cycles aren't so ordered, the chances for renewal are not annual. In real life, it can take many seasons to see the patterns that ran you into the ground, and many more for you to do something about it. When I finally pulled out of the downward spiral of self-doubt that marked my shift from youth to adulthood, several years had elapsed. My child was a toddler. I emerged not with any profound wisdom or clarion truths. I emerged only with a determination to begin this book; to raise my daughter well; to teach; and to search for others who can keep their students from wandering too far afield.

9

Sometimes as I drift off to sleep here is what I see: a batter digging into the box, a righty, his eyes on me, bat cocked above his shoulder, awaiting my offering. I see my right arm as it reaches the apex of its arc, my index and middle fingers pressed together along one seam of the ball. My front foot hits the mound, and I see the catcher bouncing on his heels. I see— I feel—the flick of my wrist, the bite of the seams as I release the ball. I see the batter pivot his hips. The ball heads down the middle. The batter starts his swing, eyes greedy with anticipation. But in the final ten feet the ball begins to tail sharply down and away, the red seams in a tight, self-reinforcing spin. I see his arms extend desperately, his face a grimace as he swats at the pitch, which has slid suddenly out of reach. As good sliders do. I see myself smiling, and perhaps, as I drift off to sleep, I do in fact smile. And in the morning, when I am awakened by the cub who's climbed in my bed, whose face fills my field of vision, I imagine that the image in my head might float like mist into hers; that one person's dream, caught at just the right moment, might become another's.

My daughter was literally born into baseball. I was with my wife, Carroll, who was thirty-nine weeks pregnant, in the third row of the bleachers at Fenway. Red Sox–Yankees. It was only May but there was a playoff-level intensity. The bleachers, usually raucous, were surreally wild. Chants rolled through the ancient stadium in overlapping waves: "Let's-go-Red-Sox" "Let's-go-Yan-kees" "Yan-kees Suck"—and, from the New York partisans, the taunting "Nine-teen-eigh-teen" (the last year of a Boston championship). Pedro pitching for the Sox, Orlando Hernandez for the Yanks. Serendipity: one of the baby names we'd toyed with was Orlando. So Carroll and I made a pact en route to the park that if El Duque pitched a no-hitter and the baby was a boy, we'd name him Orlando.

The first four innings were crisp and scoreless. Twilight stole into night, and we settled in for a classic. But in the fifth, Carroll turned to me and observed that she'd had three contractions in the last half hour. I said: Can you make it to the end? She said: I think so. Behind us, the people were a swarm, a fantastic pattern of navy blue and bloodred whorls. Fistfights broke out like volcanic eruptions, inducing warlike roars. It was awesome to behold, and the vibrations shaking the stands surely stirred the fetus. *What's going on out there?* After seven innings, we realized El Duque hadn't allowed a hit. In the eighth, though, Hernandez coughed up a single, and in the ninth, Mariano Rivera allowed a hit. As the game ended we pushed our way through the mob, rushed home, got our labor and delivery bag, and drove to the hospital. Thirty hours later, a baby girl arrived. Olivia, we like to say, was two hits and one Y chromosome away from being Orlando.

Of course, being born into something is no assurance that the inheritance will be valued, that the imprint will take. When Olivia turned two I tried to teach her how to pitch. She watched me perform a slow-motion delivery, and as she imitated me it was clear she had picked up the essentials: arms up, leg kick, reach back, and throw. But someone who knows to hold a violin in the left hand and tuck it under the chin, to hold the bow in the right and pull it across a string, doesn't therefore know how to play the violin. My daughter took the essentials of my delivery and bolted them together into a comical Frankenstein dance, in which the leg kick preceded the raising of the arms and the throw was uncorked only after the lower body had stopped moving, which rather defeated the purpose of the windup. It's not something we're born knowing how to do, pitching, and though many may learn to do it passably, the gulf between passable and professional is perhaps even wider than that between zero and passable.

Still, I'd like nothing more than for Olivia one day to become a starting pitcher for the Mariners. She's only four as I write this, but she is a lefty and she's very crafty. She and I have played catch and hit off a tee, and just as important, I've been steeping her since birth in the *religion* of baseball. The first time she ever heard me raise my voice, in disgust or in delight, was during a playoff game. One of her first stuffed animals was the Mariner Moose. She recognized the Seattle outfielder Ichiro long before she recognized Barney. When she was two, I decorated her room with banners and bobbleheads from the All-Star game, which was in Seattle that year. And to this day, the only time she gets to watch television at night is when a ball game is on.

Yet I fear this indoctrination is going to be a lost cause. For one thing, there is the first law of parental thermodynamics: what the father pushes, the child will eventually deem to be dorky. For another, Olivia's hand-eye coordination isn't exactly prodigy-level. But there's the broader environment as well. The culture. In Seattle, all the new fields are crowded, green soccer fields and all the old ones are empty, dusty baseball diamonds. The talk of other parents at dinner parties and Starbucks and the store is about soccer camps and year-round traveling teams. Not Little Leagues. Girls in elementary school who are the least bit athletic want to be the next Mia Hamm, not the Jackie Robinson of the gender line.

If baseball were a real religion, I'd have no compunction about raising Olivia with the rituals and beliefs of my denomination. But because it's only a sport, I guess I don't feel I have the same permission. There are some things I intend to teach her—like how to speak Chinese to her Nai Nai, like what her great-grandmother's Jewish traditions are—so that she can find her place in the world. There are other things I want to teach her so that I can be reminded of *my* place in the world. And baseball, I confess, lies in the second category. I love baseball because I learned it at a time before sickness crept into my own father's life, and I will always associate the game with that lost innocence. But that's my little drama. Ultimately, it's not reason enough to deny Olivia the chance to run around with all the other pigtailed, cleat-wearing girls, chasing a black-and-white ball around a rectangle for ninety minutes three times a week.

Anyway, if I know my daughter, her way out of this dilemma of baseball versus soccer will be to join the tackle football team. Not because it'd be the Solomonic, Golden Mean thing to do. But because it would be neither my wish nor its opposite, and it therefore would not be defined by me. If that's ultimately what happens, if Olivia becomes a wide receiver instead of a pitcher, I think I'll be able to sleep at night. In fact, I think I'll have taught her all I needed to.

CHORALE 1

Receive Before You Transmit

We have this notion of the great teacher as the Great Communicator. But the most powerful teachers aren't those who speak, perform, and orate with the most dazzle and force. They are those who listen with full-body intensity, and customize. Teaching is not one-size-fits-all; it's one-size-fits-one. So before we transmit a single thing, we must tune in to the unique and ever-fluctuating frequency of every learner: his particular mix of temperament, skills, intelligence, and motivation. This means, as teachers, putting aside our own egos and preconceptions about what makes this particular lesson so important, or that way of saying it so sacrosanct. It means letting go of the idea of control.

In war, wrote Sun Tzu, victory is most ideally achieved before the battle has ever begun. The clash of forces on the field should be the *coup de grace,* capstone of a careful process of gathering intelligence, adjusting plans, and adapting strategy. So it is in teaching. The inner preparation, the awareness of oneself and one's students and of the traps and opportunities that lie within each, is where the critical work truly resides. The talking, the explicit transmission of knowledge, is not a mere afterthought, of course; it requires talent and concentration, passion and practice. But when we are teaching well, when we've truly encountered our students, we know that it's all over but the talking.

PART II

Unblock, Unlock

CHICKS IN CHARGE

The pursuit of happiness? Hopeless. The pursuit of meaningfulness? Even that sounded ridiculous.

Jocelyn Wong couldn't bear to think what her father would say. She had come to Procter and Gamble because that was what he wanted. Rewind. She had gone to Purdue because that was what he wanted. Northwestern was what she'd dreamt of, like so many bright children of the Chicago suburbs, but she'd never even applied. It was too daunting to imagine what he'd say when she got rejected. As surely she would have. She'd studied engineering at Purdue because that was what he'd wanted. A Purdue engineer. A Boilermaker. And then she'd come to P&G to do this, to fulfill what she knew to be the expectation. And it was terrible. The kind of terrible that felt like running underwater, wholly submerged, lungs burning, mouth sealed shut, every gesture beset unbearably by an atmosphere of compression. It wasn't just that working in manufacturing and then research and development, as Jocelyn had for more than two years now, felt stifling. What made it truly bad was that she wasn't even good at it. She was middling at best, and her ratings showed it. How would she tell her father that she had done everything he had demanded of her—and failed? Maybe, if she was lucky, he would act as if he'd expected it all along: all her successes were flukes, her setbacks the natural course. But wouldn't such faithless resignation hurt more?

It wasn't so unreasonable, what he asked of her. For what he asked of her was really only what he *wished* for her—that his child might equip herself with the skills, the practical education, the job security that would ensure that her status would never be as provisional and unrooted as that of a mere immigrant. And the Confucian severity of it all, well, that was just style; that couldn't be helped or unwound; beneath it, she was willing to believe, beneath the judgment and the sharp silent looks of reproval, was love. It was a loving family, she said. And so, how could she repay this love, this undying concern for her welfare from a man who had traveled across an ocean and half a continent to give her these chances, how could she repay it by saying—whining—that she wanted to find something that better suited her true self? What kind of indulgent talk was that?

Her last boss had seen it. It probably was not hard to see, the lines of internal monologue etching themselves across her brow; the second-guessing of second-guessing clouding her eyes. He saw in Jocelyn Wong someone on a fast track to failure at Procter and Gamble. But before he gave up, berated her, did any of the things that stressed-out middle managers do, he asked: Is there another kind of work you'd like to explore? Marketing? The question seized her. Marketing at P&G is like infantry in the Marine Corps: the intense living heart of the organization. Jocelyn was scared. But excited too, for marketing held a promise of creativity, invention. *Expression.* So she agreed to meet with a woman named Diane Dietz, then the marketing director for North American Oral Care. What would she tell her father? What did she know about marketing, marketing *toothpaste*? Well, it probably wouldn't work out anyway. Save the worry. She was ready to give up; might as well see about this. She put on her best suit, pinned back her hair, and took a deep breath. It was time to interview.

The headquarters of Procter and Gamble is Cincinnati's stolid echo of Rockefeller Center: a boxy, handsome complex of boxy, handsome buildings, structures that were agleam in the 1950s and have become just a bit dulled. Although business casual dress, and BlackBerry PDAs, and women, and people with dark skin are all to be found there today, the main building still exudes a sense of warped time, of staid anachronism.

Step into the elevators with beautiful brass doors and inlaid carved wood panels, and you might emerge, when the doors slide open, in a bygone era. Certainly in another world.

The fifth floor, where Oral Care is to be found, is organized like most other floors in the building. A large display case greets you, like the big tanks at Chinese restaurants that hold crabs and fish and grayish water, filled here with the bright cornucopia of the floor's business units: Bounty paper towels on one floor; Tide laundry detergent on another. (On nine, the senior executive floor, everything is more elegant. Instead of display cases there are tasteful alcoves set in the walls, with accent lighting. The sort of nook that might contain a Ming vase in another corporate head-quarters here cradles a never-opened, lovingly preserved package of Charmin toilet paper.)

The floor has been chopped up and reconfigured, cubicles and low walls marking the passing of the age of the three-martini lunch. Weave your way to Diane Dietz's office and here is what you'll see. On one wall, little plastic shelves full of trophies: a three-pack of Crest Whitening Effects, cinnamon rush and orange spice and mint; a larger box of Crest Whitening Effects with Scope; a CrestPro battery-run toothbrush. On another wall, signed photographs of Diane with John Pepper, former CEO and now, as chairman of the executive committee of the board, CEO emeritus. Across from that, framed articles in *The Wall Street Journal* and *AdWeek* about Diane and two of her managers; they called themselves the "Chicks in Charge." The décor is Holiday Inn, neither nice nor shabby. Her desk, tucked partially behind a wall for privacy, is unclut-tered. Her long meeting table is clear, except for a speakerphone.

What you are unlikely to find in Diane's office is Diane. She seems to prefer roaming, prowling the corner of the fifth floor occupied by North American Oral Care. She holds meetings in the doorways of her team members. She strides quickly, confidently. A Chick in Charge. She has a broad, attractive face, with more mascara on than someone in her mid-thirties usually wears, and a brassy Chicagoland voice softened by just the faintest hint of a lisp. Her brown bangs and shoulder-length hair are prac-tical. She yells to Dave and Matt and others from across halls, from room to room, her big laugh barking through the air. She works the precincts like a pol, sizing people up, hearing their complaints; or like a football coach on game day, moving from locker to locker with a stinging punch to the shoulder, an affectionate slap on the back of the head. She is managing. The whole time, Diane Dietz is managing, moving things; making everyone's office, everyone's story, her own.

Jocelyn could not believe her ears. They had spoken for less than ten minutes. Diane must not have read her file: Jocelyn was three-rated, not one-rated; she was Purdue, not Ivy League; she had no MBA or marketing experience, for heaven's sake, not even a marketing class on her transcript. Diane had hired her. Instantly. Jocelyn walked out of the interview, stunned. She expected she would get sent back the next morning, like an impulse purchase regretted and returned. Like a defective product. But she didn't. The following week she became an assistant brand manager, taking a job usually held by people several years younger and several credentials stronger. She was going to work on new toothpaste products. She could not believe this was happening.

Diane believed. She knew it the moment Jocelyn walked in. This was a girl so hungry, so achingly desperate. A girl blinded to her own passion, because up to this point the passion had all been directed to the *suppression* of passion. The denial of her own ability to desire. This was a girl who, with permission, could imagine and create great things. This was a girl who needed a safe place: a home base; an alternative idea of how to develop. Diane would take her in. She would unscrew the lid of the jar, and let time and nature run their course.

One of the remarkable things about Procter and Gamble is that it asks people in their early twenties to run billion-dollar brands. They do so without fanfare. While many of their B-school classmates chased the Internet rainbow in the late nineties, the brand managers at P&G kept chugging along, steering the grand old juggernauts of Tide or Crest or Ivory through global waters. New-economy types may scorn the creeping and marginal nature of innovation in these massive, mature products, products rescued from total commoditization by the alchemy of brand marketing. But what they overlook is the intense pressure that comes with piloting a billion-dollar supertanker: the slightest drift off course, one-tenth of one degree, compounds itself with such momentum that it becomes excruciating and costly to correct. And that doesn't even account for the risk of unseen icebergs.

Bottom line: it is daunting to run a brand at P&G. It was especially scary for Jocelyn. Her first assignment, as an assistant brand manager at the bottom rung of the marketing ladder, was to plan the launch of a new brand. Crest Rejuvenating Effects with Scope was to be the company's maiden entry into a relatively new category of toothpastes marketed to freshen breath. (If it seems odd that toothpaste, which was invented to banish bad breath, should be considered innovative if it *really* freshens breath, see above re: the alchemy of brand marketing.) This wasn't just a cosmetic paste (it whitens), and not just an oral hygiene product (dentists recommend it); it was also going to give you that clean, confident feeling that only a mouthwash—a trusted, familiar mouthwash like Scope—can confer.

Jocelyn had it all planned out. Her plan was this: she'd try, fail, quit, and return to school. How else could she think? She looked at this project and decided the only way to get past the fear—the distraught feeling over what her family would think about her abandoning engineering, the bottomed-out self-esteem that she brought to this work, the terror of not knowing anything about it—was to throw herself into the project and let the chips fall as they would. So she studied the market research data. She worked late tweaking the mock-ups of the package design. She read magazine articles about her competitors. She conferred with Matt Barresi, her immediate boss and the brand manager, on every little detail.

Diane's strategy was to give Jocelyn little wins, one after another. She indicated to Jocelyn early on: "You don't have to prove to me that you're good. I already think you are." She took her recommendations seriously, praised them publicly. One day Diane told her she was going to bring her into a meeting with A. G. Lafely, the CEO. *A meeting with A.G.?* Marketing directors usually coveted such face time, hogged it for themselves. Why bring lowly Jocelyn in? Well, Diane said, you did do all the work, didn't you? You know this stuff better than anyone else in the room, don't you? I need you there. In fact, Diane said, why don't you present? I'll be there for you, watching your back. I know you can do it. You're going to rock. And Jocelyn did it.

Diane built the nest, searching for just the right twigs to bring back. She admitted that, like Jocelyn, she didn't consider herself so strong on the number-crunching and data analysis. She confided to Jocelyn that too often at the company newcomers were set up to fail: *Let's see how smart they are.* She treated Jocelyn from the start like one of the gang, dragging her to drinks with everyone, making fun of her anal little habits. She set an example of total emotional authenticity. She cried in front of Jocelyn. She yelled in front of Jocelyn. She called Jocelyn at home ten times, just to check in, after Jocelyn and her husband had had a fight. At first Jocelyn donned a very male style of interaction at work: buttoned up, very P&G, very engineering. Diane didn't call it out; she just kept on wearing her own hair long, putting on skirts, sneaking out to shop, drawing little hearts on her little Post-it notes. At the same time Diane could be all business when she needed to and frankly, she could be a real bitch when she was angry. She would run through walls for Jocelyn and for all the others on the team, fighting with her bosses and people in other departments to get the resources and time and numbers *her people needed to win.*

But the most important thing she did, the thing that unlocked it all, had nothing to do with business. It happened when Jocelyn's grandfather died. The whole extended family was there for the wake, which was held outside Chicago. Wave upon wave of bad feelings engulfed Jocelyn as she stood there in the murmuring: the grief, the loss, the inability of this family to express grief, the discomfort she felt upon returning to face her father, the enervating sense of inadequacy. Then she turned and saw, amidst this sea of funereal Chinese and Korean faces, the face of Diane Dietz. The sight was like a life preserver. Diane and Matt had driven eight hours in the snow from Cincinnati to Chicago, without telling Jocelyn they were coming, and soon they would turn around and drive eight hours back so they could make a Monday meeting. They had wanted to be there, because that was what family did. That day, Jocelyn grasped the meaning of loyalty and trust. Of love. That day, she knew she was going to stay at the company, stay with this team, and that the business results she delivered there would not be the thing she or anyone else would ultimately remember about it.

The launch of Crest Rejuvenating Effects with Scope was a success.

.   .   .

John Pepper sat across from Jocelyn, and was, perhaps, a bit bemused. Here was an assistant brand manager, new to the group, having her big moment to impress the legendary outgoing CEO, the man who'd revived P&G's fortunes and was retiring now to encomiums, and all she could do was talk about how great Diane was. Well, Diane had set up this lunch, of course, to spread the benefits of her high-powered relationships to her junior employees. It was a savvy gesture. It made Jocelyn feel grateful. It made John feel necessary and engaged still. It enrolled him in the success of Diane's team. In the success of Diane herself.

John is classic P&G: Yale '53, U.S. Navy, joined the company thirty-five years ago, held senior marketing roles in Laundry Care, then Health Care, did a stint in Asia, came back to Cincinnati to rise to the top of the company, became a pillar of civic life. He is lean, compact, with rectangular wire glasses, close-cropped silver hair, and an air of impatience. But beneath the Cartesian mien, he's always had a nonrational intuition about what he liked in people. If someone with the right credentials or look lacked it, or if someone with the wrong ones had it, so what; he'd track the "it" rather than what the "it" was wrapped in. A mind-set that allowed him to see Diane clearly.

In many ways Diane is unbelievably un-P&G. She is brash. Spontaneous. Absolutely disdains convention for its own sake. She cannot suffer insecure, controlling managers. *No one is the boss of me; the task is the boss.* She smashes façades of invulnerability. It's a running joke how many times the tough guys and taskmasters on the team have cried with their colleagues. *The way to be is to be me.* She once urged a high-performer on her team, a friend, to leave the company because his heart clearly was elsewhere; then she helped him get into the music business. *How can I help you find your passion?* She is fearless about creating a safe haven, an island, for her team to succeed and celebrate. When one person gets a promotion, it's a tradition that the others make a video, with action figures and cheap props, to roast the (un)lucky employee. The videos make wicked fun of the roastee—and of the hypocrisies, petty and grand, of "The P&G Way." *I don't wait for someone to change the culture here; that's a cop-out.* All of this cuts against the company's grain of near-cultish conformity; of high-strung perfectionism and data-driven empiricism; of reflexive conservatism.

At the same time, what's made this company so successful and durable for nearly a century and a half has been that its obsessiveness is channeled into teaching and learning. P&G is a "promote-from-within" company. Excluding entry-level employees and some specialty Ph.D.s, *98 percent* of the company's workforce comes from inside. That is a staggering proportion. Sustaining it means being obsessive about unlocking the talent of the people you've got. So P&G has world-class training programs and systems for measuring mentorship (bosses rate employees as learners, employees rate bosses as coaches). More important, though, it has a powerful informal ethos, passed on dyad by dyad, in which the most esteemed leaders are the ones who teach with a light touch; who tell tales of past campaigns and who scaffold their apprentices with apt questions and well-chosen work.

John Pepper remembers an early boss this way, Jack Claggett. He doesn't recall a substantive thing Jack ever said; only that he conveyed to him the belief that John would one day run the company. In this deeper sense, few are more P&G than Diane. She has attended to the growth of each individual on her team, tailoring, tucking, pushing, pulling; aware the whole time of another of her slogans: *People love to learn but hate to be taught.* She has woven them into a group more passionate about one another (and their work) than any I've ever seen, in business, politics, the military, education, *anywhere.* And they win: profits for North American Oral Care are up 290 percent in three years.

Diane was not always as cocksure as she appears to be today. In fact, there are many layers even to today's cocksureness: she once told me proudly how her mother and father had raised her to be confident and to feel special; it was someone else who told me that she was adopted. When she first joined the company, she had her convictions, of course. But as she found the courage to express them, her boss at the time didn't take well to it. He bristled when she told him straight up, *No, you're wrong on this.* She knew then she needed a teacher, a guide who could make it safe for her to find her voice. She wondered if this place could ever produce such a guide. Then she met John Pepper, introducing him at a health care event with the surgeon general, and on that day she knew. She saw that he saw. She began to seek out his advice on strategy, and he offered it. He wrote avuncular note cards to her team, praising a successful quarter or a well-executed launch, cards that ended up posted on everyone's doors and walls. He told her, when asked, that she was doing right. And the more he encouraged her, the more willing she became to step out and express her true self.

One evening John came to dinner with Diane's whole team. Here he was, the patriarch, the wise man. Here he was, he realized, with so much still to learn. He looked at them as they bantered and spoke of one another's flaws and laughed raucously and argued about work. This was a family she had made. John himself hadn't been anything like this when he was Diane's age. He'd been so much more private; guarded and opaque. He hadn't known how to reach out, the way they both do now. It took him years to grow into that man, to become a bridge that could link the old P&G, the one that had formed him, to the emerging one that would be formed by the likes of Diane. It stirred him to see, and she could see that. I asked her once what she valued most about John's friendship. "He gives me the feeling," she said, "that I could do *anything* in this company."

Diane and Jocelyn sit at the meeting table in Diane's office, ready for their regular one-on-one. Jocelyn is dressed almost exactly like her boss: a bright blazer with a turtleneck, smart black slacks, hip black shoes. She's put-together, with a glossy professional allure. They're joking around, and Jocelyn lets out a deep, surprisingly throaty laugh. Jocelyn was promoted recently to brand manager, up from assistant brand manager. Now she owns the marketing and profit and loss for rinses like Scope and a few "upstream" products in development, as well as a new portfolio, brand architecture. Brand architecture is both creative and analytical. You get to imagine a completely new look and feel for Crest, say, but you have to fit it into a coherent, fully realized strategic framework. What emblems or colors will signify the high-end product? What packaging and tubing will say to the consumer that a product is fun? Where does *fun* fit into the brand attributes we want to hit? How are we positioned against Colgate?

As Jocelyn drafted an architecture for Crest, developing a feel for what would be compelling, impressing A. G. Lafely and other top players, she began to think: "Maybe I'm halfway decent at this stuff." She could admit that she was in fact creative, not just, as she'd once put it, "Forrest Gump dumb-but-lucky." She could admit too that she had some business sense, that her judgment was sound. The butterfly, Diane said, was coming out of the jar.

But the metamorphosis is not yet complete. Jocelyn is prepping today for a Global Franchise Team meeting, an upcoming powwow of twenty executives, all men, who will pepper her about her strategy for a new Crest rinse product. In meetings like this, Diane observes, "every VP becomes an ABM," pretending to know more than you do about the details. The GFT is fraternity hazing plus Supreme Court oral argument: presentations never unfold as planned because random harsh questions start falling like mortars. The self-assurance that Jocelyn exuded as she came in is receding now, as is the sense when they were kidding around that this was a meeting of equals. Jocelyn is nervous; Diane is coaching her. Diane looks over a fifteen-page PowerPoint deck Jocelyn has drafted, and as she flips through she offers a stream of commentary: *Don't give them a chance to wordsmith; lead with "here's our goals for this presentation." Less is more with these guys. I'll open it up and tell them what a star you are. I'll manage the people if they get out of hand; you worry about the substance. Here's who you have to focus on and win over.*

Diane talks and Jocelyn scribbles, and it becomes clear that this is just like the A.G. meeting: a meeting that Diane, as marketing director on the way to general manager/VP status, should be presenting at. Once again, Jocelyn is wondering if she should even be in the room. Once again, Diane is putting her out there to show her she can do it (and to show these guys that Oral Care has brand managers who're as good as most marketing directors). Jocelyn asks whether she should use, as a template, the slides and pitch that Matt had created for a previous GFT meeting. "You should do what works for you, Matt should do what works for him," Diane replies without hesitation. She isn't going to get hung up on format consistency or intellectual elegance. There *is* no standard template. Jocelyn nods. After a few more comments, Diane flips the slide deck shut and with a convincing smile announces, "I think this is fantastic! I'm going to be right there with you." Jocelyn smiles back and lets out a deep breath.

.   .   .

Diane told them, as she always does, that a headhunter had come calling. This one was more serious than the others, though: a big job, a chief marketing officer job for a major global company based in California. She didn't think she'd do it, but you know what, this time she did want to think about it. Everyone on the team buzzed. A couple of them sat down with their spouses, had serious conferences, and knocked on Diane's door the next morning: if she decided to do it, they'd be willing to pick up their families and join her in California. So what if they weren't the ones being offered jobs. So what if the company was a technology company, had nothing to do with packaged consumer goods. They knew they had something good here, something rare, and they'd go West with her to keep it alive. Diane looked at them, stunned.

The world she has made here on the fifth floor is a cocoon, or a womb. It is an unnatural natural thing: something that must be made in order to create and nurture life, and something that must then fall away. It is temporary, a crossing to some other state of being. Even if Diane decides to pass on this job offer, as she ultimately will, it's dawning on everyone that this little family can't stay together forever. Already things are changing. People on the team are getting promoted, some are moving to other divisions, some are going to graduate school. And increasingly, Diane tells the story of the group a new way. She foreshadows the chapters to come. She speaks of the group as an incubator, a seedbed: each of them will leave, in time, join another part of the company, become their best selves, change everyone around them, and in twenty years they will meet again when they are all running a new Procter and Gamble.

Jocelyn knows the time is coming. Every now and then she can feel the chafe. She has her own opinions now, about how to do the work, about strategy, about how Diane should be managing her. A funny example: One night they were all talking about who from human history they'd like to have over for dinner; Jocelyn said Jesus and Hitler, and Diane freaked out—really freaked out—about Hitler, about the very idea of being interested in pure evil. And Jocelyn finally had to say, in a raised voice, "I shouldn't have to explain myself!" She has her own opinions too about what kind of career she wants. She gets invited now to join the VPs for dinner after meetings like the GFT. But now when she asks Diane "Should I go?" she means something other than "Am I worthy?" Diane is a rocket ship, but Jocelyn is not sure she needs to be on board. Title and influence and power are not the measure of her ambition. She wants to do something creative, find satisfaction in the experience, perhaps work abroad.

"I'm sure Diane has a path that she thinks is right for me, something more strategic," Jocelyn muses. "I'm going to have to say I need to go and do different things. And that's going to be a very difficult conversation." She knows she is seen as Diane's protégée. She knows she still relies too much on Diane for the pep talk, the comforting litany, the protective word and gesture. Her goal is to be able to give herself the pep talk. Her goal is to be able to recognize in others what Diane recognized in her. Her goal is to be able to prove that she can do it herself.

But not just yet. Not before she surveys the distance she's traveled. Sometimes, in her office late at night, lost in thought and pulsating with excitement about the Crest architecture or a new idea for selling rinses, Jocelyn will suddenly imagine how surprised her father would be if he could see her at work. He has no concept, really. He doesn't acknowledge being proud of her, and when she goes home she doesn't talk about work much. "It's not the happy ending of hugs and all that," she says, "but that's okay." Sometimes she will indulge a cinematic train of thought, totally corny, but one she keeps returning to. She'll unspool a counterfactual narrative in the style of *It's a Wonderful Life:* What if she'd never met Diane? What if she'd never joined this team? What if she had fled P&G in defeat three years ago? What kind of student, or wife, or daughter would she be now? With what kind of voice? And how, Jocelyn wonders, how would she ever have thought to measure something as flimsy and far away as happiness?

INCH BY INCH

Before Tom Brown entered his life, Quinzzy Pratt would never have acknowledged that he needed rescuing. He relied on no one. He would wake up before five, alone. The buzzing of the alarm would reverberate off the bare walls of the room. There wasn't much furniture. That was okay. He didn't need much. A table. A bed. It was okay because it was all his, no one else to mess with it. Get up, shower. The first order of business, every day, was the newspaper route. Here in Hyattsville, many miles from where he'd come from, the tree-named streets and cul-de-sacs, each only barely different from the last, presented a spaghetti bowl of a map. It had taken him some time to learn that map, but now it was second nature in the undeveloping dark of earliest dawn for Quinzzy to find his way from house to house, to contemplate them from a distance, consider the coziness of a single lamp left on, and throw to those who lived inside—families? happy ones?—this, their daily news. It was fine if he was tired after the paper route because what he had ahead of him was a three-hour bus ride. Actually, two bus rides, the F1 and the B2. To go from the suburbs of Prince George's County, Maryland, to Anacostia, in Southeast D.C., couldn't possibly be as simple as one bus ride. Three hours to catch a few winks, to open a book and do the homework he hadn't had time to do the night before when he got off the swing shift, four to midnight, at the Convention Center. Got to stay on honor roll.

Three hours to look out the window as the sky shed its morning haze and as the landscape faded, the green—the thick tropical green that reminded you, if life wasn't reminder enough, that Washington was in the South—yielding to browns, to grays, to the color of cement. Into the District. The passengers emptied out. Who rode the early bus? Working folks. Who rode the bus deep into Anacostia? Not too many folks. (Even many cabdrivers didn't know the streets in Southeast. Or at least that's what they claimed.) He'd get off the bus and walk a few blocks to the old brick building, a building of a burnt deep red that under other circumstances might look handsome, even dignified. Through the portal he went, putting his bag onto the X-ray machine, walking through the screening machinery like a tourist at a backwater airport. "Good morning students," began a greeting over the PA that was from that point on unintelligible through the static. As the bell for first period rang—not a bell, really, but a high synthesized electronic whine, like a security alarm—Quinzzy Pratt would walk down the wide, gloomy halls of Anacostia Senior High School and find Tom Brown's broken-down old classroom. Those desk/chair contraptions, rigid half-exposed cages of metal and plastic, would be scattered about desultorily. He would sit down, strike the pose of a bored teenager. But inside there would be a stirring; he'd begun to sense something interesting about this class, this man. As Tom acknowledged him, Quinzzy would look up. And at that moment he would utter his first words of this already very old day.

Halfway to Anacostia High School, Tom Brown stops his car in front of a take-out food mart. The gold-green SUV holds Tom's big, softening frame just fine. He double-parks, without blinkers, perfectly unconcerned that he's hogging the middle of the road. What is it here? Is it that Anacostia is a close-knit community where people overlook a double-park because everyone knows everyone else? Or is it that no one enforces the rules here, the big ones, so they figure there's no harm in disregarding the small ones? Inside the Korean-owned market, Tom orders his usual: the special breakfast sandwich, wrapped in wax paper, and a jumbo plastic-foam cup of green tea. Other folks mill about waiting for their orders, African Americans all, old and young, a few on the way to work. Tom looks around, preoccupied, already thinking about class today. It's been a long week. He's had to move from room to room all year. The administration can't get it straight. Once I'd come to see Tom at school and waited in the main office for forty minutes while someone tried, halfheartedly, to locate him. He's had to switch classrooms twice more since then, and each time they move him it seems one or two students leak through, silent casualties of the school's incompetence. There is a culture of no culture here: a building; some people; accidents.

It's odd that someone of such imposing bulk, and such cuddly bald-headed charm, would be reduced to an itinerant, a figment floating in the machinery. Tom works at Anacostia only in the mornings, teaching two periods of a class on how to start and run a business, a class he developed over the last two years with the National Foundation for Teaching Entrepreneurship. Afternoons, he goes to the KIPP Academy, a charter middle school where he's the gym teacher and a beloved figure. KIPP—the Knowledge Is Power Program—is a few blocks from Anacostia High, and is on another planet. Everything at KIPP works. The halls are brightly painted. The children (his youngest son among them) walk purposefully in single file, in colorful school T-shirts. Students who got suspended, rather than being sent home, must sit on the margins of class and are forbidden to speak; the chairs reserved for them tend to be empty. These children test above grade level. They greet the President of the United States for photo ops. They are changelings, thirteen and fourteen and fifteen, and seem an order of magnitude more awake and inquisitive than their siblings at Anacostia High (the kids they are scheduled to become).

Every day, Tom shuttles between these buildings; between these conceptions of what a school for poor black children in one of the most segregated square miles in America can be. A day's circuit takes him through the dimmest quadrants, then back again to a kind of brightness. But what is the sum of all this shuttling? He owns all of it, he knows. He cannot preserve one, call it home, and discard the other. They are both home, both him. The best Tom Brown can do is to be the bridge, reminding himself as he goes that the bridge, often more than the places it connects, will reveal the essence of our travels.

Quinzzy remembers: He took the class for an easy A. Entrepreneurship? How hard could it be? He'd been selling candy since he was nine; sold it right out in front of the high school. He'd figured out multiple ways to earn money. But he was struck by the way Tom spoke to him, in a natural tone, without the distance of authority or station. Tom spoke what Quinzzy imagined to be the language of home. Tom told stories. He was like a motivational speaker, but without the speeches. These children— and technically that is what they were still—these children who sat languidly in class, wearing their baggy jeans and basketball jerseys (but no caps; Mr. Brown made them remove the caps), were all one or zero degrees removed from numbing litanies of familial devastation. Tom did not ignore that. He got their attention by telling the students how screwed up he himself has been. He told them about his crack-addicted father and the shame of seeing his father on TV in a drug bust. He told them about the fight he'd gotten into his last year of high school, just to live up to what he thought the code of the 'hood was; only to get expelled when it turned out the kid he'd beaten was epileptic and had crumpled into seizures. He told them how everyone back on his block, the older jobless men, the weary mothers and grandmothers, had welcomed him back with disgust and disappointment: he was supposed to be the one to break the cycle. He told them about why each one of his prior business ventures had failed: The Shrimp Pimp (the class titters), which brought up fresh shrimp from North Carolina to Southeast D.C., didn't anticipate the huge demand and collapsed; the Request Savings Card, a cooperative purchasing club, suffered from poor market analysis. Quinzzy had never seen a man of Tom's age, a father's age, speak like this of failure and defeat. (And this was just the very surface.) Now he began to see the work as relevant, to who he was and could become. The National Foundation for Teaching Entrepreneurship had developed a remarkable curriculum, about income statements and revenue and expense, about wholesaling and retailing. Quinzzy avidly absorbed all the NFTE (nif-tee) stuff from Tom. What he learned, in the process, was that there might be another being on this planet to whom he could connect.

Tom remembers: At first glance Quinzzy was just another boy, but it became clear almost immediately that he was different. He addressed Tom as "Tom" rather than "Mr. Brown." That took Tom aback, not the insubordination but the child's belief (no insult intended) that they were of equal rank. Tom watched this one closely. As he talked in class about how Bill Gates started Microsoft, about how Ray Kroc made McDonald's, he could see the talent, the skill Quinzzy had for taking the cases and principles and applying them to his own life. The boy was building something in his mind. Quinzzy had an idea, and he started to hang around after class to talk about it. By and by, Tom learned about this boy: that he was asthmatic; that he took two buses to get to school; that he once lived with an absent brother and before that with a grandmother who kicked him out on a cold winter night with just the shirt on his back; that he had raised himself since age fourteen, in an independent living program approved by family court as an alternative to foster care. The more Tom learned, the more he understood. He coached Quinzzy on business, on school, on life. The conversation was the same in each instance: *Set a goal.* I will. *Plan ahead.* I will. He opened a space for Quinzzy, and it did not need to be said. They both were arriving at the same conclusion: *I will save you.*

Everyone hated walking to the Laundromat; trudging all those blocks in the rain and sleet, the flimsy plastic basket grinding against the hip with each step. And yet most everyone had to, because how many people actually had a washer and dryer? So why not create a service to pick up, wash, and deliver the laundry? Old folks, single mothers with too many other things to take care of. Think of all the people who'd rather pay a little extra to have someone else do it. Think of how liberating it would be to not have to do it yourself.

It was ironic that Quinzzy had come up with the idea; he, who had come to do everything himself. But here it was, a niche well found. Now the problem was how and where to begin. How to make it work. Tom helped him think it through. He worked with Quinzzy on naming the elements of a successful business plan, flipping through the NFTE workbooks for the spreadsheets and template documents. The plan was not just the required product of the class; it was something that could be entered into NFTE competitions. Which Laundromat? Who would provide and drive the van? At what cost, in labor and equipment? What would be the fee structure? What would be the profit margin? He stayed nearby as Quinzzy tried to work it all out in one of those dank, echoey classrooms, the cinder block walls festooned with little NFTE posters: "KEEP GOOD RECORDS." "YOUR MARKET is people who might buy your product or service." "For OPERATING COSTS, remember 'USAIIR': Utilities, Salaries, Advertising, Insurance, Interest, Rent." "INCH BY INCH, ANYTHING'S A CINCH." Earlier those slogans and mnemonics had seemed inconsequential, to a motivated student patronizingly obvious and to a hopeless one cruelly irrelevant. No longer. Now those posters were alive, watching.

What Quinzzy realized, as he started putting it together, was that he could not do it alone. Quinzzy was so accustomed to being on his own. He had developed not only the steel of self-reliance but the traps: he did not enjoy, he did not see the need for—indeed, he had learned to fear—any situation where he would have to depend on others. But this business plan would test all that. He would have to persuade potential partners in the neighborhood, the laundries and the car services and so on, why it would be to their benefit to work with him. He would have to talk to potential customers, up and down each block of rundown row houses, about why the time they'd save was worth the money they'd spend. He would have to discover the value of being respectful, even solicitous, to all these strangers, and attend to all the little ways his prickly poise might give offense. He would have to learn, against every impulse he knew, how to ask for help. What Tom realized, as the plan took shape, was that he would have to show the way; that all his life experience seemed written, by a hand greater than his own, to bring him to this point.

Here it all was, then: the failures, the histories, the inescapable destiny. Here, staring up at him from what seemed a cold, practical distance. In a way, he could now see, it was far worse that he'd had ambition, that he'd had enough of a spark to try to better himself. That, it turned out, only sharpened the pain of each setback. Each venture had followed the same pattern: great idea, burst of excitement, overreaching, in over his head. The latest, a concert promotion business, had collapsed of its own weight as well. But this one had gotten ugly. He didn't have the money he owed his partners; he'd been kidnapped at gunpoint, taken all the way to North Carolina (not far, it happens, from where he used to get the shrimp). He survived that, managed to resolve it, but the encounter kicked the bottom out. The businesses had all gone south. His wife had left him. And a wall had come down between him and the world, an imprisoning and measureless depression that swallowed his whole field of vision.

This was foreordained, he knew. As Tom stood on the narrow parapet of the Fourteenth Street Bridge, the crumbling little link between Anacostia and the D.C. of lore, of power and awed tourists and grand dreams, he thought of his uncle. Michael Harper, his mother's youngest brother, had been a father to him. Michael, the can-do uncle, the one who'd taught himself to read, was where he got the entrepreneurial bug from. It was his uncle's freelance moving company that Tom had worked for after the air force, after Hampton College. The same uncle who'd tried to start an exterminating business, then a tow-truck company. Michael had never said *Be like me.* He didn't need to. It was understood. Tom would be his partner and protégé; Michael would be Tom's biggest champion. But his uncle's businesses never lasted. His marriage fell apart. He alienated his family, falling out with Tom over, of course, a busted business deal. He became consumed by drugs. At thirty-six, Michael took his own life. That was only a few months ago. And here, here on the bridge as the wind stung his face, Tom was preparing to follow in his uncle's footsteps.

But now he heard the helicopter. He saw the camera protruding from the bay of the chopper before a blinding spotlight swept over him, and now a different feeling descended upon him. Shame. Shame over shame over shame. He looked down and made out a motorboat. Now, to his left and to his right he saw the uniforms. The police had come, the television news had come, the divers had come. Not even this worked out right. He heard the cops talking to him, and it began, the courting, the coaxing. It was hard to hear, but harder still to listen. He couldn't process what they were saying to him. The thunderous grind, his whole recursive life drawing in upon itself, was too great. Nothing got through to him until, minutes or hours or days into the ordeal, he heard one of the cops say it: "The Lord is not finished with your life yet."

That's what Tom Brown remembers most distinctly. The rest was a blur: coming off the bridge, the grip of those gently coaxing cops now deadly firm; being rushed to St. Elizabeth's for psych evaluation, then the next day to D.C. General, where he'd once worked the late shift to earn a paycheck, and where his former coworkers now saw him wrapped in a straitjacket; coming home to stay with his mother; laying low in her house, fearing the averted or pitying eyes in the neighborhood, for everyone knew he'd tried; hiding, and hiding; and at last acknowledging that awaiting him were a daughter of seven and a son of four, and knowing then that he had to snap out of his stupor.

Within two months, as Tom tells it, a new business idea had seized him, the Request Savings Card. He and a friend spent the next four years, till 1999, consumed by this venture, a fund-raising club through which preferred merchants gave discounts that put money into savings accounts for college or charity or whatever. It was a sophisticated idea. It failed, just too much for two of them to pull off, and the cycle seemed set to start again. But he had returned to the church after the bridge, had in fact become ordained in '97, and this time the bulwark—the faith and responsibility both—steadied him. It was time to get a regular job, he decided, and from there things began to flow in a way they never had before. That summer he was asked to run a workshop at a camp for inner-city teen entrepreneurs. He loved it, discovered a talent for speaking to these young souls. Then he bumped into an acquaintance, a local bank executive and a graduate of Anacostia High School, and the banker suggested that Tom check out NFTE. Tom did, and he loved it: the discipline, the system, the implied promise of self-improvement. Soon the banker decided to underwrite a NFTE after-school program at Anacostia for Tom to run. The next year, the program became part of the day curriculum. The year after that, Tom was named one of the best NFTE teachers in the country. The fall after that—two years into the teaching, six years after his walk on the bridge—Tom looked over his new class and saw that a gentle, wary, big-framed young man named Quinzzy had enrolled.

When he was nine, Quinzzy and his brother made a pact: they would take care of themselves and each other, they would steer clear of the drugs and drinking destroying their family, and they would finish high school. The spring of junior year, Quinzzy took his laundry delivery service business plan to the NFTE regional competition. He stood in his borrowed suit, before executives and lawyers and bankers, and made a solid presentation, a PowerPoint he and Tom had toiled over. He took second place and he was proud. Now Tom was helping him make it happen, trying to raise the money to get the thing started for real.

That fall, he moved in with Tom. It was senior year at last. Tom had remarried, and with his kids, his wife's kids, and now Quinzzy, there were seven children in the house, from three to seventeen. Quinzzy had never been in a household where someone asked about your well-being, told you to do your homework, got on you about slacking off. Tom was all over his sons and daughters, and as Quinzzy watched them, he could not help thinking of his brother, who'd started with weed and gone downhill from there, and he would tell his new siblings-of-a-sort how lucky they were that someone was riding them so hard. Tom knew those kids would listen more to Quinzzy, their new eldest brother, than they would to him. And Quinzzy could feel it emanating from Tom, this regard; this expectation. One time he and Tom's son got into a fistfight over something stupid, and Tom chastised him, in sorrow rather than anger. *I open my door to you and make this a family and I can't leave without you being responsible. If this was your household what would you do?* And Quinzzy just shut up, because Tom was right. He had a responsibility now, to Tom, to himself, to everyone.

He'd changed so much. He'd become less antisocial, he admitted. He'd become more planful, less impetuous. But he still needed Tom, he realized. He still had the impulses that needed curbing. The spring of senior year, his brother, now living down in Fayetteville, got in an argument with his wife and they left their toddlers in the car on a hot afternoon and one of the kids had died of heatstroke and seizure. First thing Quinzzy did was try to scrape up every penny he could to catch a Greyhound to see his brother. And Tom stopped him. *What are you doing? Be rational.* They made a plan. Tom would miss work and they would drive to Fayetteville together. They spent four days there. They saved a lot of money and time that way. Mainly, Quinzzy said, Tom's presence just soothed him. "Whenever anything happens," he said, "I look for Tom. He tells me to slow down, calm down. First thing he does, he gives me a story from his life. And I listen to him, and after a while I know I'm going to be okay, like Tom is okay now."

Until the NFTE experience, Quinzzy had never seen himself as college material. But here he was, at Johnson C. Smith College in Charlotte, North Carolina. Here he was, at a fabled historically black college, so far

from the bus line from Hyattsville and Anacostia, crossing green quadrangles to class, writing papers on the IBM laptop that every student re-
ceived, planning to major in criminal justice or maybe management. He
and Tom had found a program through which Child and Family Services
would pay for his first two years of school. After that, it'd be up to him.
Tom talked to him on the phone almost every day. He was still teaching,
two classes a day, but now he had other plans too. He had a dream to
build a continuing education center for NFTE graduates, offering in-
ternships and extra classes for young people who want to develop business ideas for the neighborhood. He was thinking it'd have a coffee shop,
maybe a day care.

That November a shooting in front of the school left a boy named
Deven dead. The boy, a sophomore, had had nothing to do with gangs.
He just happened to be standing there when someone, in retaliation for
something, retrieved a .44 stashed away in a hole on school grounds and
started firing at someone else. The boy was going to be in Tom's class the
next semester. The Monday after the incident Tom gave his class a chance
to vent. They were preparing that week for a field trip to the wholesale
markets in New York, and Tom spoke with them about Deven's death;
about the future; about getting a ticket out of Anacostia, a chance to de-
part, and maybe come back someday and be part of the solution.

This, in fact, is Quinzzy's plan. College is an adjustment, but he
knows he can adjust. He has the skills now, the PowerPoint and computer
know-how, the public speaking, the good study habits. He knows how to
navigate the bureaucracy. He knows how to take care of himself. What he
doesn't know, for so long hasn't needed to know, is what to do with the
ache you get when you see your roommates and classmates with their parents and uncles and grandparents and you realize, at least for that moment, that you are alone. That your aloneness sets you apart. Quinzzy
had heard about the shooting back at Anacostia, of course, and it led him
to think of Tom, to consider the abyss his life might have fallen into;
could still, with so little warning. "If there was no Tom, I'd be . . . I don't
even want to think about it," he says. "And I don't want to think about the
fact he won't be around forever either." A chill tightens his voice. "What I
don't think about don't bother me." It is mid-November and what
Quinzzy thinks about, as he sits in the library at all hours, is how Tom
will not be happy unless he gets his grades up. He thinks about whether

the laundry service is something he could make happen next summer. He thinks about the sounds of all those siblings running around Tom's house. He thinks of Tom shaving his head on a Saturday morning. He sees that little patch on the back of the neck that Tom always misses. It's a couple of weeks to Thanksgiving. Quinzzy will be home soon enough.

THE FEEL TEACHER

His entire life, Eric Barnhill had tried to keep it together. And he had. He had willed himself to walk a certain way, to talk a certain way. But he sensed something long before he could say it: that eventually, he would have to let things fall apart. And he would need someone to show him how.

A studio in New York City. By the end, Eric was sweating, nearly out of breath. His hands were locked in stiff aggression, the pads of his fingertips flattened into submission. The tremors emanating from the piano's open cavity of cords echoed throughout the studio. He stood up, pushing back the bench, and lorded over the instrument, over the music staring back at him. Ha! Nothing Chopin could throw at him, none of the acrobatics Tchaikovsky or Rachmaninoff required, could stop Eric today. These concertos were nothing if not muscular, and practicing them—practicing eight, nine hours a day—was downright athletic. He had lifted a great weight today, more than ever before.

This is what Juilliard had taught him. This is what Juilliard had made of him. He was a pianist who knew how to attack, treating every piece that came his way as something to dominate. To control. For so long, well before Juilliard, he had kept things in check, had by force of will converted his least controllable impulses, the random electrical charges that sent gestures flying from his limbs and spasms across his face, into a single powerful current. Sometimes, like today, that current was the full measure of Eric's expression, and he could launch it like a lightning bolt and smash right through the composition. Other times, though, he was in terror that things could fall apart at any moment. And the control he exercised became so overpowering, it so overcompensated for the tics and fidgets and the sheer *speed* of everything threatening to escape his body, that he played as if he and the piano alike were crammed into a tiny box.

Now Eric's breath returned, and the sweat gleaming on his forehead began to evaporate. His thoughts cooled, and as the feeling returned to his fingertips, he asked: Is this all that Juilliard has taught me? Is this what Juilliard has made of me? He had fought his way through so much to reach this point, but the result was that he played music—indeed, lived life—as if he were constantly fighting his way through something. His jaw, his fingers, his brow, his shoulders: cramped. And yet his mind, his dreams, his spirit: yearning to be unclenched, free. There was a teacher at Juilliard he had heard of, Bob Abramson, reputed to have a gift for liberation, for making freedom safe, even necessary. Some of his former classmates swore by Bob. It was time, Eric decided, to see what this Bob Abramson was like, what he might do to harness—or was it to unharness?—all the tumult and sensation and impulse swirling within.

Bob Abramson uses someone's sneakers to mark the middle of the floor. At one end of the long, narrow dance studio half the class stands in a line; at the other end, the other. Everyone is in socks. Bob stands at the piano and plays a mincing little melody, playfully accelerating and decelerating. The two lines of students (and I, for he has roped me in) tiptoe toward the middle, speeding or slowing to the music. With a few yards to go, his fingers suddenly storm across the keys, sending the two lines into a sprint. He stops at the last possible second, and so do we, sliding into one another on the hardwood, noses nearly touching, the exuberance of it all surprising us—thrilling us!—as we teeter breathlessly.

In the room are about twenty-five people, from their twenties to their sixties: musicians and dancers; students and graduates of Juilliard, the Manhattan School of Music, the Tisch School; music teachers from all five boroughs. Another way to put it: in the room are twenty-five children. We are at play, remembering a language of movement we have not spoken since kindergarten. Still another way to put it: in the room are twenty-five converts. This is a reprogramming camp, compulsory re-education. This is phys ed. Bob Abramson is not a gym teacher; he is a *feel* teacher. His job is to restore to his students—musicians mainly, though over the decades he has worked with the Oklahoma University football team, trial lawyers, painters, neurosurgeons—a sense of their senses. The method he uses, eurhythmics, was developed by a nineteenth-century Swiss musician named Émile Jaques-Dalcroze, and it teaches people to move their bodies anew, to excavate their primal ability to connect sensation and expression. To find and release their inner musician.

As we move around the studio, responding to his directions, we listen intently. Bob's voice rarely rises above a labored whisper, the result of smoking and major throat surgery. Hearing him on the phone when we first spoke, I pictured an ailing, bedridden man tethered to a respirator. What I found, when we met, was a sixty-nine-year-old who dances and prances like a boy, a campy performer who plays his one remaining vocal cord like an instrument of great range and sonority. Mostly, though, he chooses to be silent. He makes stylized hand and wrist gestures like a Balinese dancer. He flops and bends like a vaudevillian. He wriggles his brow and lips, his full complement of facial muscles, like a newborn testing all systems. He regulates the flash and light of his eyes like a naval Morse code operator manipulating mirrors. The more I watch him, the more I realize that this man's office is not the airy dance studio we stand in now or the crowded apartment where he conducts private lessons. Bob Abramson's office is his own *body,* each limb and line containing every possible form of human articulation; each pose calculated to draw us into heightened awareness. Wherever he walks, this man makes a classroom.

One of the first things Bob had to do was teach Eric how to walk. Hard enough that he was a prim, inhibited Midwesterner. Even tougher that he was a Type-A Juilliard product. But he also had been wrestling with Tourette's syndrome since childhood. Eric walked stiffly, in fear of chaos, with a pole up his butt, Bob thought. Bob zeroed in on this, and figured it would be as good a place to start as any. He began by teaching Eric to swivel his hips, something men under most circumstances aren't shown to do, at least in a school setting. He did this by telling Eric to pretend he had a piece of chalk tucked into his belly button. Good. Now go up to the blackboard to write your name. *What?* First in print. Then in cursive. Eric looked at him, comprehending but not quite wanting to admit it. Bob wordlessly egged him on, with an illustrative thrust of the pelvis and dip of the knees. And to the front of the invisible classroom walked the student, pressing the chalk to the board, pulling it slowly across the slate.

The very first time Eric went to Bob's Thursday morning eurhythmics class, he was marching around the room with the group, doing a rhythm exercise. Bob silently watched one circuit. Then, as Eric passed again, Bob forced out a few words over the raspy frequency of his exhalations: "You're too careful. [inhale] Too afraid you're going to fuck up. [inhale] Let go more." It was bracing, the way Bob had come at him hard without warning, after only thirty minutes. "He had already sensed that with me there was no need to sugarcoat," Eric recalls, "and that the F-word would help to wake me up, and I would respect that I was getting honest advice, without putting me off. I am quite certain all these aspects were quite conscious on his part."

Another time, Bob asked Eric for a long step, a fencing lunge. In front of the class he called, "Eric, I want your ding-dong to hang down!" (He said "ding-dong," with uncharacteristic politeness, because there were guests present.) The image had the desired effect: Eric's stride lengthened dramatically. But as Eric wrote to me later, "Lest the class think this was a frivolity, he talked shortly afterwards about the broader picture here, how I needed to learn to walk like a big cowboy, and that this is a style of movement that had its counterpart in music. And he's right: there's music where to capture the spirit, you have to know what it's like to throw your dick around." He added: "Also everyone thought it hilarious." Eric Barnhill was learning what it feels like to walk.

Eric's teacher at Juilliard had been a good person and a stunningly good pianist, but someone to whom piano playing came so easily that he had a difficult time relating to someone of lesser ability. Juilliard, like all the top-tier conservatories, attracts and produces students of incredible technical virtuosity. It feeds and feeds off a brittle culture, prevalent in elite music-making, of surface perfectionism: at auditions and competitions young musicians are critiqued on minor deviations from the score—on their errors—rather than on their capacity for telling a story with the music; rather than, God forbid, on their power to create beauty. As if figure skating judges were to offer only technical scores and no artistic ones. All this focus on technique, of course, never accounts for the simple question Bob Abramson asks: *Why?* Why do you play? To please whom?

When Bob saw what Eric Barnhill, M.A., Juilliard 1998, was capable of technically—the muscularity, the aggressive brilliance—he knew this would make things only more difficult. First came reintroducing the boy to his kinesthetic self: to the walking; the ability to express a crescendo or a diminuendo in the length of his stride; the ability to use his hands to replicate the rhythm of his name—e-ric BARN-hill, pop-pop-POP-pop—by clapping, by rubbing a sofa, by snapping, by flicking a finger. Now came the truly tricky part: teaching the boy to meet his mistakes; to welcome them and get to know them. It would all have to unfold in stepwise fashion, even though to Eric it would have to appear random. For the idea of *embracing* error was too direct, too frontal an assault on the bastions of high academic conservatory training. The traditional methods have as their locomotive force the power of moral judgment. *You are bad if you play badly: you are lazy or undedicated or weak.* Bob has many students who, as they play for him and flub a note or botch a chord, will mumble "sorry." And Bob will ask them, as they play, "Who you talkin' to? Is someone on your shoulder?" And they will smile nervously, keep playing—and keep on saying "sorry" as they play.

So he gave Eric exercises that he'd *have* to screw up. Little exercises, like what you'd do with preschoolers. Drawing a triangle in the air with one hand while drawing a circle or a line or a square with the other. Disordination, he calls it. Making Eric clap along while Bob played the piano—and then stopped—and then started—then stopped. Eric had to, after a while, laugh. To laugh at his mistakes. And then Bob began to train Eric to keep on playing. Whenever Eric played a piece, he had the habit of stopping after a mistake, resetting, then picking up from there. Bob broke him of the habit, demanded that Eric keep playing, no matter what the error, that he remain in the stream of unconsciousness that ran beneath the notes.

Not long after I'd met Bob, I went to visit a class. A student sitting at the piano was playing a Bach sonata. He played like a robot, literally: every note was struck accurately and none was articulated with spirit. The grammar was correct, the phonemes pitch-perfect, and all of it devoid of meaning, pacing, color, nuance. It.was.as.if.the.notes.were.written.like.this. "Phonics without rhythm," Bob huffed. "It's like you've forgotten how to breathe." The student blushed, tried again. Failed. That poor kid left an impression, and made me realize that Bob's criticisms of conservatory-trained musicians were not hyperbole. It wasn't until a year later that I saw that student again, and was introduced to him formally. Eric Barnhill. Bob was following the boot camp plan: break down the recruit to build him back up. By now, Eric was already in the midst of the reconstitution. He was still struggling, to be sure. Still trying to form a pattern from the fragments of experience, of sensation, that Bob was throwing at him; trying to make them cohere into a philosophy of learning. But he knew his work now. He reflected on this, with a knowingness that still seemed freshly issued: "Once you get to a certain point of proficiency," he said, "what you can and can't do musically is directly related to what you can and can't do as a person."

You can see it in the way Bob teaches now—the stretch, the reach, the strain of being the living bridge. You can hear it in what he spends more and more of class time talking about. First principles of Dalcroze. Not so much of the technique or the exercises. Increasingly, Bob's classes are imaginary dialogues. He pretends he is a parent, or a principal. He asks his students to tell him about the plight of children today, about the need to explain Dalcroze's theories to a general public. First principles: *music is life, everything you do is music, feel the rhythm in every gesture.* He tries to draw it out of them, like Socrates. He has to. What will happen when he's not around anymore? Who will defend Dalcroze? There are already too many people who think it's kids' stuff. They have no idea their humanity is at stake. They have no idea what they cannot feel. Even within the Dalcroze community there are some now who question whether there is truly a method there. What insolence! He has studied the writings more than anyone alive. He has done more to spread and revive the gospel of eurhythmics across the continents. And there is so much more to do. For so long he has been the guardian, the one who could span the eras. But will anyone want to enter this realm when he is gone? There is so much more to do.

Too excited everything spilling out all at once fast getting faster his voice his thoughts. Always had been this way. He'd learned to deal with it. No, that's not it, quite. He had known nothing else. As a boy he was diagnosed, but what was that going to change? It was a diagnosis, mild. He and his parents thought he'd grow out of it. Never medicated. Never had therapy. Stuttered at five, probably related. Didn't grow out of it. In a sense, he grew *into* it, filled the mold as it was given. The wiring of his brain, the electric grid, maybe it was off somehow, maybe it sent some quarters of town blinking like a strobe and left others dark and others lit twenty-four/seven: but that was the city he would learn to walk. He tightened his jaw, forced out his words, held his back straight. And he walked.

Now, he asserts, it's hard to tell he has Tourette's at all. And it's true: I would not have guessed it when I first met him. At the same time, he did strike me from the start as intensely coiled, his diction and presentation studied and precise, his pate and palms adew with the sweat of unseen exertion. He crackled with a subdermal nervous energy that in trying to hide itself only announced itself. But with Bob and the Dalcroze exercises sending a different kind of magnetic force through him, realigning the polarity of his muscles, his nerves—down, it seemed, to his cells—there was more stillness, and now Eric was able to do something new. The speed remained; you could hear it in his speech. But now he could split his attention. He could cleave off a quiet space apart from the buzzing. He could keep one eye on himself, on his balance; find a neutral reference point.

The achievement of consciousness; the interior diplomacy that made self-awareness his ally and agent rather than a hostile insurgent—this was great progress. The next phase of work that he and Bob were entering was about liberation. Improvisation. All the way through the nineteenth century it was common practice in teaching a piece to ask the student to make up his own. "Make me a happy piece, a troubled one, a piece about Romeo and Juliet," Bob tells it. "And they could do it." In classical music the skill of invention fell away as the cult of technical virtuosity ascended.

(In jazz, of course, it lives still.) Dalcroze says little about improvisation, so Bob has had to take what he can find, plus ideas from the Baroque, when the lowliest church organist could riff for hours, and ideas from modern dance and theater, and bring it all to his students.

First Bob had helped Eric rediscover his limbs, the sense that movement and meaning are connected; that music is the movement of sound. Now it was time to rediscover his inner ear. No repertoire for a year, Eric decided; back to square one. Today he spends three hours a day on musical games and exercises. He takes a headline in the *Times* and tries to convey its rhythm and mood on the piano. He'll bang out the cadence of his name in random chords, and by adding my name or Bob's or anyone else's, presto, he is creating a kind of song. He practices sight-singing, something he'd never done before. He'll take a tune he heard in the cab and try playing it in every key. It is radical: a professional pianist, at the stage in his career when he should be deepening his repertoire, adding to the list of great concertos he has mastered, deciding instead to play games all day. But he knows this is not frivolity; it's about becoming a performer. Bob will give him a piece he's played hundreds of times before, a Bach two-part invention, say, and ask him to make new versions. Add a trill, an ornament. Extend a motif, rewrite it. Play with it. Like blocks. Build a teetering tower and knock it over. Eric hesitates, flubs it, but Bob joyfully praises his mistakes—they too are invention—and the more Eric experiments, the more aware he becomes of the composer's intentions. He senses what the composer was trying to say, and what *he* must now try to say to an audience. It's this: *Feel it.* What do you have right now? Not what are you trying to accumulate, what does your résumé list, what does everyone think. What can you do *right now* with what you've got? This moment—experience—is not ephemeral; it is all you have. It is all you are.

"Question: How do you get someone's attention?"

The way Bob asks it is, of course, part of the answer. But no words are allowed now. The spirit of a five-year-old suddenly inhabits Bob; his shoulders and face slump into stupor, his bored gaze drifts across the ceiling. Eric starts to answer the question and Bob cuts him off—"Don't talk to me! Use your—" and he points to his eyes, his hands, his huge ears. He puts a smile on, coaxing the comprehension out. Now Eric tries again. He walks to the piano and plays a tune, then stops. Then starts. Then stops again, all out of sync with the expected phrasing and pauses. Bob perks up, nodding vigorously. He is pleased. "How do you know what you already know? That's the first problem of teaching," Bob says. Eric now has begun to teach Dalcroze classes to children, and he's come to the apartment an hour early, before Bob's weekly class for educators, to seek out some counseling. Early on Eric played a game with the children called "the candle melts." Instead of doing a musically analogical thing, like playing a slowly descending scale, he produced one big crash of notes; the kids, confused, just fell to the ground. And Eric was confused as well, not understanding at first how his choice of improvisation had killed the exercise. "Remember this rule," Bob says. "It's always the teacher's fault."

Twice a week now Eric takes a train out to Long Island and works with twelve Alzheimer's patients in a nursing facility. At first only three of them seemed at all present. The others were in a daze, or at best, totally off-rhythm, as if listening and responding underwater. Eric didn't rely just on Dalcroze drills—he borrowed from the Feldenkrais method, a therapy of extremely slow physical motions; from martial arts; from traditional Chinese concepts of *qi,* or breath. Through trial and error he started to find pathways that could reach his distant students. He would conduct a phrase, giving them five different ways to say "Good afternoon" together. He discovered he could get them clapping by standing in front of them and clapping, but once he moved over to the piano they'd stop. So he tried to get them to clap on without him—calling out, "Clap/clap/keep it/going"—and they made the transition. Gradually he removed that scaffold altogether. "The goal is to take away the model," he said. Now, after only four months, all twelve of his elderly, childlike students have awakened. Now they clap in time. Their lips move as he counts. They can keep their left and right straight. Now they retain ideas from class to class. Now some who have been silent for years, their tongues stilled by the darkening, will experience sudden verbal outbursts: a flash of light; an echo of Eric's own Tourette's, but something here to celebrate.

As his teaching takes him farther afield, Eric spends less and less time studying with Bob. He perceives, without words being exchanged, that Bob is not pleased. What can he say? Bob's Dalcroze classes, though powerful, are meant for novices. But there's something else too. Bob's dedication to the method, to the sacred principles, to the milking of every last moment and gesture and phenomenon, is so all-consuming, so total, that it can be a bit oppressive. So much obligation. Eric knows there's so much more he has to work on still, as a student, a teacher, a student of teaching. He needs to be able to make an audience feel like moving, he has to get kids to want to hop and gallop. He needs to be able to read a story to children using wildly different voices, and to play the piano the same way. Eric knows. He can hear his teacher saying it. "Bob has given me my fundamental orientation," he says. Now it's time to feel his way forward.

AMENDMENT

The lights were so hot. How had I never noticed them before? Now they were all I could see. They bore down on me from the gallery, producing an accusatory, burning white beam. The whole of the room, the ornate ceiling, the ancient wooden desks, the American flags and the plush navy blue carpet, the wainscoting, the great seal, the men in fine dark suits, the whispering tourists above, all seemed to be closing in on me, liquefying, converging as if down a drain: the drain, my throat; my mouth hanging dumbly open.

"You did take care of that, didn't you, Eric?" the senator asked, a little loudly.

He was standing. I was seated, like a schoolboy, next to his desk. It had been Harry Truman's desk, Huey Long's desk, and now David Boren's desk. All their initials were carved inside. He'd once shown me this, with childlike, conspiratorial wonder. "You took care of that, didn't you, before we came down here?" His eyes widened. I was silent, but my boss and I both knew the answer.

Just hours earlier I'd had it all figured out. I was a brand-new legislative assistant in Boren's office. I'd just come from the staff of the Intelligence Committee, where he was chairman and I'd been a research assistant. Now I was in charge of foreign policy for one of the most respected members of the United States Senate. I had recently turned twenty-three.

There were six legislative assistants, or LAs. We shared a single office, three desks down one side and three down the other. We didn't feel cramped, partly because of the high ceilings and windows, partly because the commotion was part of the appeal. Phones were ever ringing and the TV was always on, showing CNN or C-SPAN's live feed from the Senate floor (hence the bright lights). We were all young, especially by Senate staff standards. The office of Daniel Patrick Moynihan, the legendary New York senator and fellow Democrat, was next door. His aides generally had fifteen years and several advanced degrees on us. But we got at least as much done. We took pride in being a young, smart, aggressive team. Boren knew what he was getting. He was happy to trade our youthful inexperience for our youthful intensity and resourcefulness.

Each of us sat at our desks, working the phones, cajoling a colleague from another office, laughing loudly at a joke, listening to the appeals of a lobbyist or a constituent. Each of us, that is, except for me. I was still the new guy. I didn't have a Rolodex yet. I was not in on the inside jokes. I watched them work. In this room of smooth-talking, shrewd Oklahomans, I was a wonky Yankee and a Yalie. The only obvious thing we had in common was our employer, a smooth-talking, shrewd Oklahoman *and* a Yalie.

One morning I was at my desk, quietly reading a report, when the phone rang. It was the senator's intercom line. I cleared my throat and picked up the phone. "Eric, how're youuuu?" Boren said, in his pleasantly orotund accent.

"Hi, Boss," I said. We all called him that.

"Eric," he said, "I was talking to Sam today, and we were worrying about the winter the Soviets have ahead of them."

"Uh-huh," I said. Sam was Sam Nunn, I deduced, a Democrat from Georgia, chair of the Armed Services Committee. It was November 1991. The USSR was on the brink of disintegration. Gorbachev had barely survived a coup attempt and the country now faced a winter of privation and political uncertainty.

"And we were thinking," Boren continued, "that we need to do something to provide for the people there. To make sure there isn't the kind of chaos that could make things worse. We should be sending humanitarian aid."

"That's a great idea, Boss," I said, cringing immediately. What a lame thing to say.

"So we agreed we'd offer an amendment to the defense appropriations bill that's on the floor now. We want to set aside two hundred million dollars to airlift emergency food and medicine into the country. I think we can get some other cosponsors. Do you think you can draw that up by three today?"

"You bet," I replied, with false cheer. I hung up the phone. My pulse pounded. I looked around. Everyone was doing their own thing. No one had any idea that I had no idea what to do next. Good. This is the way I wanted it. I was supposed to be the smarty-pants. I'd been eyed a little warily when I arrived, and no one had offered to show me the ropes. I sure wasn't going to admit that I needed help. That wasn't my way. I was going to prove that I was worthy. I was going to do it on my own.

I set to work. First I took a cut at writing the amendment myself. I took out a *Congressional Record* and looked at other recent amendments. When I had a rough sketch, I gave it to Legislative Counsel, the office that draws up or revises proposed legislation for all the senators. I told them how urgent it was, then set about looking to collect cosponsors. I thought about whom to seek out. First other names in foreign affairs: Lugar, Bradley, Dole, Pell. Then some other respected members from both parties: Republicans like Cohen and Rudman, Democrats like Lieberman and Levin. For the first time, I was working the phones. I called my counterparts in other offices, laid out the amendment, cajoled them into signing on for their bosses.

Boren called me about two hours in to see how it was going. Great, I said, everything's under control. I suggested that we make this a Boren-Cohen amendment, rather than Boren-Nunn, so as to have bipartisan lead sponsorship. Good idea, he said. Leg Counsel got back to me with the appropriate legislative language. And when three o'clock approached, I was feeling pretty proud of myself. I had a very official-looking amendment in my hand, with fourteen A-list cosponsors, and this little piece of legislation was going to do a lot of good in the world. I'd written a nice floor speech for Boren and as we strode purposefully down the marble corridors and bustling tunnels from the Russell Building to the Capitol, I felt like I was floating a foot off the ground.

We got to the Senate chamber and waited while other amendments worked their way up for consideration. I'd been on the floor once or twice before, but just to deliver a document, never as the aide on the line. Boren dropped me off at the chair beside his desk and went to chitchat with his colleagues. I took in the view. It was awesome. Senators, the great gods of American politics, walked all around me in their calm, unperturbable way. I was more thrilled, more nervous than I'd ever been. My palms and soles were icy and damp.

Then it was Boren's turn. He rose, and began reading the speech I'd written. "Mr. President," he said, "the distinguished senator from Maine and I offer the following amendment today. . . ." I sat beside him, looking up occasionally as he spoke, scanning the room. "These conditions could lead to the return of hostile, anti-American leaders in the Soviet Union . . ." This was history in the making, I thought. Boren spoke of how the measure would authorize up to two hundred million dollars. At this, three heads from across the chamber suddenly swiveled in our direction. The heads belonged to James Sasser, Democrat from Tennessee and chair of the Budget Committee, and his two senior aides. Sasser listened to a few more of the Boss's words, and then, unbelievably, he began to gesticulate. He waved both hands sideways, catching Boren's eye. Boren's speech grew a little uncertain, but he kept reading. When Sasser began to pull a finger across his throat repeatedly, signaling either *Stop!* or, it seemed from the look in his eyes, *I will kill you!,* Boren stopped cold. He asked for a quorum call, a parliamentary time-out, and Sasser marched over.

"David, what in God's name do you think you're doing?" Sasser hissed.

"Well, Jim, I, it's an amendment to provide emergency aid to the Soviets," Boren said. This was the first time I had ever seen him flustered.

"I *know* that. I mean, what do you think you're doing offering this up without clearing it with me first?"

The idea that ignorance is bliss is so terribly misleading. It's bliss while it lasts. But no one gets to stay ignorant forever. And the longer it takes to end, the more painful the result. Boren looked down at me and back up at Sasser. "What do you mean?" he asked.

"I mean," Sasser said acidly, "that you don't have authorization to break the caps." What his words meant was, "You are attempting to take more cookies from the jar than we are allowed." What the acid meant was, "You damn fool. Nobody circumvents process like this." Sasser added, "This is the first I've heard of this amendment." I was now acutely aware of the lights. "Nobody from your staff," he said past me, "ever cleared this with us."

Boren's eyes begged me for reassurance: *Please, please don't tell me you made such a gigantic mistake. Please don't tell me you've sent me out like this before all my colleagues.* What could I say? I'd been too proud to seek guidance. I'd been too afraid to appear uncertain or to admit weakness. Now my world was about to collapse, completely. My bright shining career was about to shrink to the dark density of a black hole.

And then Senator Byrd arrived. As I remember it, he didn't have wings. But in every other respect, as Robert Byrd approached us, he was like an angel descending from heaven. Byrd, the iconic senior senator from West Virginia, master of obscure Senate rules, partial to old-fashioned hour-long floor speeches that mixed homespun witticisms with the history of the Roman republic, was the all-powerful chairman of the Appropriations Committee. The cookie jar that Sasser was defending so vigorously was really Byrd's. As Boren and Sasser and Sasser's aides stood in a circle arguing about the situation, and as I stood among them helplessly, Byrd hovered. He listened closely. Just when it seemed Sasser was about to administer the death blow, Byrd draped one arm over Sasser's shoulder and one over Boren's. He leaned in; instinctively, we did too. He eyed Sasser and his aides and whispered, "Let's see what we can do to help David fix this one." Then he drifted away.

It took me a moment to understand, but Sasser's men got it immediately. The looks they shot me said it all. An ignorant newcomer—a *kid*—had broken the most basic rules, and now, on Byrd's word, not only was he going to live; he was going to be rewarded. Sasser shook his head slowly with a forced smile. His men grimaced, suppressing their annoyance. But they were professionals, and after a moment they conferred in code on the proper fix.

For the next fifteen minutes the five of us huddled over Boren's desk on the floor of the Senate and furiously rewrote the amendment. One of Sasser's men ran over to get some boilerplate language for us to insert.

He dictated, and Boren himself began scribbling on a separate sheet of paper, which he then tore off: "The Congress designates all funds in this Section as 'emergency requirements' for all purposes of the Balanced Budget and Emergency Deficit Control Act of 1985. . . ." I noticed that one of the changes he'd made needed to be repeated in another section, so I scribbled some words in as well. When we were done we had a three-page document that was the typographical equivalent of uncased sausage. We handed the mess to the clerk. Boren resumed his speech and asked for a roll call vote. As other members strolled in, Boren again left me at his desk so he could gather up votes. Amendment 1441 was approved 87 to 7.

As we walked back to Boren's office afterward, he was in a fine mood. He greeted passersby and chatted about other ideas he had for legislation and what else he had on his schedule that week. I was pretty quiet. I figured this was the way executions happened in Washington: with a smile.

Four days passed and I hadn't been fired or even reprimanded. On the fifth day there was a long, flat package on my desk, wrapped in brown paper. I carefully opened it. It was the three pages of the amendment put under glass, framed handsomely and inscribed: "To Eric— Congratulations on your performance during your baptism under fire—David Boren." Beneath his signature, he added, "87–7 isn't bad on your first outing." The other LAs came to my desk and were impressed. They patted me on the back. They ribbed me. *Don't think you're gonna get one of these every time something passes!* The next day, the lead LA announced that the Boss wanted all staff, no matter how senior, to take a review course on the ins and outs of the budget and appropriations process. I scanned the room but no one was staring at me. A couple of LAs nodded, as if admitting they could use the refresher.

When I saw the Boss later that day, I thanked him for the gift. I left tacit the other 95 percent of my gratitude. "I'm proud of you," he said, smiling. From that day, I was unafraid to ask questions—of him or my fellow staffers—and to admit when I thought I could use a hand. I was in a safe space now. I could dispense with the façade and put aside the anxiety about proving myself: my failure that day, and the way he'd turned it into a work of art, proved enough. Two years later I would leave Washington to go to law school. Two years after that David Boren would leave as well, retiring from the Senate to become president of Oklahoma University.

Since then he has likely had many students like me; I can say with certainty I have not had another teacher like him. The inscription is fading now and so that framed amendment no longer hangs on my wall. But I carry it around in my head, and now whenever I step into an unfamiliar chamber, the memory of it is enough to calm my pounding pulse.

CHORALE 2

Unblock, Unlock

What keeps so many people from learning—learning *anything*—is not their ineptitude or deficits of talent. It is their insecurity. They assume they are inherently unable to do something or to be someone. They fear failure and humiliation. They cannot imagine that growth or change could be possible, and they live down to their expectations. When we are being good teachers by receiving before we transmit, we get ourselves out of the way. The next step—unblocking and unlocking—is to help the learners get out of their *own* way.

Powerful teachers have a decongestant effect, clearing clogged heads of mental blocks and maladaptive self-images. We teach students to see the obstacles their undernourished or overnourished egos have put in their own paths. We teach them how to take inventory of their fears and delusions and, in the process, demystify them. We train them to believe that anxiety about not having "the right stuff" is always misplaced—that the stuff we are made of is, in truth, stuff we can make more of. This happens subtly, usually invisibly. When we do these things well, we may not have much that is tangible to show for our efforts. All we will have done is make it possible for someone to learn.

PART III

Zoom In, Zoom Out

THE SAMMIE AND TUDIE SHOW

1

What do you do when you and your partner are in a rut? When it's the same old beats, the same old shtick? If you're smart, you look for a teacher, someone to show you what you've got. Someone who can break down your routines and help you discover within even the most basic gag all the possibilities you had overlooked, or had never even known to search for.

2

Sammie and Tudie had been coasting along with the same clown act for years. They'd never written it down. They'd just started winging it and it had grown. Sammie was the gaunt sad-faced boy, eyes turned sweetly down at the corners, so obviously needy; Tudie was more serious, fleshier, motherly in a way that hinted at sternness, frayed patience. They worked birthday parties, mainly, with balloons and magic and face-painting for the distracted kids, parents chitchatting all the while, as if there weren't a performance going on, as if this weren't something worthy of respectful quiet. They had more talent than this. But the talent didn't matter, did it? Or at least, wasn't the point here. All those years of theater: not the point. This was a job. Clowning. It was also a life, they knew. And it did have its points of satisfaction: the look of wonder in a child's eyes when he finally yielded to the idea that wonder could be conjured this way, by a gesture; the joy of being able to read your partner's eyes and to know, silently, what gesture should come next. But even on the good days they knew, Sammie and Tudie both, that it would become only more unsatisfying to remain in this routine.

Dick Monday, for his part, was on guard. When he gets students who've been amateur clowns, doing parties and the like, it is a mixed blessing. Such students come in with some experience, yes, but too often they come in so set in their half-formed ways. What a pain in the ass it can be to deprogram a know-it-all, shortcut-seeking second-rate hack. What a thin line separates the buffoons who are witting from those who are not; as thin as the border between water and ice. With these two, though, there was something encouraging: a willingness—maybe even a hunger—to learn and to unlearn. Liquid still. Steve Brown and Susan Estes—Sammie and Tudie—knew they needed change. That's why they'd sought Dick out. They'd known him by reputation, of course: he'd directed the Ringling Brothers Barnum and Bailey Clown College in Miami for three years before it folded in 1998; had toured with the Big Apple Circus; then with his wife, Tiffany, he'd started NY Goofs, a celebrated troupe and "playground" offering workshops for clowns. Not long after Sammie and Tudie moved to New York from San Francisco in 2001, they saw Dick at the Big Apple and signed up for a summer workshop with him.

Dick has the wiry build, elastic face, and attentive eyes of a circus professional. But take off the makeup and costume and put a white coat on him, and with his wispy gray hair he could pass for a trusted family doc. First thing Dick did, like a physician, was ask them about their usual routine. He watched them do their birthday-party thing, and he saw it immediately. His eyes read their act the way a grand master's eyes read a chessboard, with the sort of insight that is developed by seeing thousands upon thousands of patterns and routines, a knowledge of position and advantage and exposure that eventually becomes as automated and unconscious and miraculous as sight itself. He could see all that formal training seeping out: their love of theatrical time, as opposed to real time. Kids can smell theatrical time, the fakeness. They can smell emotional contrivance as well. The relationship between these two seemed over-scripted, when in fact it wasn't scripted at all. The way Sammie behaved, all passive-aggressive, interrupting Tudie whenever she tried to lead; the way she sighed and huffed and kept it in: there was tension there, and it sort of kept you watching, but it was the tension of dishonesty. Inauthenticity. That's the difference between acting and clowning: actors must try to be someone else; clowns must be no one but themselves. Dick saw it at once. They'd have to take their routine apart, bit by bit, and ask why. They'd have to ask themselves who they were, truly, and whether they might ever express it in the beats and strokes of this craft.

3

Funny thing about Steve and Susan: when they speak of their characters they speak in the first person. They invoke Sammie and Tudie not as an act, not as fictions or creations. They invoke them as second, unseparated selves. He says: "I'm hyper and I wanted to please everyone. I'd be afraid of *not* pleasing everyone. So I would always try to be the center of attention. I adore Tudie but I'd step over her to get attention." She says: "And I would get so frustrated with Sammie but I wouldn't express it with my full voice and everything I can bring that's powerful. I was scared of the anger, and I just wanted to play it safe."

I'm talking to two people but six entities: Steve, Susan, Sammie, Tudie, the couple called "Steve and Susan," and the act called "Sammie and Tudie." They've been married since 1994, an act since 1995. And they know exactly who is speaking when, to whom, for whom—though their brains, like those of the bilingual, long ago stopped making conscious distinctions between tongues, long ago started treating every utterance as drawn from a single pool of thought and experience. Only when a stranger enters their realm do they recall that they are speaking a private language of shifting, intermingled identities; only then do they recognize how disconcerting it is for a listener not to know which *I* is speaking, which *We*.

The act they'd been doing before they met Dick was a hodgepodge of classic gags, drawn from circus clownplay, from *I Love Lucy* reruns, from fading books of burlesque. Gags like "meet and greet": they come onstage, stride toward each other for a handshake but miss, then look confused and turn around and try it again. Or the "telephone" bit (use an uninflated balloon as a telephone cord, start a tug-of-war over who gets the phone, he insisting "Let me have it, let me have it!" until finally she, releasing the cord like a slingshot, lets him have it). They cooked up variations on these basic bits, and they'd improvise their way to an entertaining enough performance. The act had many echoes of other people's ideas of a relationship. What it didn't have was their own idea. What it didn't have either was a beginning, middle, or end. A sense of progression.

The thing Dick knew from practicing with the greats of the last generation, old-timers like Hovey Burgess whose names are uttered at all today only because of the devotion of the Dick Mondays of the world; what he knew from immersing himself in centuries of tradition— the Harlequins, commedia dell'arte, itinerant troubadours and minstrels, street jugglers and carnival performers, vaudeville—was that you can't teach someone how to clown. You just can't. It's like teaching them how to be human. The best you can do, Dick knew, is to remind them. Lead them to discovery. With Steve/Susan/Sammie/Tudie/etc., Dick was a matchmaker, a dating service for personas "real" and "fake." He gave them exercises to do in class and the exercises teletyped out a concise summary, like a rough-draft personal ad, of the people they were and wanted to be: *MWF, mid-thirties, responsible but resentful, the grown-up in the house, the enforcer, a little tightly wound, seething with unseen passion; MWM, mid-thirties but wishing he were nine, insecure, overcompensating, but lovable and sweet; together, we seek a new identity as a couple in balance, in harmony even if not in unison.*

Usually the kids liked Sammie and didn't like Tudie. Naturally: Sammie was clearly a kid, a goof. Which made Tudie only more inclined to stifle her frustration with his manic, spotlight-hogging antics. Poor Tudie, always bearing the burden. She's the one who books the gigs, puts the brochures together, takes care of the props and the logistics. She's the one who knows that the comfort level she's achieved in this act is her prison, yet still is unwilling to break free. Dick intuited something about Tudie's hidden heaviness of heart, so for a stretch he gave her exercises to play nothing but lonely, sad people. But even then, she was too clever, too verbally nimble: this was her crutch, diverting wordplay that could paper over the gaps in the act, in her own expressiveness. So he put her in situations where she had to shut up. He put her in situations where a save wasn't possible. Where the improvisation would just fall flat.

And Sammie. Sammie, the moody, tyrannical boy. He knew he was most appealing as a child but felt a certain shame about it too, a sense he picked up in the eyes of kids and adults alike that someone his age shouldn't really know the names and histories of all the Pokémon characters. Grow up? Why? Why not, instead, just exercise the control of the child? Mess up the perfect little world of the adults. What Dick needed to do first was disarm. Make it fine, completely uncharged (and a bit uninteresting) to be a child. You want to be a kid? Go for it. The next thing was to get Sammie to clue in more to Tudie. He gave him listening exercises to stir his awareness—of his partner, of anyone around him, really. Let someone else into your sandbox. Think of how to relate to them instead of how to impress or assert yourself to them. Feed off of her, see her gestures, her outbursts, as a *gift*. Learn to wait. Find the power in waiting.

As he reintroduced this pair to themselves, Dick acquainted them as well with a sense of flow. How to get in and out. He gave Tudie the loosest and sparest little bit to work with, an "entrance and exit" piece. It's simple. You're going to work, or to a restaurant, a hospital, whatever—you enter, stay a few minutes, leave. What Tudie found was that she was comfortable only in the middle. The anticipation of the entrance, the resolve of the exit: these she found unnerving. She didn't trust herself enough to think freely about how to get into the hospital. She found it hard to conceive of why she would leave. And the discomfort, the ache, of determining where the joke was in this bit, defining the punch line in her own choices; of being wrested from the safety of the moment, *this* moment, and jolted into a matrix of before-and-after that extended all around her: it was disorienting, even distressing. But this was story, wasn't it? The discovery of story. Turning random bits—of lives, of selves—into something more.

4

Dick could feel their pain. He knew a little something about married clown teams. When Tiffany, his wife, started clowning he'd already been at it for fifteen years. When they started doing routines together—and when she started getting good—Dick sensed he wasn't getting noticed, at least not in the way he'd been used to. It took him quite some time to realize he wasn't a solo performer anymore, even when he was doing one-man shows. It took him longer to learn how to convert his insecurity into art. And longer still to convert it into teaching. But now he knows: The teacher is the straight man. You have to be willing not to be at the center. You've got to stop talking so much. Simplify your exercises. Give the learners more freedom and release them from the imperative of pleasing you.

Sammie and Tudie are creating a new show now. For adults, not for children. In a theater. Less than half will be drawn from their old routine. They're writing it together, at least the outline, though they haven't decided yet how much to script and how much to improvise. It's been eighteen months since they started Dick's workshops. Eighteen months of watching Dick and other brilliant clowns crash and burn in class, then rise again. Eighteen months of stripping away the tinny skin of their old act. They're still doing parties, of course. But even there, everything has shifted. For Tudie, the biggest change has come in playing the honesty of a scene. One time Sammie interrupted her, like he always used to, started wrecking all her careful planning, but this time she cut loose. She screamed at him, a full-throated scolding yell: "Sammie! Stop it!" And guess what? The kids loved it. There was a thrill in hearing someone *else* get in trouble. Sammie came back, chastened. It was okay. The act didn't collapse. In fact, the yelling, the troubles, only made it more meaningful when later they were playful again and loving. Now she can follow with sassiness, silliness, silence: she's broadening her choices. She doesn't have to be the solemn, controlling superego. She can be the one having fun, making a mess. She can be Lucy. Let *him* be Ricky.

And how does it affect Sammie for her to be slipping the ropes off the moorings? His impulses for attention are still there. But he's finding better ways to express them. He's learning to hang back more, to let the action unfold. And he's found that by doing so, by standing expectantly to the side with great interest in his eyes, he actually draws the kids' attention in a different way. He doesn't have to jump up and down and say "Look at me!" They'll look at him. That's affected his confidence. For years he'd been doing balloon tricks as a crowd-pleaser, but lately he's been learning how to throw a top with a string. Pretty cool. He's doing it not to please anyone or to show off, but just to do a skillful thing for its own sake. This is more adult, Tudie says. And Sammie nods, still a little reluctant to say it. He's become interested in exploring the edges. There's a little nastiness now when he pulls a prank on Tudie. Offstage, he's been going to the Lucky Stiff some nights, a darker and hipper burlesque performance space, lots of piercings and tattoos in the audience, no kids around. He's been doing a lot of his usual clown routine there and finding, to his amazement, that it goes over well.

Before, their act just happened. It was like dumping out a box of toddler toys. Now they feel they've got Lego pieces they can assemble any way they choose. It's why they feel ready to take their relationship to another level. Doing this new show, moving from living rooms to a well-lit stage, is a big step. Dick has warned them and reassured them about that. It's going to mean more than writing new material; it's going to mean redefining character. Even as Tudie describes it, Sammie admits, "Gosh this scares me!" He purses his lips. "We're often asked whether we're adults or kids," Tudie says. "We don't know, to be honest, but we're definitely expanding the adult version more." Sammie nods again. "Yeah," he says. "We're going to be the cool adults."

FOOTSTEPS

1

A Creole recipe. Open up the storehouse, see what you've got. Start with a good blues, and let it simmer. You can feel that bass. A little Jelly Roll now. Just begging for some other sounds. Drop in a Gershwin quotation, some rangy octaves. Now how about some funk? Stevie Wonder syncopation? That's interesting. Some Elton John chords? Can you get with it? Sprinkle in some Monk. Oh yes. Isn't it amazing how that calls out the other flavors? Do you dare add a little Prokofiev, something just as off-center as Monk? Will anyone taste that Old World essence? What the hell. You can learn later what we're cooking, the proportions and recipes. You can learn later that it's made of mixolydian scales and G7 diminished chords and 5/8 time and the rest. For now, see what you've got. Keep getting more. Keep stirring that pot.

2

There are some things so fundamental that they are best passed on from blood to blood, father to son. Things like how to cut through someone else's idea of who you are. How to know when you are trying to be some-one you aren't. The fundamentals. It took Branford a while to hear it, but the chord chart of his life was written in great measure by his father, Ellis.

It wasn't like Ellis Marsalis stood at the front of the living room each evening and held forth, offering lectures on the history of jazz, enumer-ating the academic taxonomies that cleanly divide bebop from post-bop, cool jazz from modern. He didn't pace the floor with a willow switch clasped behind him, waiting to strike the child who deviated from his plan of instruction. He didn't preach a gospel of self-determination or self-respect, of the great richness of their cultural heritage ... of, well, of any kind, really. Truth be told, he didn't even expect them to be musi-cians. Wynton he thought would be a scientist; Branford, he didn't know. Ellis had come of age in such a different time, colored in a segregated New Orleans. He saw early on that he wasn't likely to end up a brain sur-geon or president of a bank. He knew circumstance had so much to do with what opportunities he'd have. So be it. If life is a bowl of shit, Ellis's own father had said, make a shit sandwich. It was what it was. Now it was something different. So when the time came he didn't push his sons toward music or away from it. He did his thing, which was to play music. And when their chromosomes began to unfold, each activating its allot-ment of gifts; and when each of those gifts was amplified by the environ-ment; when, you could say, a certain destiny became imaginable, all he did was agree with his wife, the force of the household, who said we ought to at least get them the best instruction we can.

Ellis Marsalis is a jazz pianist and teacher, father of six sons, four of them musicians: Branford, saxophonist and Grammy winner, former *Tonight Show* bandleader; Wynton, trumpet virtuoso, jazz and classical Grammy winner and head of Jazz at Lincoln Center; Delfeayo, a trom-bonist and producer; and Jason, a drummer. Ellis is sometimes described, worshipfully, as a patriarch. And he is: he sits atop a famously able family, one of the great musical families this country has ever yielded. But the idea that he's the Joe Kennedy of jazz, mastermind of an intergenera-tional dynasty? He snorts at that. At the inevitable whispered subplots too: that the father is jealous of the sons, or the sons of one another. If that's a story someone needs to tell, well, that's their problem. He knows how unorchestrated this all was, remembers how uncertain he was of what it even meant to be a father, how to speak to children except as small adults. There was no grand plan. Even today, past seventy, Ellis carries himself more like a question than a declarative. He has a hunched, bearish gait that hides how big he is and how perceptive, and he has the round, cool, quizzical face of a cartoon owl, eyebrows ever raised in languid surprise (a set of features that reverberates through his sons).

In the Marsalis household in Uptown New Orleans, on Hickory Street, there were a few fundamental aspects to the routine. Practice was one. Relentless, never-ending practice. Ellis himself set the tone. Not by saying so, just by doing it. He was playing gigs, was out at this club or that, on the road, whatever, but you could be sure when he was home he would be practicing, working out some kink, thinking through a better way to dance across a chord change or close out a solo. When he sat reading or conversing, his fingers would still drum out a passage on the tabletop, nearly involuntary spasms of silent melody. It was as Puritan a work ethic as you would ever find in this Bourbon Creole quarter, and all the boys absorbed it deeply. Of course, how the ethic interacted with their natures varied. Branford, the eldest, had more talent than industry in Ellis's estimation; the second child, Wynton, the reverse. But each was talented and industrious far beyond any ordinary standard, and together they were something else. Harry Connick, Jr., who was Ellis's piano student and grew up knowing the Marsalis boys like brothers, speaks reverently of the atmosphere in that house. *We were in awe of them.*

There was something else in the air there, something as ephemeral yet indelible as the din of clarinets and keyboards and horns and drums drifting through the halls. Sometimes Branford calls it "pragmatism," sometimes he calls it "being a pain in the ass." Here is how Ellis was pragmatic: He taught Branford how to play chess. He never let Branford win. He would beat him, then beat him again, then, when the boy seemed to be showing promise, or even dejection, just when the boy looked like he could use a boost, he would beat him again. Ellis wouldn't gloat or smile. He'd ask Branford why he'd lost. *Explain it. Consider the possibilities.* Here is how Ellis was a pain in the ass: At dinner, when Branford or his brothers would sound off about the Vietnam War or racism in America or LSU basketball, Ellis would stop them mid-sentence, stop them cold, and paraphrase Thomas Paine to the effect that while they had a right to free speech they had no right to an unsubstantiated opinion. "Don't come to this table and talk about what you don't know about." Those boys learned that only when they became precise in their thinking could they speak.

And not just precise. Open. The segregationists, the enforcers of the Jim Crow world that Ellis had grown up in? Don't stand in judgment of them. That's easy. See it from their point of view. Don't accept or excuse it. Just *see* it. See it and hear it and behold it with no veil. This was the painstaking pragmatism of life with Ellis. The language the father taught the son to speak was only incidentally a language of music. It was, more deeply, a language of catholicism, of an ecumenical, omnivorous search for more knowledge; a severe commitment to exploring every side of every idea; a willingness to treat music not as a vocation but as a way of taking in the world. These are the things Branford recalls when he thinks of the routines of home. The first things. The other things—the New Orleans musicians who came over to play ballads; the bands Branford joined; the rock and funk albums Branford would give Ellis to listen to and discuss; the way Ellis would improvise a blues to see if he could sneak an allusion past his sons (he could fool Wynton but not Branford); the detailed case young Branford and Wynton compiled to prove that Miles Davis, then at the peak of his aura and celebrity, was musically adrift, lost in forms; the way Branford and Wynton would do solfège together, singing ear-training exercises from Bach's *Well-Tempered Clavier* in do-re-mi, starting with ten assigned exercises but getting carried away, consumed with the beauty of the variations, until they'd made their way through all 168 exercises—these astonishing gifts, artifacts of an inheritance as nearly vast as what Bach gave his own sons, these were only the second things.

3

Branford always responded to the old-school guys. Guys like George Marx, band director at De La Salle High. Freshman year, Ellis had driven Branford to check out two Catholic high schools, De La Salle and its rival, St. Augustine. They were literally at a crossroads, an intersection where a right turn meant De La Salle and a left turn meant St. Augustine. Turn right, he told his dad. It was because of George Marx, who at the audition hadn't just asked him "Can you march?" George made him work. Let me hear you. Gotta fix that aperture. That how you play scales? Play 'em again. And that was only the audition. Branford at the time was a clarinetist, mainly because a clarinet is what Ellis had in the house. Branford at the time was also a Grade-A bullshitter. He had all the talent in the world, a knack for the instrument, an effortlessly big sound. And he knew it, was always joking around, testing boundaries. One time Marx was riding him at rehearsal and Branford uttered a sotto voce "Yes, massa." Marx shot him a look and said, "Don't lay that Uncle Tom bullshit on me." No, George Marx wasn't interested in being your friend, and Branford, well, he liked that in a teacher.

At Southern University, up in Baton Rouge, Branford could feel the tug again. He was learning the saxophone now. His teacher, Alvin Batiste, had known Ellis going back to grade school in New Orleans. His style wasn't dictatorial—he made suggestions; he liked to ask questions, as if he were the student—but he was definitely old-school in his seriousness about the life. Meantime, Branford had also joined the Southern U. Marching Band, a.k.a. "The Human Jukebox," a raucous dancing drum line that set the standard for halftime shows among the historically black colleges that played each other in football. Dr. Isaac Griggs, the famed and fiery director of the band, wasn't a mentor to Branford; he was more like a wild-ass uncle. When the band was on the road, to Alcorn State or Hampton or Louisiana Tech, there were two buses. Branford should've been on Bus One: he was a true musician, a good boy, from a serious family. But Bus Two, filled with the practical jokers and loudmouths, where the kids hazed their drivers and mocked the assistant band directors—to this day, sucking in your lips like old toothless Chet White is all it takes to send Branford and his old busmates into bellyaching laughter—that's where Branford liked to hang out.

"I was all for coasting," he says now with a smile, "for not living up to your potential." But "Bat," his teacher and his father's friend, saw it differently. There was a day sophomore year when Alvin and Ellis were driving to Baton Rouge, Branford in the back, and Alvin said to Branford, "You gotta get out of here if you want to pursue jazz. You gotta leave this place." Ellis and Branford remember it exactly the same way. Branford knew. Ellis knew too, but as was his way, he didn't say anything then. He didn't have any aversion to Branford falling on his ass, and he wanted to see what the boy would choose.

What Branford chose, halfway through his time at Southern, just as things were getting *really* fun, was to move to Boston and enroll at the Berklee School of Music. At Berklee, famous for its rigorous jazz program, Branford learned a few things. He learned that being from New Orleans meant something, and he became damn proud of it. Everything in Boston was cold, distant. There was that time, of course, he got chased through Southie by a gang of white hoodlums. Not exactly a welcome wagon. But also the time he greeted a classmate, a black kid from Philly, who stared at him and said, "I already talked to you this morning." Branford couldn't resist: "So let me get this straight. Just because we said hello this morning, we can't say it again now?" He continued to greet everyone in good, self-assured southern fashion. He asked folks why they talked the way they talked, assumed the things they assumed, and when they called him a weird cat, he wore it as a badge of honor. He learned too at Berklee that too many of his classmates were there just to get a degree and then a job. He began to appreciate more the education he'd gotten from Ellis.

Great music goes the way of the polyglot. That's what Branford understood when he met all these vocationally minded, musically monolingual students. "Growing up in the South," he says, "we knew the power of the English language." At Berklee he rediscovered the riches in his Crescent City storehouse, in his relational database of colloquialisms and slang and imagery and motif that he'd been compiling since birth. He began to understand that good improvisation is no more and no less than good conversation. The more symbols and references and idioms you have at the tip of your tongue, the more compelling your sound will be. The more capable you are of wit and color change and surprise, the more interested your audience will be. To play properly, you have to see the world. Harvest as many bits of it as you can.

After Berklee, Branford started playing with Wynton, who'd come out of Juilliard and was already making a big name for himself as a double-threat world-class trumpeter, as fluent in Haydn and Handel as in Ellington and Armstrong. For four years Branford played in a jazz band with Wynton, getting steeped in the forms and perfecting the standards to a high polish. And then he quit. To go play with Sting. His family wasn't thrilled. The timing was awkward. Why would Branford leave jazz, leave family, to play pop songs with Sting? Branford shook off the insinuations that came from inside the jazz world, that he was tired of being the eldest brother but only the second most famous. He knew what he needed to search for. Life was too short to live the dreams of others. He went his way, toured and recorded with Sting, saw the world. He made his own albums too, in all genres. He formed his own quartet. Won a Grammy for an album called *Contemporary Jazz*. A couple of years later he got the gig as the *Tonight Show* bandleader, which brought him mass-audience fame to complement the elite recognition he'd already earned. He did *The Tonight Show* for four years, smiling at Jay Leno's jokes and being more accommodating and less ornery than his nature typically allowed. In the end, the problem wasn't that he had to pretend he was an entertainer when he wanted to be a musician. In the end, the gig was unsatisfying for a simpler reason: it didn't require him to work very hard. It was coasting, and he knew it. So he left.

4

In 2002, Branford closed out his contract with Sony/Columbia Records and launched his own label, Marsalis Music. Its debut release was an album called *Footsteps of Our Fathers,* which Branford and his quartet recorded in a two-day frenzy. *Footsteps* was an unabashed homage to some of the greats of an earlier generation: Ornette Coleman, Sonny Rollins, John Coltrane, John Lewis. On the album Branford plays the entirety of "A Love Supreme," Coltrane's landmark opus, a work of spiritually inspired, mind-expanding virtuosity. It was a daring thing to do. No one is ever going to scale that peak; it's a mountain Coltrane created as he climbed it. Some of the critics asked whether Branford's attempt was sacrilege or mere folly. But the effort, Branford knew, would reveal more about him musically, about the limits and possibilities of his character. It would challenge him to discover just what was inherited and what was invented in his tenor voice. And he and his bandmates played the piece, on the recording and on tour, with the abandon, zeal, and self-assurance of people who know their instruments and don't need the "respect" of strangers to play. They were on fire.

A year later, the quartet was in Seattle and I went to hear them. The pianist, Joey Calderazzo, was unable to be there, so Branford invited a guest to fill in. The crowd at Jazz Alley went wild as Ellis walked gingerly onstage. "Rather than make him learn our book," Branford said, "we're going to play from his book." They started playing some old ballads, though with an undercurrent of impatient energy in the bass and drums. At first Ellis wasn't keeping up that well. His solos were spare, more courtly than creative. It was the first set on Thursday, and the band was still experimenting, making mistakes. They played one song composed by Ellis that they'd never done as a quartet, and it wandered off-key. "Who wrote this song, Dad?" Branford asked, provoking chuckles.

But as they got a few tunes deep into the set, Ellis warmed up, playing with more brio, his fingers ageless, his halo of white hair catching the stage light as he bobbed and leaned into the keys. He and Branford were unified in thought now, the patterns of their play interweaving. Toward the end of the performance, Branford said they were going to do a tune that the drummer, Jeff "Tain" Watts, had written and that Ellis had never played. "I'm going to enjoy killing him," Branford said, pointing the bell of his horn in the direction of his dad, "like he killed me all those years." It was an edgy piece, fast and unconventional, but Ellis was hanging in fine. He was emboldened, indeed, to shout out in the middle of the song, "Who taught who?" The bassist, Eric Revis, twanged a wry note for emphasis. Branford smiled and nodded, wet his reed, and proceeded to unwind an astounding marathon solo that left everyone, his father included, in the dust.

HER OWN PATHWAYS

1

She was an infant, lying on the changing table as I put on a fresh new diaper. Olivia would stare up at me with eyes that sometimes seemed playful and comprehending and other times seemed to be tracking an invisible bird across the ceiling. And I would repeat the four tones over and over again, a mantra as empty of meaning (or as full) as anything else I was saying:

Mā
Má
Mǎ
Mà

Four tones: the first, a high note held steady; the second, a low note rising, like an elongated, maternal *Yes?;* the third, a note dipping down, then up, like a sarcastic *Noooo;* the fourth, an emphatic downward accent, *Ha!* These are the tonal building blocks of Mandarin. In Chinese, tones make all the difference in the world—the difference, in this instance, between *mother, numb, horse,* and *scold.* Over and over again I would groove these four tones into my child's brain, hoping to redirect some of the swarming bustle of neural genesis. For several months she gave me no feedback on my litany, except a passing smile, but that could easily have been the passing of gas, or precocious sufferance of this obsessive father she'd been assigned. Then more than a year later, after she'd already begun talking, I put Olivia up on that same changing table and gave her the four tones once more. She pointed a tiny finger at my face and said in reply:

Glāsses
Glásses
Glăsses
Glàsses

A beat. And then I roared with surprise and delight. She reflected the laughter right back, her eyes widening and her legs kicking, shooting out bolts of excitement. A pattern was set.

2

Around the time Olivia showed me she could speak in four tones, I made it part of my morning ritual to go through the phonemic elements of Mandarin with her. There's a four-beat series, sort of an alphabet of sounds, that in the Romanized pinyin system of transliteration goes like this:

bo po mo fo
de te ne le
ge ke he
ji qi xi
zhi chi shi ri
zi ci si

It goes on a bit longer, but you get the idea. The entire list was branded into my memory when I was a boy, and now I was the one wielding the iron. I made it into a game. I would say *bo po mo* and wait, and then she would say *fo*. I would say *de te,* and she would answer *ne le.* For a while this amused her, and for a while she could recite all the sounds. In fact, she could say all her *bo po mo fo*'s before she nailed her ABC's. (Or at least I think so: until she was about three, she'd sing "ABCDEFG, HRJKLMNOP, QRS, DUV, WS, Y and Z" but there'd be a mischievous gleam in her eye that suggested she was doing it just to tweak me.)

After a few months, though, she lost interest in the *bo po mo fo* routine altogether. She started to sing nonsense syllables over my recitation. Instead she wanted to play other kinds of word and song games. In English. She took a tune that Carroll had made up, also at the diaper changing table, that went, "Clap, clap, clap your feet," and converted it into a ditty of her own that began, "Sheep, sheep, jumping jump." I tried Chinese flash cards with her, and again, she thought it was a fun diversion for a period, but what she paid special attention to was, for instance, the fact that *dùzi* and *tùzi* rhymed, not unlike their English counterparts, *tummy* and *bunny*. Another time, it was Halloween season. She was four now, and I'd been reading to her *The Runaway Bunny,* by Margaret Wise-Brown. We were eating breakfast and Olivia wolfed down several pieces of toast. "The most toast!" I announced. And without missing a beat, she added, "By Margaret Skeletonbones!" What could I do but burst into laughter?

I suppose one alternative would have been to burst into tears. I had grown up with the sounds of Chinese all around me and then failed to gain command of the language. Now I was pushing the tones on Olivia to atone for that lapse. But the whole time I thought I was training my child's ear for the unique sounds of Chinese, it turns out what I was truly doing was deepening her ability to play with meter. She could convert the rhythms into routines of her own now. In the process she'd traded languages. She'd slipped into the sounds that surrounded her every day, which were English, not Chinese. I'd laid down some pathways, yes. But now, so very early, it was already getting late. She was wandering off those paths.

3

My daughter and my mother. One of them sometimes uses "he" and "she" interchangeably. One of them sometimes says "incept" instead of "except." One of them says "nerve" instead of "nervous." One of them says things like "especially including me" when she's feeling enthusiastic about being part of something. One of them says, "It's mind!" when she means "It's mine!" One of them randomly drops conjunctions from sentences, as in "Please leave your name phone number" or "Let me know this is the direction you want." One of them asks, "Am I available to do that?" when she means "Am I able to do that?" One of them says, "Some unpleasant thing happen to me today." One of them asks, "Are petticoats extinct?" One of them tends to disregard tense; her verbs float between past, present, future conditional. One of them advises me that I should "think from animals' point of view." Both of them say "ya" instead of "yes." Neither of them understands what Carroll's dad means when he says, "Man, you are just *killing* those oranges."

My daughter and my mother are at a moment in their orbits when their understandings of English idiom and grammar are nearly synchronous. My daughter is finding her way at preschool and home. My mother is finding her way at work. It's always a tough call for me to figure out what is worth correcting and what isn't, what will work itself out and what won't. It's striking how often they sound like each other. But this won't last. Soon Olivia will pass my mom. Soon she will speak as flawlessly as I do. Already she understands that the accent that marks my mother's English marks her as different. *Why does she talk so funny?* True, she asked the same question about her other grandmother, whose voice was made in Mississippi, Texas, and Louisiana. But that's different, isn't it?

My mother has given me a book of Tang dynasty poems, all in Chinese. We have started to read one poem together every week, character by character, over the phone, so I can get a deeper feel for the poetry, the music and image. So that my Chinese is not so thin and Americanized. I have a plan to enroll my daughter in Chinese school, meanwhile, but I haven't found one yet that will be easy to get to, and in truth, I haven't found the time to look hard enough. For Christmas, I gave Olivia a book of Aesop's fables, and she loves them. The concept of a story having a clear lesson at the end is new to her, and intriguing. In my mind's eye, I track the trajectories. How long can my gravitational field hold the generations in phase?

4

It took me a while, but I finally figured out a way to get Olivia interested in classical music. Every morning when I drive her to the Learning Tree, her preschool, we listen to a CD in the car. Usually, it's something like the soundtrack to *Shrek*. A pretty good CD, I admit, but I wanted to diversify her musical diet. So one day I tried to sneak in Schubert's *Trout Quintet*. She howled in protest—"*Shrek* CD! *Shrek* CD!"—but then, on a whim, I started making up a story to go along with the music. "Listen," I said. "This song is all about some fish friends, some trout, who are going on an adventure together." She paused, and I kept going with the flow. "Hear them now? They're waking up, stretching and moving real slow in the morning. It's so quiet. But now the water's getting faster, and they're off! They're swimming in the stream now, playing games with each other. Hear how one of them is chasing the other one?" I saw her little head nod in the rearview mirror. "Now they're singing to each other, singing about what a great sunny day it is and how much fun they're going to have. And boy, now they're really splashing and kicking: Splash splash splash! Splash splash splash!" And on like this. Usually we got through about seven minutes of the first movement before we arrived at school. And now she loves hearing those same seven minutes many mornings. For a while she wanted my narration, but now she's kicked that scaffolding aside and just silently imagines the story as she hears the piano quintet playing.

I was pretty proud of myself for discovering a way to hook her on classics. But I can still be obtuse about making natural analogical leaps. A few months ago, we started playing a game called "secret languages." We would speak in the rhythm and cadence of normal English sentences, but all the words would be complete gobbledygook. So, for example, "Oh, so *thaaat's* how you did it!" would become something like, "Shnu, wa *slooofel* diggibut!" and would be said with all the appropriate theatrical gestures. The fun of it was to see how absurd we could make the non-sense words (and how often she could slip sounds like "butt" into the stream). One day I noticed my nonsense words seemed to derive mainly from some lost Slavic tongue. So I decided that I should sneak in some Mandarin-sounding tones. The good news: she picked up on them immediately. The bad news: she said, "No, don't make it Chinese." I was puzzling over what to do about this when another game provided the answer.

If she's recently seen *The Lion King,* Olivia likes to run around the house on all fours, pretending to be Simba, the lion cub. And if I happen to be around, I am cast in the role of Mufasa, the father of the cub. Not that I have to get on all fours, necessarily. I just have to do whatever I am doing in the house, and Olivia/Simba will copy me like a diligent cub. She'll imitate my eye movements, my walk, my face-scratching—and my speech. Noticing this, I took another shot.

E: Hey, Simba cub.
O: Hey, Simba cub.
E: What are you doing, you little buster?
O: What are you doing, you little buster?
E: Do you know what a little buster is?
O: Do you know what a little buster is?
E: It's a *xiǎo guāi guāi.*
O: It's a *xiǎo guāi guāi.*
E: *Wǒ ài nǐ, xiǎo shīzi.*
O: *Wǒ ài nǐ, xiǎo shīzi.*
E: You know what that means?
O: You know what that means?
E: It means, I love you, little lion.
O: It means, I love you, little lion.

(She doesn't quit.) The thing was, her intonation was perfect. Her ability to make sounds not usually spoken in English, like the rolled-tongue *shi,* was like that of a native speaker.

And that's when it hit me. The best way to get her to Chinese may not be through direct instruction. Not through sneaking, either, or at least not only sneaking. The way to get her there is through a set of characters that she and I can play—through a story and role of her own design, to which she, because of her nature, will be unstintingly faithful. This was such a short leap from the *Trout Quintet* principle. But it was a revelation nonetheless. And it made me realize how I was going to have to teach this child. Olivia Liu marches to her own drummer. My job now, though it goes against every instinct I have, is to be silent. My job is to listen for the beats.

CHORALE 3

Zoom In, Zoom Out

All thinking is analogy-making. All learning is analogy-finding. All teaching is analogy-showing. To teach something—how to write a legal brief, how to solve an algebra problem, how to make a piece of Pueblo pottery, how to navigate a race car around a track, how to shoot a dove out of the sky, how to draw a cathedral if you are blind—we use analogies. We reveal the hidden architecture of the subject and break it down to its core elements (*zoom in*). Then we show how those elements can be combined and recombined; and how they connect to elements from other subjects (*zoom out*). Cinder blocks, DNA, riffs of music, swatches of worn fabric, chunks of red clay, flight paths, grid maps, precedents and theorems: everything is available to explain everything else.

It's like studying Talmud: Crack each word of text, then examine context. *How does this relate to itself? How does this relate to something we already know?* When we zoom in, we explain dance, say, in terms of basic motions; relationships in terms of behavior patterns; politics in terms of interest groups. When we zoom out, we explain dance in terms of trees, relationships in terms of weather, politics in terms of war. And the whole time, we are executing a head fake. For what we are teaching, really, is not how to dance or love or win. What we are teaching is simply how to think, and how to be.

PART IV

Invisible Hands

THE SPACE BETWEEN

A Mural in Twenty-one Panels

1

A ravine, a concrete gash. She wanted to bring color to the Valley. Images and stories of neglected cultures. But the people there didn't want the murals on their block, in their neighborhood, across from their homes. Larger-than-life faces of dark-skinned ethnic people? Not in my back-yard. Not facing *me*. So the vision had floated, homeless, from zone to covenanted zone, until at last it lit in the Tujunga Wash flood control channel in Studio City. Below ground. Facing another concrete wall. You'd have to look through a chain-link fence to see it. But that was fine. In a way, Judy realized, it was perfect.

It is 1980. Midsummer. Hot, malaise-inducing hot, in that desert-dry San Fernando ravine. Jimmy Carter is president. Jerry Brown is governor. Tom Bradley is mayor. *Who?* They don't exist. Judy Baca is queen here. Matriarch, site manager, den mother, impresario, pied piper. She has spent the last decade turning her talent for painting into public art, founding the city's mural program and dotting East L.A. with Chicano murals that merge the prophetic aesthetic of Rivera and Siqueiros with the spirit of Black Power. Now she has had her greatest vision yet. A "Great Wall of Los Angeles," a half-mile-long mural depicting, in massive decade-by-decade panels, an alternate history of California and America. It will be the biggest mural on the face of the earth. Here will be the internment of Japanese Americans. Here will be the migrant workers crossing from the fields and villages of Mexico. Here will be the phoenix rising out of Watts. Here will be the Holocaust survivors, reaching for a city of angels. It took her a moment to conceive. It will take four hundred children seven summers to birth, and for all that time and all those children, Judy Baca will be the one constant. The life force. She is thirty-four.

This summer, this day, is just another sweaty, dusty afternoon in the channel. Judy patrols the area with a swagger, her dark paint-speckled T-shirt hugging her curves close, the tools and brushes dangling from a work belt hung nonchalantly. She gathers her long dark hair out of her face, out of the way, so she can take a better look. She is beautiful. And so are these children. These children are black and brown, mainly. They are teenagers from the projects, the barrios, the forgotten corners. They are children who have nothing else, nowhere else to be, no one else willing to believe that in their skinny fingers there may be more than the ability to snatch; in their large eyes, more than privation or special pleading. They are not quiet children. It is hectic. It is always teetering on the brink of chaos. Two black girls are singing songs to each other as they paint. A group of brown boys is horsing around by the scaffolding. Their taunts simmer down when they sense Judy's eye scanning past them. In ones and twos and threes and fives, the children work. They whitewash the cement walls. They consult Judy's sketches of their assigned panel. They pull tape measures and convert the lines to scale. They outline the images from each block. They mix paint in great batches. With bigger brushes, they fill the outlines with color.

And over there is Jorge, skinny Jorge Samayoa. He is eighteen but seems five years younger. He has been in America for six years but you can hardly tell. He is working by himself, so diligently. The panel he is stationed at depicts the internment. He is painting an anguished Japanese face, a huge face in the foreground of the panel. He had no idea of this. He stands there, imagining what it would have been like to have everything stripped away like that. He would like to ask someone if they knew about this already, this part of the country's history. He would like to ask so much. He is scared, though. Shy. These natives, tough city Chicanos, would probably make fun of him for asking. How long, he wonders, before you are no longer an immigrant? He is here because he can paint, and paint well. He is here because this is doing something big, because he doesn't want the generations after to think he was just a do-nothing. He gives the small stipend he earns here to his mother. Judy watches him, and he feels her gaze. She asks him to go back and repaint the eye, the fold of the lid. Go back, get it right. He does.

2

"What is it *for*?"

How to answer a question like that? "It is to awaken the consciousness of the people." "It is for the movement." "It is for inspiring children to be something greater than what they know." How to begin to explain to her mother's mother that art, abstract painting, even mural-making, is work? And work that matters?

Judy's grandmother was born in Mexico at the turn of the century. She raised Judy's mother, who worked for years on the floor at the Goodyear Tire plant in Riverside. Her mother was a strong woman, using her hands to operate machines, to make useful things. She had no time for things like art.

One day Judy found a sheaf of aging black-and-white photographs of her parents and their friends. She looked closely. It wasn't a trick of the eye. The sky bore a hue, and the hue was sky blue. The cheeks were rouged. The grass was unnaturally green. Who had added these secret patches of color? Who, amid the practicalities of raising kids and bringing home a paycheck and counting the hours, could have found the time? Something stirred inside Judy. Who, holding a tiny brush plump with liquid, could have released the tint of life into these fraying documents?

Who, Judy Baca thought, but her own mother?

3

You lean into the wall. Your shoulder sockets, the ropes of muscle in your neck, ache from all the brushstrokes and the craning. Your fingers sting where the turpentine seeps in. Your lips taste of dried salt. Your eyes pulsate with the heat and the whiteness, the blinding whiteness, of the freshly coated walls.

Judy once had a teacher, a master muralist, who literally asked her to dance with him as he painted. *Feel it. Feel the movement of the painting. Swim in it.* Earlier, probably a decade earlier, she had a drawing teacher named Hans who stood over her shoulder as she sketched a still life. He stayed her hand, slipped the pencil from her grasp. Without hesitation, he made two small marks that transformed the image, the weight and the line. When will I learn to draw, she asked. Hans smiled. In eleven years, he said. Earlier still, when she was in first grade, Judy's teacher let her sit in the back of the room and paint while the other children read stories. Judy could not yet speak English.

4

Angelica is curious. It is 1994, her sophomore year at UCLA. She has heard about this woman by word of mouth and decides to go to her class. It is an art class: "Whose Monument Where?" The students and teacher arrive on the day of the first session to find the classroom door locked. Judy Baca walks them outside, as if she knew it would be locked, and finds a tree for all to sit beneath.

The first thing Angelica remembers Judy saying under that tree: "I have a lot of opinions and I will tell you what they are and make no apologies. I've worked so long and hard just to have them." This takes her breath away. It is a different way of being, such an unfamiliar posture for a woman. Yet the language Judy speaks is so familiar. It comforts. Angelica, who came from Mexico at age four and learned English in the first grade, thought she was fluent in both tongues. One day she took a psychological test as part of a study on bilingualism. In the test she had to resolve two unfinished sentences, one in Spanish and one in English. She couldn't complete the Spanish one. She realized then that her academic mind, her logical and problem-solving mind, operated in English. Spanish was for family and spiritual life and poetry. Spanish was for home.

Judy speaks English in this class, not Spanish. But she speaks a language of home. She speaks of her mother, her aunt, the kids on her block. Angelica can envision them, hear their lilting voices. Judy talks about moving from Compton to the Valley when her father found work with Lockheed, and she muses about the ways that great economic and social trends buffet the lives of everyday people. Angelica considers the sweep of it all, and her own family's place. In describing the coolness that a certain painting evokes, Judy describes the great fanlike wheels with large grass panels that she would pour water into, a poor family's air conditioner. Angelica grew up with one of those in her own home.

The course is a progression: art history to art-making to community-making. They will study narrative painting and public art across cultures. They will learn how the Great Wall of L.A. came to be. They will make plans to create new monuments, murals rich in the symbols and colors of home, for the most blighted precincts of the city. They will touch the people who live there, seek out their stories, and use those stories to reveal the unseen scale of things. To Angelica Pereyra, an inquisitive, soft-spoken girl in her first college art class, this is all revelation. Angelica studies math. Her first love is geometry, the fit and form of the shapes. But she is seeing lines now that were only hinted at before. She is sensing how many more ways there might be to take the measure of the world.

5

It is 2003. Late summer. It is stifling hot outside but cool in this high-ceilinged studio. Concrete floors, brushed steel counters, track lighting. The lights are off. We are in Venice, California. This is the UCLA Cesar Chavez Digital Mural Lab, a few miles from campus. Judy slumps on a couch next to me, drinking a Diet Coke. The air conditioners hum. There are several elaborate multimedia workstations behind her, where her young acolytes, masters of the Avid editing machines and iCube computers and Quicktime encoders, are documenting the creations and the legacy of their leader. They work with urgency, as if in fear of forgetting. Huge digitally crafted montages, her students' latest work, hang like championship banners from the rafters. This is the next generation of mural-making. Indian faces, Catholic shrines, American ghettos: the mestizo motif is everywhere. Around the walls, at eye level, runs a horizontal band of blueprints and storyboards for the hoped-for next phase of the Wall (which stopped with the 1984 Olympics). A screen is pulled down in front of the couch, and on it is projected an unnarrated slide show, each image holding for one second, then fading. Is there a techno beat pulsing along too, or do I only imagine it? Mexican murals. Mayan monuments. A Kahlo portrait. Renaissance frescoes. Florid graffiti. Gilt objects. The Great Wall. Images of a younger Judy, a sepia phantom. It is a dreamscape, and I sit, mesmerized, lost in time, unsure of my own medium. For a long time we are silent. Then the older Judy, the Judy of today, speaks, and returns me to the moment. Her voice has been deepened by time. She has taken on a handsome heaviness. It becomes her. What was lithesome once is now fleshy, substantial. There is a slower flow. Her face has broadened, though her mouth remains small, even dainty. Her hair is still long and dark. You could imagine her wrapped in velvet capes now, fuchsia and bloodred and darkest night. She speaks now, and tells me of a boy who was painting the Holocaust panel of the Great Wall, a panel that morphs from the ovens and gray striped shirts of Auschwitz to the verdant irrigated plains of California. He asked her: "Is this a movie?"

6

Jorge introduces himself as George. He wears a tan checkered shirt, short sleeves, and tan slacks. He is trim, circumspect. His face is still unlined. In his entire manner he leaves little trace, his Guatemalan accent nearly gone. In profile, he looks just like the boy who helped paint the Great Wall. He is still shy. He is forty-one now, living in Pomona with his wife and three children. He averts his eyes as he describes his job, saying he has been in the auto industry for twenty years. He works in maintenance at a Chrysler dealership. He is more enthusiastic when he describes his side job, running a collectibles business from home. He buys and resells Star Wars paraphernalia, Hot Wheels toy cars. He sells sometimes over eBay. He goes to shows to buy and sell and swap. The money is irregular but he keeps track of every cent.

Jorge, all his life, has been a good boy. He has done all that was asked of him. He worked hard. He never did drugs. He never drank alcohol. He still goes to church. He has raised a family. He tries his best to support them. He attributes it all to Judy, to his summer at the Wall. That summer taught him to be responsible, he says. That summer taught him to be with other people, to express himself and be a better person. For the first years after the Wall, Jorge tried to keep painting on his own. He thought of being a commercial artist. But there was a child, then another, then another. He did not finish college. He needed to earn a steady living. His hours and his obligations did not leave time, and it has been a while now since he has painted. It has been over ten years. He'll look sometimes at paintings and imagine a brush between his fingers. He'll imagine the resistance, the soft wet scrape, as he pulls the brush across the canvas. He has been a good man. He has done all that was asked of him.

7

When you go to university and you are the first, you bring everyone to school with you. Your relatives and neighbors. You carry their hopes in your knapsack. Their expectations are your chaperone. Everyone is asking after you, wanting to know how you are doing, what you are learning. What you will become. You want to do something to repay them. You want to become something worthy of all that unrequited wondering.

Angelica had an uncle and two other relatives who'd gone to college, who were in fact teachers. But she was the first in her immediate family to go. Her father was so proud of her, especially because she was a math major. She would do work that was truly of the mind and not the hands. Every family, it seems, delegates its roles. Angelica, this placid loving child, who could see the way everything added up—she was the academic. She was the master of numbers. And it was a unique identity: how many Latina math majors do you know? He wanted everything good for her. Her father did not say anything when she told him she was taking an art course. He did not have to. She could feel it.

Judy once said to the class: "The same education that can bring communities and families together, you have to fight to not let it separate you." Angelica wrote this down. In her mind, a question formed: *A healthy tear?*

8

One afternoon Judy saw herself. One of the girls at the Wall, Esther, was playing around during a break, cracking jokes and doing impersonations. She hooked her key chain on her belt, like a janitor, and walked around with a shoulder-swaying swagger. The other kids burst out laughing. Judy, who spied this from out of view, understood immediately: Esther was doing *her.* A pretty good her. And all this time Judy had thought it was the kids who were transparent. She asked herself: What to do with this transparency? What, that swagger alone might not achieve?

Another afternoon. A torrential rain had fallen somewhere in Los Angeles, and now the waters were running down the sides of slopes off the flats and into every draw and canyon. A child screamed that the water was coming. They clambered up and out of the channel, leaving paints and scaffolds and tools rattling in the emptiness. Judy was not on-site. She was in her beat-up pickup truck, clear across town. She heard the flash flood warnings on the radio. She drove into the sprawl, inching her way through constipated freeways, fearing the absolute worst. It took what seemed like hours to get there. As she pulled up by the channel, she could see a river rushing through it. Her stomach collapsed. She could see a helicopter overhead. And now she could see one of the girls, on her back, carried along briskly by the current. The girl was peaceful. Her eyes were fixed on the helicopter, which was lowering a rope. The girl reached up and held the rope. From a distance, it appeared umbilical. Afterward, Judy was so shaken by the near-tragedy that she considered shutting the project down. She called a meeting of the kids to talk it through. She spoke. One of them called her a hypocrite for wanting to quit when things got hard. The project went on.

There were two boys working on the Wall, brothers. Their parents were drunks, abusers. Judy took them into her home for a time. The boys were freewheeling, hard to control. Every day Judy feared they would erupt in violence. It was true of so many of the kids. They were wild creatures. Once she was directing a crew of forty ninth-grade boys, and thought, *They could devour me. The only thing between me and them is my will.* But the main thing about these kids was that they were, down to the cellular level, unloved. Anyone could sense that. And she, at least for a time, could do something about it. She could give them structure and direction. Also, she could need them. She could indicate in subtle ways that here, she was nothing without them. She could ask their permission to create something together. Her will, their permission: these two, she understood, would keep things in balance. It was the first summer of the project. Everything was in chaos, nothing worked. Judy was in way over her head. She sensed even then it would be all right.

9

His friend runs a day care center. It has Winnie the Pooh and Mickey Mouse painted on the walls. It is in East Los Angeles. Every child there is Latino and poor and has likely never seen much of the world beyond East Los Angeles or Mexico. When Jorge sees the place, he realizes this is it. These children deserve more than badly drawn Disney knockoffs, an imitation Pooh telling the children that even their fantasies are secondhand. They should see something of themselves here. He will paint a mural, he decides, a work of scope and beauty that has images and icons and *memory*. This will be where he returns to the work he began twenty years ago. There will be a story to the mural, a moral to the story, that reflects the center's name: *Nuevo Día por Latinos*. A new day.

10

From the Great Wall many things emerged. One was fame. Judy became known throughout the city, the country, the continent, as a visionary: a heroic Great Latina who, with a company of discarded children, took an empty gulley and made one of the largest, most stunning public art projects in the world. *Twenty-five hundred feet of muscular, brilliant, iconic story. Half a mile.* Many admiring articles were written, Bill Moyers did a short documentary. But the hubbub subsided eventually, and then it became clear what had truly emerged from the Wall: a process. And in the years that followed, the process evolved into the Process. It became the lifeblood of Judy's studio and of her school, which called itself the Social and Public Art Resource Center (SPARC). Stare at a mural as long as you like; when you close your eyes the afterimage eventually fades. But the Process, to those who have been touched by it, is indelible.

This is the Process: There is the image that forms in your mind, the horizontal sweep and aspect that suggests the idiom of film but is really the idiom of dream. There are choices to make about symbols and icons and idols from the story. There are the sketches, the early efforts to breathe the visions into tangible form. These must be done with careful attention to scale. One square inch equals one square foot. There will be deep consideration of the palette, and what meaning each shade will have. Every element of the mural must advance the story, even if the story is oblique to the uninitiated. The physical exertion of making the mural must itself advance the story: the raising of the scaffolds, the churn of great vats of paint, the selection and enrollment of the rollers. Or, if we are working digitally, the bleeding of one scanned image into another, the manipulation of screen objects into luminous electronic tableaux that—

But wait. Wait. This is getting ahead of things. For this is storytelling, and storytelling is where the process ends. It begins somewhere else. It begins with story-*listening*. The artist doesn't sit in an empty studio with only the mad voices of her own demon genius for company. She goes into the world. She asks childlike questions. She asks people to tell about things or moments that have shaped their lives. She teases out of them the plainest, simplest details. *When you were deported, who took care of your garden? What happened to your children's toys?* She harvests fact and metaphor. She grabs hold of the unexpected. She knows this much: when she holds a community meeting to explain the mural she is going to make in a gymnasium, and introduces one of the graffiti artists from the block who is going to help paint the mural, and is interrupted by a woman in the audience who rants that *this kid is no artist he is a hoodlum he is a destructive gangster a disgrace,* and when the boy after the meeting confesses *yeah that was my moms*—she knows when something like this happens, you must take it not as a disruption of your perfect little plan, but as the plan itself. She knows story will rush all around you if you let it. She seeks out nodes where the segments and rays and trajectories converge. She hunts for that tightly folded fragment of memory—a sad song, a smell of grease, a cold bullet—that can open out into a pathway to empathy. She finds affinity. Then, only then, will she begin considering how to combine the colors.

11

Angelica is as her name suggests: she has a round cherubic face draped with short curly chestnut locks; her brown skin, like her wide smile, belongs to a child; her eyes sparkle a startling green. It's her manner, though, that makes the name so apt. She has a serene, intuitive way of asking questions—even when she is the one being asked. Judy saw this, this innate spiritual understanding of how things relate. Angelica was still so very tentative about art-making, uncertain of her vision and unsure of her hand. The way through to her, Judy sensed, would be community. By seeing others, Angelica would see herself.

Her early experiences were as part of a team assisting Judy. One mural they did was an image of Life and Death, for a community theater. Angelica painted Life. She also learned the way that Judy worked, which meant that she—Angelica—painted nothing. *They* painted everything. *They* owned it: the woman's face, the water gushing from her open palms, droplets in the shape of sacred serpents. Angelica remembers that she worked on a feathered serpent.

Angelica was now taking a second course with Judy, one called "Muralism and Community Development." She made her way, at her teacher's behest, to Estrada Courts, in East L.A., one of the oldest public housing projects in the country. Estrada Courts has a long history of mural-making within its walls. The next logical step was to go digital, to use new technologies as the medium for storytelling. She met a family there. She met a fourteen-year-old girl named Isabel who, at the very end of their time together, revealed an extraordinary story, made more extraordinary by its matter-of-fact telling. She noticed the girl rarely told the full story herself; others told it for her. Angelica absorbed it. She ate Sunday dinner with this family. She saw, in their preparation of the meal and in their figures of speech at the table, how they dreamed. It was a story for others. Angelica took note of every knickknack on the mantel, every framed photo. She asked first, then used her digital camera to capture images of the children and the low-slung building and the asphalt walks. When she was done, Isabel gave her a clipping of the chayote vine that

grew outside the door. Angelica accepted the clipping. The vine continued to grow.

12

The mural Angelica made is called *La Familia*. This is what it looks like:

A light blue window frame. Up near the left center, a bullet hole, radiating shards outward like beams of light. Caught in one shard is a
street sign: Lorena 1330 S. Across another shard is a distorted image
of a girl running. In the upper left corner, the image of a young man
and woman painting over graffiti. At the center, an alcove, altarlike,
with a teenage girl, seated. She holds a pencil in her right hand and a
book in her left. Her gaze is cast downward. To the right stand her father, mother, sister, brothers. Behind them, in black and white, sit
four children: those same siblings, only younger. Around the bottom
and side of the window frame creeps a green vine, its leaves reaching
upward.

This is what the mural says:

I was in my bedroom. I was studying, reading a book at my desk.
Okay, I was asleep on my book. It was night. It was so dark that you
could not even see the vines growing outside our door. Somewhere
across the street somebody tried to shoot somebody else. But they
missed. And that bullet, it ricocheted off a tree and came right
through the window and into my left foot. It didn't stop there, though.
It rattled around my bones and up into my spine. It rode my bones like
a train on a track. When it finally stopped I hurt so bad. My mother
and father came running in. The rest was like a dream. They took me
to the hospital. They did all kinds of operations. The doctors said I
wouldn't be able to walk. But my family, my neighbors, they prayed
and prayed for a miracle. And while they waited for me to heal, they

started to clean up the block. They decided enough was enough. And I got better. Today, it is like it never happened. I can run.

13

The sandstone Art Deco building SPARC has occupied since 1976 was once the Venice jail. (In fact, the building was borrowed to serve as the police station in the cop film *L.A. Confidential.*) The layout makes for an excellent art space. The booking desk is the welcome center and gift shop. The holding cells are galleries. Some of the barred iron doors have been preserved, left open, and painted light pink. Judy's murals, reproductions and originals, are everywhere. They follow you down halls, up stairwells, behind doors. Even if you don't track their narratives, her murals have a visceral, primeval effect. Nearly religious. The images make your throat tighten, your temples burn. They hit you in the solar plexus. The fevered acrylic assertiveness of her oranges and reds and blues and greens; the flat, stylized faces that speak an emotional syntax as elaborate as Kabuki; the bare limbs carved in exertion and anguish; the supernatural imagery set beside the most commonplace objects; the masterly modulation of perspective to create dramatic illusions of depth: all these add up to a uniquely compelling visual signature. A *Baca*.

But those are the obvious elements. There is something else at work that draws the eye and vaults the viewer irresistibly into the scene. It is Fibonacci. The medieval mathematician Leonardo Fibonacci discovered a sequence in which each number is the sum of the previous two: 0, 1, 1, 2, 3, 5, 8, 13, 21, etc. What makes this sequence more than a curiosity is that it appears repeatedly in nature. The sequence is everywhere. It is *us:* the proportion of knuckles to fingers to hands to arms. When plotted as a graph, it traces the curl of a conch, the pattern of plates on a pineapple's armor, the eternal spiral of the Milky Way. Many painters have incorporated the sequence into their work. Da Vinci's *Last Supper* is filled with objects placed strategically to create implied lines in Fibonacci-derived ratios of 3:5 or 8:13 or the like. Judy puts an image of a Siqueiros on the projector. With a click of the mouse, a web of crisscrossing meridians appears. Fibonacci. It is the internal logic that gives a static art form its dynamism. Judy's murals are made with the same calculated asymmetry. Every icon, every outstretched hand, is placed to send a chord from one harmonic node to another.

When she first discovered the Fibonacci sequence, years ago, Judy fell into a trance. She studied sunflowers and rosebushes and counted the number of turns the petals and thorns made. She reopened all her art books and looked at the paintings and buildings with new eyes. The discovery changed the way she painted and the way she taught painting. She understood that in both cases, her task was to use these numbers like magnets. Their pulse was the pulse of human yearning; their primal imbalance a call for release. She wondered, as the sequence appeared before her wherever she walked: *Is this God?*

14

His oldest child is now the age he was at the Great Wall. His other children are four and fourteen. One early autumn afternoon he took them to see the Wall. He explained it to them, the histories and the meaning of the imagery. He wanted to teach them about the value of their heritage. He took them there, as well, to expose them to an old-fashioned way of looking at things, something richer and deeper than the history-free eye candy of the entertainment world. He could see that his middle child, who is already dabbling with art, was interested. "It felt good to be there," he told me. "Everything gets so methodical. You sleep, eat, go to your job, watch TV, and that's it. It's nice to have places like that to feed your senses." He paused. "I wanted to show them something I finished."

15

Angelica had always had such strong, mysterious convictions about the "rightness" of images she liked. Now she knew why. There was a cosmic satisfaction to the knowledge that a sequence of numbers girded her inchoate artistic sensibilities. But each layer yields another. This was the beginning.

One time, when they were redesigning the gallery to display a series of new murals, she and Judy developed a way of working together. Judy would describe how she envisioned the space, free associating, thinking aloud in random metaphors, as Angelica followed her around the room. Then she would exit, leaving Angelica to figure out the implementation. At first it was disorienting. But the more they worked together, the more Angelica caught on. Before long, her intuition mutated into skill. Judy would be explaining the proportions she wanted and the ideal relation of things, and even as she was speaking, Angelica would say, "Okay, I get it. I get it."

16

Jorge is back to see Judy, for the first time. He has convinced his friend at the children's center to hire him, and now Jorge has made his way from Pomona to Venice to ask for advice. For guidance. It's one thing to have executed someone else's vision two decades ago. It is another thing, *now,* to have to conceive it yourself. How did she do it? Where did she begin? He remembers the numbered blocks on the wall. He remembers applying the primer, then moving from left to right. He remembers her advice not to get too consumed with detail too early. He remembers the way she would follow up his part of the work with finishing touches that gave the whole its stylistic consistency. But how did she plan the whole? How did she know how to divide the project? And what was the magic that made people tell her their stories? There is so much still to learn.

17

Angelica was grateful. It had seemed natural to her, the switch, but she knew of course it might seem preposterous to others. When she told her father that she was becoming an art major, he could not hide his anxiety. But he did not lose his temper. He did not become angry. She sensed something in him, a yielding. She was the oldest child. She had always been logical. And as she explained it to him, this seemed the most logical choice she could possibly make.

18

Jorge still has a vivid memory of the panel he helped paint. He remembers the tents lined up at the internment camps. He remembers the face of the woman crying. He remembers the man next to her, closer to the viewer, looking up at the hot sun with a sad expression. He remembers the barbed wire fence.

What is the use of regret? He has a sense of pride about what he did at the Great Wall. What does it help to dwell on the possibility that he might never feel such satisfaction again in his life? That he accomplished more in those two months than he had in the twenty years since? When he was eighteen he had no notion that what seemed the beginning of an ascent to awareness might actually have been the peak. At forty-one, what could he do but give himself a chance to paint again? There were things he had acquired that summer—a sense of scale, a belief that you did not have to give people a picture of yourself but only needed to be yourself—

things that it was still not too late to retrieve. But first he had to give himself the chance.

19

She shows her paintings at a gallery in L.A. once or twice a year. She just did a piece for a Tibetan Buddhist group, to sell at a fund-raiser. Her paintings have become more abstract and more openly geometric. This is recent; she didn't used to call out the internal logic or make the numerical structure so evident. If you weren't looking for it, you would only perceive the art to be pleasing in a general sense. "But I finally gave myself permission to go with it," Angelica said. "Honor the shapes, use vertical stripes, use the Fibonacci properties."

It has been five years since she graduated from UCLA. She is a teacher now, at Palisades Charter High School in a suburb outside L.A. She teaches geometry to ninth and tenth graders. On weekends, she takes it upon herself to show some of the students how to make murals. In her free time, she paints.

What had Angelica sensed in her father that day? Yielding, she thought. Trust. But perhaps not only the trust that she would make good choices and that she was capable enough to make it on her own. Perhaps also the trust that in time, her choices would carry her closer to where she began.

20

The little mural crew she has assembled is just five girls. The boys lost interest after the first Saturday work session. The girls enjoy the painting, but Angelica tries to convey to them that the process before is what's key.

They have no idea about murals, about Chicano art or the Mexican tradition. Originally they were going to paint a mural at a HUD retirement home in West L.A. But that fell through. It didn't faze her. She had too much SPARC in her now. Now they will paint a homeless shelter. She won a grant from the Cesar E. Chavez Foundation, under a program to create spaces for people to maintain their dignity. Angelica has a vision. There is a Buddhist notion, she learned, that meditation is meant to mark the space between your thoughts; that to practice Buddhism is to find that space, wedge yourself in, expand it into bliss. Angelica decided to make this the theme of the mural. She looked high and low for such spaces: between teeth, toes, eyes. Between the fibers in Chavez's flannel. Between the bird and the flag in the United Farm Workers logo.

It's the first time she's ever had to lead a crew. The hardest thing, she finds, is resisting the impulse to do everything for them. Judy is on her mind constantly. Angelica tells these girls the place Judy occupies in the history of mural-making. She tells these girls she has opinions and worked hard to earn them. She tells them that painting, like geometry, has a logical structure for validating your opinions. She uses processes that Judy taught her, like passing out index cards and asking everyone to write down ten things, ten pivot points in your life, like the first time you could hold a pencil. It becomes hard, after five or six, after you get past the cute ones, to get deep and more personal. That's when trust begins. More fundamentally, she sees from her new vantage how hard it is to give students confidence when you are letting them figure things out for themselves: how hard it was for Judy to do that. She sees now that with every mural, Judy had a game plan, obscured from view. "Before you knew it," Angelica said, "she'd been there and back." The images would resolve.

It took her some time to be willing to say, "I am an artist." If introduced that way, she would throw up a disclaimer—"Oh, I dabble"—but only because she took the title so seriously. She was not sure yet whether she was worthy of it. It's the same now with another title she is given—*maestra*, "teacher." Does she truly have mastery? Is she masterful? Angelica has been teaching geometry for five years. At first she was itinerant, floating from room to room with her rolling bag, but now she has her own class. She is becoming comfortable. And she realizes, "I'm not so comfortable being so comfortable." She needs to mix it up. Recently she had a tough day with her students. She went out for some air and asked,

What am I doing here? Never had she posed the question in that tone. She pressed: *What got me here that got me here that got me here?* And that unwinding led her to recall something Judy had said many years ago: for an artist to change things is a lifetime of work.

21

There was only one time when Judy was ever really in danger. She was striding across the planks atop the scaffolding, surveying the work. She was the only one up there; the children were at another section and the day was coming to a close. To either side of her the flood control channel stretched out in a line of perfect perspective, and she could see now that the color the children had put on the wall was not an aberration; it was, in fact, all the eye could take in. The scaffolding, like everything else, was secondhand and shaky, but usually it held up fine. Not this day. She was mid-stride when she realized the whole skeletal contraption was tipping; that her own steps were swaying the rigging side-to-side, like a parallelogram about to collapse into a line. As the scaffolding fell away beneath her, she yelled, to herself more than anyone else, "Jump!" And she did.

FAITH'S FATHERS

1

PRELUDES

Can you help me? It was dark already when Johnny Ortega flagged him down. He'd seen Father Greg around Dolores Mission and the 'hood but usually avoided him. He could no longer. Everything was collapsing. The coke, the drinking binges, the gangbanging: he knew how this story was going to end. At that very moment, Greg Boyle's car was coming down First. Johnny decided right there to ask. He stepped into the street, flailed his arms, made Greg stop. He walked up to the window, unsure what to say. "Father," he asked, "can you help me?" Greg studied Johnny. Stopping the car had been the leap of faith, and that was done now. Whatever came next would have to be redemption.

Can you show me? It was the school's first year. New Jewish High School, founded on the promise of pluralism. Orthodox, Conservative, Liberal, Reform—all were welcome. It was on that promise that Rachel Burstein quit her public school and signed up. Her mom, not born a Jew but converted, was all for it; her dad, raised a traditional Jew and skeptical ever since, was perplexed. She had insisted. She'd wanted to define Jewishness on her terms. Now, irony of it all, she sat before Rabbi Lehmann. Another student had complained that Rachel was not under traditional law a Jew, her descent being patrilineal, and that her participation in services was therefore offensive. "What are we supposed to do?" she asked. Danny Lehmann understood that this was indeed the question.

Can you steer me? He was drunk. You could smell it. You could hear it in his slurry belligerence. Hugo Jimenez was getting off the elevator to see the girl who had just delivered his baby. Father Greg was coming onto the elevator, having just visited yet another boy who'd been shot. Hugo recognized him. He had heard of this priest who took in gangsters from all over East L.A. and got them jobs. Homeboy Industries. Hugo stood unsteadily, listing. He was tired of this life, waking up at one every day with no aim. "Are you Father Greg?" Hugo asked. Greg said he was and spoke with him. He handed him a card and said "Call me." Just before the elevator doors closed, he got Hugo's number too.

Can you guide me? When she had walked into his office, Shulamit Izen did not know how the rabbi would respond. Now, alas, she had a sense. She had just told the headmaster of her school that she was lesbian. She was coming out to an Orthodox rabbi. What was she hoping for? She needed him to know. She wanted him to help her find her way, to help her reconcile this knowledge with her faith. Could she? Could he? Rabbi Lehmann sat silently for a long, uncomfortable moment and rubbed his eyes. He opened his mouth to answer.

2

TIME

He is always in motion. His eyes scan. He paces. He sits at his desk for a moment, comes out from behind, sits in a different chair, rocks in the chair. He gets up. He moves through the corridors in a hurry. He looks at his watch. He is late. He comes to the main lobby, as the students exit classrooms and search for the next. Sukkot, the Feast of the Tabernacles, is approaching. He stands at a table set up in the middle of the traffic. He stays there, his weight shifting from foot to foot. His hands busily tie palm fronds. He is there to be seen. To be seen working, in devotion.

Even when he teaches, teaching Bible, he is moving. Same way. Standing behind a podium, arms around it, hands rocking it. He isn't a terribly good classroom instructor. He gives off a vibe of kinetic impatience that is hardly steadying to a group of antsy teens. He doesn't receive before transmitting. He irritably shushes the kids. He veers between fine-tooth analysis of the text and corny examples of how the lessons apply in suburban life today. He holds class in the new atrium where assembly is held, and his voice is an echoey wash, lost amidst the shuffle of chairs and paper. But the classroom is not this teacher's venue. He does his work in the halls, in doorways, on the stairwell, at the lockers. He does his work at his long meeting table, rocking impatiently, worrying over design: of the walls, the rooms, the classes; of the teaching, the faith.

A corona of gray-white hair, trim beard, wire glasses, slumping shoulders. Daniel Lehmann, in a still photograph, looks like a portly and wise grandfather, a bookish rabbi. But there is nothing still about Danny. He knows he has to keep moving at all times, because this school he has invented, this miniature society he has spawned in just five years, keeps threatening to catch up to his plans for it, to surpass them. He is a Jewish Ulysses, making and remaking his boat as he sails it, one eye on navigation and one on reconstruction. It's a wonderful problem to have, he knows: students like waves of the sea, who find in one another the force to swell and swirl and carry the vessel where they think best.

"Nothing stops a bullet like a job."

You see the slogan once you walk into Homeboy's nondescript office. First and State, across from the 98 Cent Store and the Iglesia Bethesda, right next to the LAPD's Hollenbeck substation and the Felipe Baguez Mortuary. Walk in and look straight ahead, and there's Father Greg's fishbowl. Or is it everyone else who's in the fishbowl? His office is all the way to the rear, separated from the chaos of the referral desk and waiting area by a thin wall of glass. His office is painted a violent shade of mango that keeps you alert no matter the hour. He positions his chair and desk to peer straight through that glass, and he sits there, calmly, eyes on patrol. The intercom will ring and he won't leap up to answer it. He'll lean over, conserving energy. The stack of messages in front of him doesn't appear to trouble him. No point in wasted anxiety. Greg is efficient to the core. He has to be. A touch, a word, a look: he communicates with a disciplined economy of gesture. Sometimes, if he has a moment to breathe, he remembers when he was a freshly frocked priest who could devote three hours listening to a young couple listing their troubles. It would be nice to have that kind of time now.

Time seems to have slipped or warped its way past the lives of these gangbangers. They are so lost. They wear nearly identical close-cropped hair, baggy pants, flannels and hooded sweatshirts, tattoos. It might appear that their studied tribal insignia give them order and solidity, center them somehow. But it's only an illusion. Their brief life histories are fractured, jumbled affairs. *Three years in the pen, six months probation, last worked five years ago (or six?), finished ninth grade, haven't seen my dad since I was eight, went to school on and off for two years, got shot in '98.* Time, for these men, is an overspliced stream of noise; compressed then elongated, random without rhythm.

And there are so many of them, these homies who want to become ex-homies and can't even find the words to confess it. Once word got around that Father Greg was the man to see, everyone started knocking. They looked at the photos on the wall of friends and former enemies, people who'd pulled it together. They milled about in threes and fours in the waiting area, eyeing each other warily, knowing they were from rival crews but knowing this was neutral space. Sanctuary. Sometimes there'd be an eruption. But usually not. Usually Greg saw the portents—the emphatic hands, the jutting jaws, people coming at each other crazy—and that would be enough for him to snap suddenly into motion, to spring from his chair and bark through the doorway: "Carlos, watch yourself!" His children would separate. For a moment, at least, order would be restored.

3

CALLING

Pico Gardens, Aliso Village. Two of the loveliest names to grace the roll of failed twentieth-century public housing experiments. These projects on the city's eastern edge make up the largest zone of subsidized housing west of the Mississippi. Within them, ten thousand Latino and black gangsters, clumped into sixty gangs, live a littered, empty-calorie imitation of life. For six years, starting in 1986, Father Greg Boyle, SJ, was the pastor at Dolores Mission, in the heart of Pico/Aliso. It wasn't long before he saw how much more he needed to do than help the helpless mothers, or pray for their boys, or bury them. He started an alternative elementary school. Then he created Jobs for a Future, a program to teach these youth how to find and hold a job. Then he created Homeboy Industries, to help the hardest cases get work by running their own nonprofit businesses—first a bakery, then a silkscreening shop, now landscaping and graffiti-removal businesses. After his rotation in the parish ended, Greg returned to the neighborhood to run Homeboy. This would now be his ministry.

He looks, in some ways, like an Irish Danny Lehmann: gray beard, balding pate, spectacles, thickening midsection. He's a bit more bemused, though, as if he knows he is becoming a persona. The saga of Homeboy Industries is something out of an after-school special. *The Jesuit homeboy, the gangland priest: didn't we see that one on cable?* Indeed, Greg has gotten a lot of media attention, particularly as he's criticized the LAPD's approach of hammering the gangs. He speaks with the polish of both a clergyman and a minor celebrity. Some of the lines he uses are, well, recycled. I'd read them in his clips. The stories of the founding, of the rescues and acts of salvation, gleam like stones many times held. Yet what made them refreshing still is that they were never meant to be anything more. They are like stories from the Bible. They are a daily record, a matter-of-fact accounting of the volume of flotsamed lives flowing past. They are a reminder of constant inadequacy. The day I met him he told me he had just buried his 114th child. Greg is free of pretense that what he does is visionary or saintly or world-changing. He is a single human, distributing sandbags against the flood; called to imagine that his labors, in the end, will matter.

Rabbi Lehmann's name is pronounced *layman.* It's fitting. He is an unorthodox Orthodox. Ecumenical in his curiosity, he has ever searched for inspiration in realms beyond his expertise. He delighted in the Jewish idiom of lively textual debate and believed that *hevruta,* interpreting sacred passages with a partner, was a powerful way to learn. So he was naturally drawn to the Great Books curriculum at colleges like St. John's, which treated education as a conversation with the canon. He thought the Buddhists could teach the Talmudists a few things about meditation. He felt that the distinction between schooling and camping should be broken down; that time in the field, away from the classroom, would most effectively transmit culture. This he got not only from decades of Jewish summer camps but also from the high-WASP boarding schools of New England. As he came to know the priests at nearby Catholic high schools, he became interested in their notion of "spiritual formation": that a religious education should not only pass down tradition but also enable people to attain deep spirituality. This idea came not from the idiom he knew. That was good.

He'd taught for years at a Jewish day school in Baltimore. Then he'd moved to Boston, where the only such school was Orthodox. He had seen how many Jewish children in the public schools were losing their already thin connection to the faith. He'd also seen how children at the Orthodox schools were getting only one strand of the faith. What troubled him in both instances was the evaporating commitment to pluralism. Assimilation and isolation each bespoke a rush to escape the pain, the discomfort and insult—even within one's own heart—of confronting competing ideas of how to believe, and to be. In their hurry for pure schooling, students were missing the point of learning.

In 1996, he found a second-story office space in Waltham, above a bank. Within those walls he and a few like-minded teachers and parents began an experiment. The New Jewish High School. Danny wanted it to combine all the methods of teaching he'd encountered. It would have to. For the questions that called this school into being were huge: Could different conceptions of a single faith coexist usefully? Was mere tolerance enough? Did traditional and liberal ideas of Jewish identity cancel each other out? The answers, he knew, would lie in how the children were taught. The texts would be their teacher. The experience would be their teacher. The rituals would be their teacher. The building would be their teacher. And the teachers themselves—the flesh and blood—would be there to coax that knowledge out; to be embodiments of devotion. Pluralism would be the animating faith of this place.

Danny had a sense, corny as it was, that this sounded a little bit like America. What he didn't know yet, as the idea rumbled to life, was that only through *challenges* to the idea would the idea ever be achieved. A little bit like America.

4

ATTACHMENT

It was Groucho Marx who brought her there. Rachel Burstein was attending a play, a one-man Groucho act, and saw an ad in the program for a new pluralistic Jewish day school seeking students for its first class. When she went home she told her parents. Home was Winchester, a Catholic suburb with very few Jews. Home was the public schools. Home was a mother who was once a practicing Christian and now a Jew and a father who was once an observant Jew and now lapsed. Home meant Hebrew school up till the bat mitzvah, but also Christmas trees and gifts every year. Home meant a diluted sense of Jewishness but a thirst for something more. Home meant taking commuter rail all the way to North Station and then the T all the way back out to Waltham, just to get to New Jew.

New Jew: that's what the kids called it, nearly from the start. They painted it on the sides of their yellow school buses, advertising their irreverent ethnic pride. There was something about the newness of it all, the spirit, the chance to create the culture of a school, that compelled Rachel to go. That first year, 1997, there were only fifty or so kids in all grades combined. Only about a third came from public schools, the rest from the Schechters, traditional middle schools. She had always been a secular Jew, but a Jew all the same. Now she was determined to define that identity more fully. Never did she imagine that the primary basis for her identity, her line of Jewish descent, would be challenged.

When it was, when someone complained that she technically was not Jewish and that her presence lessened their experience, she was shaken.

She'd given up everything to come to this school. And now, sitting across from Rabbi Lehmann, she could scarcely believe her ears. *Conversion?* It was suggested that she convert? Danny took pains to say this was just one possibility, but she was insulted, and they both were surprised how quickly the welt of offense appeared. Politely and firmly, she rejected that possibility.

Danny could tell, just from this minutes-old encounter, that Rachel was a force. He'd never worried that the issue of matrilineal versus patrilineal descent might become crippling; it seemed natural that a pluralistic school would welcome both. But now the meaning of all those words was subject to parsing: "natural" assumed the very thing it meant to define, open-mindedness; "pluralistic school" implied that everyone there shared the same sense of what pluralism meant; "welcome" elided the question of whether merely accepting someone's presence or accommodating them in ritual was the truer form of reception. Rachel had no interest in backing down. Sure, she wasn't as observant as others, but did that make her less religious? She was every bit as Jewish as any other student. Put another way: What had she been until now, if *not* Jewish?

The issue at hand was *tefilah,* or prayer. There were two different services in the morning, both traditional, one allowing women a speaking role and one not. She'd been going to the egalitarian service, so called because it permitted women, when the complaint was lodged. So Rachel said she would make her own service. And she did. There were others at New Jew who felt, for one reason or another, alienated by the prayer options and who welcomed a third alternative as well. Rachel didn't go down this path lightly. It was hard to take on this work. It felt, moreover, like a concession to some anonymous other person's determination of right and rule. This was the thing about pluralistic settings, she realized: things will revert to the highest common denominator. Rachel didn't have texts she could ever point to that said she or anyone else needed to do this or that in order to fulfill an obligation to God. What she had was her own voice.

The service she invented and led, a hodgepodge of prayers and Hebrew songs that today seems embarrassingly conservative to her, marked at the time a small revolution. It re-formed the nascent school's sense of itself. Danny didn't help her create the third service but he encouraged her and told her he respected what she was doing. His approval sent a message. For he was an Orthodox rabbi. The traditional students and parents looked to him to be a bulwark, and some began to grumble that he was undermining them. In Bible class, Rachel remembers, he pointedly said one day that "ritual should never trump morality." She took this as a coded message for both her and her critics.

The issue came to a head that spring, when the students and faculty gathered for one of the religious retreats that would become a regular feature of school life. The conversation swiftly clustered around the question of *Who is a Jew?* It was a cathartic, emotional, intense discussion that lasted the whole weekend. Danny let it unfold, knowing this was a critical moment. Students of every mind spoke passionately about why they believed what they believed. For the traditional and the liberal alike, the answers were inseparable from their personal histories and deepest values. They cried and argued and declaimed. At the end of it all, there was no conclusion. No one tried to force a consensus. After a full two days of this kind of interchange, everyone knew well that consensus was not the point.

Rachel came away from that retreat changed in this sense: she knew she could now be whatever kind of Jew she had the confidence and seriousness to be. And she now had a totally changed idea of what an Orthodox rabbi was. Danny had not been interested in good feelings. He'd been interested in honesty. In that first face-to-face, he'd told her bluntly that if he were a student he would've had a problem too with her participation in services—but that the aim of this school was to get people to be able to see things from several perspectives. In later years, Rachel would speak for the school at events, and she would speak of having been taken seriously—as a person, as a Jew. She would speak of having been given the tools to converse with her tradition, even with its problems. She would say that what made that retreat so powerful was precisely that no one changed their minds. Pluralism didn't mean altering what you thought; it meant learning to live together. And whenever she'd be at the podium, Rabbi Lehmann would nod his fast nod, silently thanking this girl for helping his school grow up.

.   .   .

With his shaved head and goatee, his unfocused drunken eyes, and his stump of a right arm (a birth defect), Hugo Jimenez was a picture of menace. The words he had for Father Greg at the elevator were hostile too. He said, "I know you—you're the one who doesn't help anyone from our neighborhood." It wasn't just cynicism. It was a geopolitical comment that Greg understood well. Hugo was a member of the Marvelosos, a "Mara Villa" gang at war with the "Sorrenos," gangs of the Mexican mafia, whom Greg more often worked with. He was a gang veteran, his compact body filled with scars and screws and rods from the three times he'd been shot (at thirteen, fifteen, and twenty; in the arm, stomach, and femur). Greg was taken aback by Hugo's hostility but quickly recovered. This was a chance to build a bridge to the Mara Villa. That's why he made sure to get Hugo's number, why he called Hugo early the next morning. Hugo came in at nine. He was twenty-five years old. He had never held a job in his life. He was, as he put it, "allergic to work." Greg put him on the payroll that very day, putting him to work in the office— covering the phones, doing small chores and odd jobs.

One month earlier, Hugo's father had died of complications from diabetes. Greg learned that in the course of their initial interview. It shaped his handling of Hugo, as it shapes his handling of so many ex-homies. The young men who pass through Greg's parish may lack motivation and work skills and capital. But what they lack prior to all of that is a primal attachment. Their "lethal absence of hope," as he calls it, comes from the fact that so many have never been loved and have never been able to love in return. "Gangs are bastions of conditional love," he says. "Homeboy is a community of unconditional love."

Hugo was one of the lucky ones; he'd had a father, he loved his father. Greg's work was to sustain that attachment. He told Hugo at every turn, "You are exactly what God had in mind," and waited for Hugo to inhabit that truth. He didn't tell Hugo or anyone else they could be the first Latino president if they applied themselves. He told them, "You are exactly enough." He didn't woof at Hugo with lectures. He said, "You are everything I would want in a son." If Hugo showed up late, Greg wouldn't yell. He would silently wait, until Hugo hurt inside from the forgiveness. If Greg said, "You're doing a good job, son," it made Hugo want to do a better job. When Hugo decided to get custody of his son,

Angel, Greg brought the social worker to see Hugo's closets lined with baby clothes the next size up, ready to be grown into. Greg paid the three hundred dollars to file papers and accompanied Hugo to court. Hugo didn't understand what the judge was saying until he heard, "Full and sole custody to petitioner," and then the hair on the back of his neck stood on end and he looked at Greg and he wanted to cry.

At first, watching and listening to Greg, I was inclined to put some of his actions in a box called "strategic" and others in a box called "sincere." Then, gradually, the boxes became indistinguishable; or, at least, the distinction became irrelevant. Greg tells these lost sons, one after another, that they are in fact exactly enough, that they are everything he would want in a son. And he opens up something primordial in them, something that leads, almost on cue, to huge sobbing and release. The words he spoke to Hugo, the salve of unconditional love that he applied, he has applied to many others as well, often using the very same language. He knew too that Hugo's loyalty would help him broaden his reach to new gangs. What I realized after a while was: So what? So what if he wanted to reach more people? That is his job. So what if his love was produced and dispensed in large batches? Each dose felt real, and each one healed.

Hugo proved to be a diligent worker. Over the next two years he started taking on more responsibilities, using computers for data entry and record keeping, becoming more vital to the operation. The next challenge for him, Greg said, will be to assert his value in the world beyond Homeboy Industries. Every Saturday morning Hugo goes to the cemetery to visit his father. He said to Greg once, "I wish I could show him what I'm becoming. I wish I could see his face, because all I gave him when he was alive was grief." Greg answered, "He is seeing you now." And that was enough for Hugo. It was enough to keep him going that day, to get him out of bed the next morning and the morning after that, to help him take care of himself and his boy. It was enough to make Hugo resolve, silently, that he wanted to be for Angel the kind of father Greg had become for him.

5

RITUAL

The funny thing is, Father Greg has no recollection of the night fifteen years ago when Johnny flagged him down. There was so much more to come in that relationship, and at every moment, so many other Johnny Ortegas to answer.

The day after they met in the street, Johnny showed up at Greg's office. Greg got him a job as a gardener for a pastor in Santa Monica. Greg knew better than to expect linear progress from there, but even by the chaotic standards of this subculture, Johnny's next phase of life would be an utter mess. He did the gardening for a while, then got arrested on a gun charge and spent six months in jail. When he got out he worked as a laborer on a movie set and did that intermittently for nearly ten years. He and some friends then got an idea for a housecleaning business. They asked Greg for help, and Greg, for reasons that could only be called faith-based, bonded them for insurance. That business fizzled when Johnny got into an altercation with his wife and was arrested for "making a terrorist threat." He went to prison for sixteen more months. When he got out this time, there was a message from Greg to come see him. He joined the Homeboy graffiti cleanup crew, which does contract work for the city, and started working again. That ended when Greg got a call that Johnny had been gangbanging and partying using the crew truck. Johnny had no memory of it.

At the root of it all was addiction. G, or G-Dog, as Johnny and others came to call Greg, had called it. You've got to get past the drugs, he told Johnny in their first meeting. During his first three years on the crew he was still smoking pot and snorting cocaine and drinking all hours. "G would see I was losing weight from all the coke and he would ask about it and I would lie. And he would say, 'I'll take your word for it.' But he knew I was lying." After the work truck incident, Johnny agreed to go to an outpatient rehab program. He stayed clean for a month before he figured out how to cheat the system. When he got kicked out of rehab, G gave him an ultimatum: check into an inpatient program, or sever ties with Homeboy.

Johnny thought about it, and "out of respect for G," granted himself one last run. He got a motel room during a long weekend and there he filled his lungs and veins with every substance he could abuse. Tuesday morning he came to work and told G he was ready. He checked into Warm Springs for ninety days and, as of the day we met, he'd been sober for a hundred and thirty-two. Today he is back on the graffiti crew, as one of the supervisors.

I asked Greg what it was he'd seen in Johnny that justified his faith in him. Greg said, "It wasn't what I saw in Johnny; it was being a parish priest. You have to try to imitate the God you believe in. Why should I deal in a language of bitterness and disappointment?" He gave Johnny "little marks to hit." When he hit them, it was progress. When he didn't hit them, it was progress. The attitude was to declare victory at all times, even when two steps forward meant eight steps back. This was core to Father Greg's MO. He was not naïve, or blind, or a weak-willed enabler. "No hanging, no slanging, no banging" is the only clearly stated requirement for entry at Homeboy. Yet Greg could see that the troublemaking and the drug abuse and the graffiti and gunplay all continued. He simply refused to use it as an excuse. He refused to reinforce the message of failure that had shaped these boys all their impoverished lives. Their parents and siblings are addicts. Their schools are disasters. Their homes are shabby. Their gangs, ultimately, are unreliable refuges. Shame and disgrace, and shame and disgrace over the shame and disgrace, are all they have known. Greg didn't lay on the guilt. He gave Johnny a choice: you can leave this way of life, or not.

The idea of agency is powerful, but best taught in subtle, indirect ways. I never heard, or heard of, Greg delivering a sermon to these boys or even an overtly religious message about personal responsibility and personal agency. What I heard about was his birthday calendar. On his cluttered desk is a worn notebook that reminds him every day to pick up the phone and call Felipe or Jaime or Armando, homies who've already passed through his program, and say *Happy Birthday, son. I am glad you were born.* Sometimes he can't get to the call till after eleven P.M., at the end of a long day, but he will place it before the night is over. It's often the only call these young men will get. For many, it's the first time their birthday has ever been properly acknowledged. The two-minute call is something that makes them feel *firme,* proper, like they can hold their head up high. It's the feeling they get when they do their homework well for the first time and burst into Greg's office to tell him. The feeling they get after their first day on the job.

What I heard about too was Greg's visits to the hospital. "How do you communicate a sense that yours is a love that can be trusted, that there is a no-matter-whatness to your relationship?" he asks. "Go to the hospital when you find out they've been shot." It is a regular part of his routine—perhaps not as frequent as it was in the early nineties, when three kids a week were getting shot, but frequent enough. Everyone has stories of wounds. He goes to make each of these children feel their stories are something real, their wounds worth noting.

The irony of Father Greg's work is this: he tries every day to excavate individual human beings from the wreckage of their surroundings, but his work is so overwhelming in scale and in scope that he rarely makes a lasting bond with any single son. There are a thousand letters at home, and piled up on the floor of his office, from the people he has touched. His walls are plastered with fading photographs of these boys, and the boys they have since brought into the world. His work is plate-spinning, Greg says. *Here's Johnny, he's about to fall, here's Hugo, keep an eye on him.* "There are a lot of plates," Greg says, "and some have fallen. Not five, but five thousand." Those are the odds.

Johnny Ortega has a routine now. He gets up every day at five, while Greg and the city still sleep. He and his four-man crew, ex-homies from rival gangs, will cruise through Boyle Heights and try to take down last night's tags before the sun is up. He has three or four pages of "hot spots" they have to hit. It'll take them till early afternoon. He drives and scans the city. He searches the blocks, the walls and corners, for the telltale signs of this gang or that. He reads the coded language of assertion and aggression and insult painted on every surface. Sometimes, he will remember what it was like to belong, to color these walls and not erase them. Primera Flats was his gang. Sometimes, naturally, the memory of demons now dormant will clutch his innards. But the pangs eventually pass. He will remind himself, "I don't want to die over a neighborhood." He will think of Father Greg and remember, "I don't want to let G down."

·   ·   ·

Every day at nine, the students and staff gather for assembly. On this Wednesday morning, Danny stands at the podium and tries to be heard over the din of gathering, chattering teenagers. The noise fills the two-story atrium. It's been five years since the New Jewish High School opened above that bank in Waltham. Now the school, renamed Gann Academy after a benefactor (though "New Jew" still sticks), occupies a brand-new 120,000-square-foot building on a twenty acre campus. Inside, the handsome brick and fresh carpet and matte steel fixtures give it the feel of a fancy new house, a house too big for the family (even though the family has now grown to nearly three hundred). Danny waits, rocking slightly, holding his microphone in both hands. On his head, in place of the skullcap, is a Red Sox cap. Tonight will be the first game of the 2003 American League Championship, a series against the Yankees destined to add another chapter to Boston's near-biblical record of suffering. But it is morning, the series has not yet begun, and there is only hope in the air, electric anticipation.

Danny settles the crowd down and begins his remarks. It is a rabbinical talk, serious and carefully phrased. He knows I am visiting, and it seems his words are for me as much as for the students. "I want to remind you all what our school is here for," he begins. "This is a place for pluralism. A place where Orthodox, Conservative, Reform, and secular can create community." He scans the audience. "Sometimes, though, we must confront the limits of Jewish pluralism. Even among us today are people who test the limits of our tolerance." A solemn hush falls over the room. "Even among us are a few wayward souls who prefer a heretical, intolerable allegiance . . . to the New York Yankees." With that kicker, the ten kids in Yankee caps uncoil huge, defiant grins, and the rest of the student body erupts in a spontaneous chant: "Let's-go-Red-Sox! *Clap clap clap-clap-clap.* Let's-go-Red-Sox! *Clap clap clap-clap-clap.*" The rabbi continues, raising his voice over the pandemonium: "I don't want to predict the outcome of this perennial battle between good and evil, but we do not believe in curses." Huzzah huzzah. "So in honor of this momentous occasion, all homework due on Thursday"—the noise level rises expectantly—"all homework due on Thursday," he repeats with a pause, "is due on Thursday." A loud groan, followed by the usual student announcements: meetings, rehearsals, notices. Back to business.

Four years earlier, assembly was different. Four years earlier, when Shulamit Izen was still a student there, nothing seemed solid enough yet to bear such mock-serious mockery. She remembers vividly the day she came into Danny Lehmann's office. She was a junior and the school was in its second year. Shulamit had grown up in Lexington, cradle of the Revolution, going to public schools where it often seemed she was the only Jew. By the end of middle school she felt she was being robbed of her heritage. By the end of middle school she also knew she was gay. She came to New Jew at the recommendation of a friend: Rachel Burstein. She arrived at school "out," but people there didn't quite get it, or want to. "They thought I was just being 'creative,'" she says.

And so that day she met with Danny Lehmann, her aim was to convey to him that she didn't feel that sexual orientation was being taken seriously at the school. She wanted to establish a personal connection with him and enlist him in an effort to create a gay-lesbian-bi-transsexual forum at the school. It was hard for her to do this; she was always a shy girl. Here is what she remembers the rabbi saying to her: "I think it's sick to look at the world in terms of sexuality." She tried to tell him not only that she was lesbian, but why, and why it mattered. He told her he did not want to hear the story, and that she did not need to tell it. He was visibly ill at ease. She left the room in tears.

Danny is the one who first told me of this encounter, and he recalled it with a pained expression. He handled it terribly, he admits. "When she wanted to say why she was gay, I didn't want her to go there," he said. "Partly because I didn't feel she needed to justify it and partly because I was scared about what else she was going to reveal about herself." How much should a teacher know about a student? "This is a plane," he said of intimacy, "that is not my strength." His awkward phrasing proved the point. And unlike the issue of descent that Rachel had presented, the issue of how to square homosexuality with religious law—or, for that matter, with an avowed commitment to pluralism—was not something he'd spent much time considering. One of the things he'd blurted to Shulamit during their session was, "You can't change three thousand years of tradition overnight." But as she left the room, he realized he might have to do just that.

At first, Shulamit was so disturbed that she began to question whether it was even okay to be gay. She called her friends from a gay Jewish support group in Boston. When she was done with those conversations, she decided there was one thing to do. Keep pushing. She asked Rabbi Lehmann for permission to do an assembly on GLBT issues. For reasons he never explained, he granted it. Weeks later, she organized the assembly. Before the whole school, she spoke of why she felt it was important to acknowledge this part of one's identity. Two rabbis spoke of how it was a worthy question whether the text could accommodate homosexuality—a question they all could learn from. Then, unscripted, one of the most popular teachers came out, giving a powerful speech about the pain of her hiding.

In the days after the assembly, Danny wrote Shulamit a note: "I'm proud of you." Shulamit had become a powerful figure in the school community. Her presence, over time, changed the tenor and content of that community. "I began to relate to her," Danny said, "as a person who had something serious to contribute." Not as a grandstander. When she proposed that the school create a gay-straight alliance called Open House, Danny suggested she present the idea to the school's board of directors. She did. The directors considered the idea and worried whether support for such a group meant advocacy or even "recruitment." Shulamit sat before the directors, who were well intentioned but uncomfortable, and made her case with poise. She wanted dialogue, searching inquiry. She wasn't trying to "force" anything on anyone. Danny, watching her, felt immense pride in her ability to speak to strangers about this. The board approved her proposal.

What helped make Rabbi Lehmann so supportive of Shulamit's efforts was that all the while, she was emerging into a serious, even passionate student of Judaism. Shulamit had been raised in a Reform household. Now, in an unlikely counterpoint to her emerging gay voice, she was becoming increasingly traditional in her religious observance. She adhered strictly to dietary laws. She attended traditional services. She studied Torah with fierce attention. She even went to an Orthodox kibbutz. She decided she could no longer be Reform: "I hold Jewish law in great esteem. I see the Torah as divine," she said. "Reform Judaism disregards the law and I couldn't do that." What of the Torah's prohibitions on homosexual relationships? She didn't miss a beat: "The Torah also says you cannot put a law on a community that a community cannot follow."

Through it all, Danny got grief from traditional students and their families. When Shulamit invited a gay Orthodox rabbi to be a guest speaker, he got calls from parents angry that this person had even represented himself as Orthodox. As he'd revealed in his initial encounter with Shulamit, his own views were also quite traditional. But as it had been with Rachel, his own views were beside the point. He had created a space for debate. And now, the students who had populated that space were creating the debate. How could he deny someone like Shulamit the opportunity to live a core Jewish value: to grapple with the text and with who she was? He was steadfast. As graduation approached, Shulamit composed a letter to tell Danny she was proud of him—for his exploration of the issue, for creating the school. She never sent it, though: she was never satisfied that the language she'd chosen was articulate enough to convey her gratitude.

6

DA CAPO

The classes at Gann Academy, the New Jewish High School, are as varied and vibrant as Danny had envisioned seven years ago. In Harry Sinoff's ninth grade Talmud class, the kids are paired off in *hevruta;* they argue over the meaning of every word in the passage, shouting and laughing like it's a party. Except their language is exacting: one of the mantras here is *There's no such thing as casual speech.* Two boys ask Rabbi Sinoff to translate a Hebrew phrase and he says, "I can tell you, but how will you know what I say is correct?" In Yoni Kadden's history class, a seemingly standard seminar, the teacher asks why the Industrial Revolution didn't happen two thousand years sooner than it did and the students, instead of answering, ask why that is even a relevant question and the teacher, unfazed, explains it is to get them to see how religion and economics and other tectonic plates of history move and the students, satisfied, offer hypotheses. In Rabbi Lehmann's rabbinical literature class, the students ask why there appears to be conflict between a simple reading of the assigned text and the commentaries. They want resolution: one of these is wrong, right? Danny says, "Pluralism means holding contradictory ideas in your head and appreciating the compelling parts of both, even defending them." A student: "Like three sides of a two-sided argument." Danny: "Like one hundred sides."

There is a line from the Babylonian Talmud: "I learned much from my rabbi, even more from my *hevruta,* but most of all from my students." I once asked Danny to tell me about students whose lives he had changed during his years as headmaster. Instead he told me about students who had changed *him;* who had breathed meaning and imperfect truth into his words about pluralism. He provided the philosophy; they made it a way of life: a living commitment. Shulamit Izen today is a student at Smith, active in Hillel, studying Jewish education, considering the rabbinate. The question is, under what banner. She may have reconciled her sexuality with traditionalism, but most traditionalists have not. "I'm going to have to find or create something else," she says. Rachel Burstein went to Swarthmore after her years at New Jew. She has not been as observant but she is still as probing and inquisitive. "Sometimes," she says with a smile, "I think I have more in common with Unitarians than with Orthodox Jews."

What will become of these two and their classmates? What identities will they don as they enter the world, what codes and rites? Open questions. Which is appropriate. For what they learned to worship at this school was not one strand of Judaism or another; what they learned to worship was the question mark. How do you reconcile passages? On what basis can you remake tradition? What tools must you acquire to have the right to state who you are? How do you form a question? To ask and accept plural answers; to live securely in the midst of paradox; to know that it is from the sharp jostle of contradiction that belief arises unseen: this is the heart of a Jewish education. Whatever forms their faith may take, Rabbi Lehmann's students have already taught him that much.

When Johnny first came to G he was a teenager. Now he is thirty-four, with lines in his face and three children in his home. He is, for now at least, sober and clean. His children know the difference. "They're happy to see me now." What time he lost, what time he has left—these don't matter. He is present today. Three years ago, before Hugo came to Homeboy, he would never have spoken to me, let alone told of his father and his hopes and fears. He could never have imagined working all week and earning a paycheck and buying a Happy Meal for a homeless man at the on-ramp, as he did the other day. He knows God brought him and Greg together in that elevator. God did it for a reason. He does everything for a reason.

For a long while, Father Greg stopped returning my calls. I knew he was busy, but this was unusual. Months later, he called back. "I'm sorry about that," he said. "I was getting treatment for my cancer." When Greg was diagnosed with leukemia, the news seemed to rock everyone around him but not him. "People here have been able to ask me, 'How are you feeling?' " he marvels. "And that is remarkable for people whose own burdens are more than they can possibly bear." As he began chemo, Johnny and Hugo and a thousand other souls walked in and all asked the same question: *What do I have that you need? Organs? Blood? Anything— tell me.* They did the very thing he had done for them: they came to the hospital. Johnny brought him a little porcelain dog. "My dog is the one who has my back," he explained. "You're my dog, G."

His voice fades more quickly now; his skin seems tender, a bit blotchier. He tires more easily. But the beard is still thick and the hair on his head has not thinned much more since I last saw him. You wouldn't be able to tell just by looking at him that there is an 85 percent chance of recurrence. For Greg, the experience has been "like being awake at your own funeral, or sitting up in your coffin," he says, smiling. "It has been a graced experience." He recalls the old Ignatian monks whose mantra was *Today.* He finds God in all things now—a multicolored leaf, a Flannery O'Connor story, a group of fellow chemo patients. Chemo itself was "interesting" more than frightening. He understands more deeply now that the opposite of love is not hate but fear, and that he cannot live in fear. And by his example, this is what he wants to show those around him. "You have to be careful what people will project onto you in terms of their fear of death," he observes. Indeed, none of the ex-homies, these hardened toughs who have seen their share of blanched lifeless faces, seem to want to speak of "Greg" and "death" in the same breath.

The grace has come, perhaps most perceptibly, in his sense that spinning the plates and keeping the tally sheets and planning what's next aren't so important anymore. "I used to think my job was to save," Greg says. "Now I don't think I can save anyone. The focus ought to be on how to stay faithful to an approach you believe in and to your principles. Anyone can do this work if you have a pulse and your head together." He tells me a story about a kid he'd once helped, whose brother had just killed himself. The kid had a dream: He was with Greg in a dark and silent room. He knew Greg was there. He knew Greg had a flashlight. Greg turned it on, and aimed the beam at the light switch. And the kid thought to himself, *I'm the only one who can flip the switch.* This child's dream has been on Father Greg's mind a lot. "It's freed me from wanting to turn the light switches on for people. I feel content to have a flashlight and to know where to aim it. Because then, it's who saved whom? Hugo saved himself when he came in to work at nine." He draws a breath. "To say nothing of God's role."

FRESH FIELDS

One of the first things I noticed about Alice Waters was her hands. They are strong. She welcomed me into the cottage where she was staying, and as she walked across the kitchen to prepare us some tea, she reached into a vase filled with long stems of peppermint and other herbs. Alice is petite, her short tousled gray-brown hair framing a youthful, nearly childlike face. With a swift and easy snap, she broke off two branches and dropped them into glasses. Cellists, carpenters, archers—I'd seen others before with such graceful force coiled in their fingers, and it made sense that a chef famous for planting and harvesting her own ingredients would have it as well. But I was surprised nonetheless.

Alice Waters is the founder of the Berkeley restaurant Chez Panisse, a famous bistro and a shrine to lovingly prepared organic cuisine. She is the author of best-selling cookbooks, and a leading voice of the "slow food" movement. I came to talk with her about teaching, and thought she'd want to muse about apprenticeships of the kitchen. Instead, she wanted to talk only about the Edible Schoolyard.

She created the Edible Schoolyard, at Martin Luther King, Jr., Middle School in South Berkeley, in 1999. The vision was simple: convert a parking lot into a garden and enable children of the asphalt city—poor black and Hispanic children whose faces, voices, palates, and hands aren't part of the yuppie organic milieu—to grow and prepare food for themselves. In conceiving the Edible Schoolyard, Alice was influenced strongly by Montessori preschools—one from her own childhood, and one her daughter had attended. Waters talked about Montessori with reverence—unsurprising for someone who in her work pays eloquent homage to the tactile experiences of a country market and the social rituals of home-cooked meals. "It's all about sensory teaching," she said, "and a hands-on emphasis."

But as with Montessori, the Edible Schoolyard's simple vision masks a sophisticated agenda. This program exists not just to do good or to grow food. It exists to teach children how to be fully realized citizens. "In this culture we just grab things to get a good life quick," she explained. "It's fast food. Everything is prepackaged. We graze and we get desensitized. We forget that everything flows from food. We can get to history, economics, politics, music. When we go to market and prepare the food, we learn how to share and work in a group. We learn how to plan ahead. We learn that pleasure and work can go together."

A few weeks later I went to see it for myself. The garden at the Edible Schoolyard is a lush, impossibly green rectangle, bursting with plants I hardly recognize. The kids, who built the garden, work together in small groups. Some are at the compost heap, others sit in a circle talking with their teacher about an Aztec grain called amarand and about the role of grain in civilization. I walk over to the ramada, a domelike shade structure fashioned out of kiwi vines that is the spiritual hub of the garden. There's a little whiteboard assigning tasks and pointing out interesting plants and birds to be on the lookout for. It's all very Berkeley, and at first I have some doubts about the rigor of the enterprise.

Then I walk into the kitchen, a trailer just off the garden. It's like a Montessori school on steroids: a maelstrom of activity as seemingly chaotic—and in fact deeply self-regulated—as an anthill. Over here four kids are chopping vegetables from the garden with huge sharp knives; to their right two other kids are rinsing utensils in the metallic sink; over next to them are a few other kids checking on biscuits baking in the oven. The kids are exuberantly talking to one another. The kitchen manager, a former chef, is directing traffic and answering questions but mainly just hovering from group to group. Across the room, another pair of kids is taking tablecloths they've just washed, dried, and ironed and setting them up on the long cafeteria tables, while three other kids set the table and put flowers from the garden in glass vases. Bethanie Hines, one of the teachers, tells me what she is doing here: "We are trusting them, giving them power. We're not following them around, and that's not something they are used to," she says. "But they always rise to the occasion." It is the meta-skills more than the kitchen skills that matter here. They're learning what to do when you make a mistake, like putting a half cup of baking soda into the cookie mix, instead of a half teaspoon. How do you ask for help? How do you set things right for people who are counting on you? How do you see a recipe through from start to finish? Cooking is only a fraction of what they are teaching.

In a short while, when the meal is prepared at last, the bustle will subside and these young teenagers will have perhaps the most satisfying and refined ritual of their week. They will eat together. As they express thanks for their meal, they probably won't think to credit Alice Waters. She isn't anywhere to be seen, and her name is never spoken. From afar, though, she has shaped every last aspect of the experience. She selected the seeds and the greens, mapped the parameters of the garden, articulated the customs of the kitchen. She created the understandings: about the rules of proper behavior (how to pass food across a table), and about the *meaning* of proper behavior (why we share meals at all). With invisible hands, she made the garden. And then she let things grow.

It had been fifteen years since I'd first marched across the searing hot asphalt of the parade deck, fifteen years since I'd eaten the dust and mud of the roads and trails that burrowed deep into the wood. What amazed me was how immediately every sensation rushed back: the stabbing pain of blisters between the toes; the load of a pack that was half my body weight; the fierce thirst that snuck up and wouldn't let go; the haze of the midday sky; the iconic beauty of the large "F" and small "2"—Fox Company, Second Platoon—stenciled on the backs of forty yellow PT shirts; the hypnotic whirring of industrial fans inside the darkened barracks. My memory was as vivid as first contact. Except now my voice didn't quaver when I spoke to the drill instructors. This time they addressed me as "Mr. Liu," politely, instead of spitting out *Liu!* or *Little one!* or, my favorite, *Glasses!*

For two summers when I was in college, I made my way to the sprawling Marine Corps base in Quantico, Virginia, for Officer Candidates School. I'd signed up at the suggestion of a friend, a former officer. The appeal was multilayered: it was a pure form of patriotism and service; it was a pure form, as well, of the kind of assimilation I then sought; and it was a call to chart the territory of my manhood. I loved it. Well, actually, I hated it until the minute I finished. Then I loved it. All told, I spent twelve weeks there, six each summer. I completed Platoon Leaders Class and earned a second lieutenant's commission. I got fitted for a uniform the fall of senior year, and was on a path to sign up for a four-year commitment.

Not very long afterward, I turned down the commission. Seeing my reflection in dress blues had done it. It had brought home just how many sides of myself, how many possible lives, I would be foreclosing. Four years suddenly seemed like forty. I was too young, I decided. With that, I ended my formal tie to the Marines. I never served a day as an officer. I eventually stopped wearing my hair so short, stopped writing dates and times in military fashion, stopped affecting the clipped manner of a professional order-giver. Surface evidence of my time there has faded. Yet a week has rarely passed without my thinking in some way about Quantico and the little channels it carved into my psyche.

Now I was back. A September morning in 2003. I'd returned to OCS to meet some of their best teachers. One of them was Gunnery Sergeant Tyrone Horton. Horton was from Cleveland, had enlisted after high school and been in the Corps seventeen years. He was straight out of a recruitment video: intense eyes, rich baritone voice, dark brown skin, neck and arms cabled with muscles, haircut high and tight, uniform perfectly creased. This was one squared-away Marine. Horton had been a drill instructor at Parris Island, then a senior DI, then a series gunnery sergeant. He came to OCS, where he was a sergeant-instructor, then a platoon sergeant, now a company gunnery sergeant. Over his career he'd taught twenty cycles of enlisted or officer boot camp.

As we talked, I did a quick calculation: at my age, I would by now be a major or even a lieutenant colonel had I gone in and stayed in. A battalion commander, leading nearly a thousand Marines. I looked around, taking in the familiar walls and signs and colors of the mess hall where we were meeting. I took the measure of the officers and enlisted Marines walking through. The captains and majors, people who back then had seemed so experienced and wise, were younger than I now. It was disconcertingly easy to imagine the quantum me in that parallel universe: the self that had decided that the black-and-white thinking of the military was more appealing than not; the self that had stayed on a single path and had yielded to the Way of the Corps. That was the appeal, wasn't it? Having a "Way" laid out for me? Having a culture to belong to unambiguously?

Horton started telling me stories about people he'd taught. There was the one officer candidate Horton called "The Preacher," a shy, religious young man who was painfully homesick. Horton made him a deal: give me a week. Horton watched him closely, coached him, told the other instructors to lay off, and he kept renewing the deal each week until the guy got through. Then there was the high school football coach who was a massive, hulking man, a specimen, but who had no idea how to carry himself; he was trying to combine too many leadership styles at once and literally could not get words out of his mouth when he was trying to command. There was the gunny sergeant with sixteen years in the Corps. Horton, his erstwhile peer, had to break him down like the rawest recruit in order to rid him of his senior enlisted mind-set. (This was a variant of a common problem. Usually the candidates are impressionable college kids, and start thinking that to be an officer is to yell and scream like an enlisted drill instructor.) There was the trial lawyer who had come to OCS to develop courtroom confidence but who, Horton chuckled, couldn't persuade a fish to swim. Back at Parris Island, there was the white supremacist who'd had a hard time taking orders from Horton. Horton eventually reached this guy, got him to open up. Just when he thought he'd made a connection, the guy dropped out.

Two things stood out about the stories Gunny Horton told. The first was just how sensitive a reader and teacher of human beings he was, capable of the most subtle tailoring. The role of the stereotypical drill instructor, for men like Horton, was only a role. "Being the stress monster all the time gets boring," he said. "You have to learn the personalities you've got and then shape people as individuals." This was something of a revelation. When I was on the receiving end of all the stress and the hazing, I figured the instructors were being completely indiscriminate in their abuse. I had no sense of how intuitive they actually are; how much they see and how carefully they use what they collect.

The second thing Horton's stories revealed was the mass scale of his work. Horton couldn't remember more than one or two names of the people he was describing. He couldn't remember the year or the class. Those he did remember he had not heard from; he had little sense of whether they were even "in the Fleet." This stood to reason. After all, each increment of OCS cycles hundreds of new people through. There is no time for deep, lasting relationships. In the moment, a master teacher like Horton can get a nuanced read on an individual candidate or recruit and provide just the right kind of instruction. The moment might last for weeks. But the moment passes. Then it's on to the next.

It is no contradiction, to be so in touch and then completely out of touch. In fact, it is perfectly apt. Someone like Gunny Horton, no matter how skilled and perceptive a mentor and instructor, is ultimately an embodiment of something else. If the Marine Corps trains its trainers well, he should be perfectly interchangeable with any other instructor. They are there to model the Marine Corps Way, to replicate it, to embody the grand design of the institution. They are there to screen newcomers and filter for the traits of the culture. But it is the culture—the rules, the rituals, the code—that truly shapes newcomers.

I do remember my instructors. Staff Sergeant Hatfield was a wiry little fireball and Staff Sergeant Graves was his tall, deadpan sidekick. But honestly, I don't remember anything in particular they said to me. What I remember is the terror of "disembarkation" on day one, followed by the joy of survival on day two; close-order drill on the parade deck and the elegance of a platoon properly executing a column right; cadence songs for slogging fifteen-mile hikes (*Mama, mama, can't you see . . . what the Marine Corps's done to me . . .*); the totemic gleam of the silver anchor and globe; the feel and weight of the M-16A2 5.56 mm rifle; the quiet crispness of our instructor's movements as he demonstrated left shoulder arms; simulating hand-to-hand combat in adrenaline-pumping pugil stick fights; keeping my knees from locking so as not to faint during company inspections under the withering sun; the names Belleau Wood and Tarawa and Khe Sanh; the words UNCOMMON VALOR painted in great red letters on the cinder-block walls of a classroom.

I was there for just twelve weeks. And it's not like I sit around and recreate that time for kicks. The memories are called up by everyday events. Seeing my daughter leave Magic Markers uncapped makes me think *at-*

tention to detail, which makes me think of how I learned to keep my foot-locker orderly. Feeling tired after a long day of writing makes me think *endurance,* which recalls those grueling runs, and *integrity.* Hearing my wife talk to her colleagues at the hospital makes me think *professional,* which reminds me how the commanding colonel once said with a smile that OCS was the world's toughest job interview. Watching a colleague throw a tantrum makes me think *bearing,* which makes me remember the unflappable calm of one of my fellow candidates as he led our squad through a small-unit tactical exercise.

After Gunny Horton and I finished chatting, we exited the chow hall. I stood there for a moment. He walked across the railroad tracks, across the empty parade deck, and toward the fields beyond, fields and forests marked with great wooden obstacles and metal ammo boxes and red-and-gold signposts. As he walked farther away, his back to me, he joined up with another Marine. Soon I could not tell who was who. My gaze returned to the fields.

CHORALE 4

Invisible Hands

Whenever we enter a bustling marketplace, we like to think that a force like Adam Smith's "invisible hand" naturally aligns all these individual agendas. But markets, we should remember, are not natural. Chaos is natural. Markets work only because of the man-made grid of rules and norms we put in place, to steer and to save people from their own worst instincts. When we become wise as teachers and mentors, we know the same is true of learning spaces. We know that what often matters most is not how we explicitly instruct or even how we listen or unblock. Our greatest impact often comes up front, in the careful design of the environment and the strategic selection of materials: in the creation and reinforcement of a culture, with rituals and role models and a pressure to belong. The environment can be a Montessori school or a Marine Corps boot camp. The materials can be kitchen toys for "practical life" or semiautomatic rifles for tactical survival. It doesn't matter. What matters is that we develop the culture; and then develop the trust to let the culture do much of the teaching for us.

PART V

Switch Shoes

THE VOICE AND THE ECHO

1

They navigated a line right through history. Amaris could sense it, eras passing and converging all around her, the churn of time and memory in swirling eddies and tugging countercurrents. They drove, just the two of them, down Auburn Avenue, through the very neighborhoods that once fed Martin Luther King, Jr.'s Atlanta congregation. And they were headed to King's church, Ebenezer Baptist. The thought of it set her mind atingle. One of Amaris's pump-up tunes, "Tom's Diner" by Suzanne Vega, was playing. It told of bells and cathedrals and voices. It was the only noise in the car. Randy didn't need to say anything. What was there to say? *Don't be nervous? Speak naturally?* Like telling Tiger Woods to relax. Besides, he could tell that Amaris was with him, only somewhere else. Her expression was absolutely placid but her limpid bluish eyes were wet, welling to the brim. Everything was rushing back. She was counting all the miles they had driven and flown together these four years, all the tournaments they had been to together, all the places he had shown her. And now they were a few minutes away from arriving. By the time the song was over, she would be in the church, at the pulpit, while Randy hid somewhere out of her sight line and listened, watched, believed.

Her brain, molded by her coach to search for parallel structure, noted this: her very first extemp speech had been at Martin Luther King, Jr.

High School in Oakland, and now her very last one would be at the church of the Reverend himself. That first speech had been, well, unforgettable. Her whole body had been shaking, her hands sweating as she clutched a small index card like a life preserver. She'd had no idea what she was saying or doing—no sense of form, rules, convention, poise, presentation. She remembered what Randy had said to her: *You're going to be just fine, kid.* She remembered that he had said it afterward, when it meant more. Now, today, *here,* if she could close her standout career with a national championship, that would be the perfect zinger (Randy-speak: a tidy ending that memorably recalls the beginning).

Of course, they both knew that as with any beautifully delivered speech, there was much more chaos and uncertainty than met the ear or eye. Just below, there was always a torrent of ideas, associations, paths of argument, rebuttals, allusions, deliciously bad puns and truly bad ones, stray statistics, quotations, all elbowing for attention and for time on the tip of the thinker's tongue. Above, only calm and self-possession. Below, the buzz and bewilderment of a mind and life on fire. And yet they both knew that the measure of the progress they'd made was this: the chaos, the madding noise, was now *beneath* the surface.

They arrived.

2

The autodidact is not inherently a good teacher. In fact, probably more often than not, he is a subpar teacher. He's come up with quirky, highly idiosyncratic ways to get himself from A to Z, which reflect the fact that he entered the subject at H and stumbled into Q and stubbed his toe on T before he figured out he ought to be starting closer to E. How would you teach someone else that kind of jerry-rigged, kick-the-jukebox-here-to-start-the-music kind of cognition? Why would you inflict that on someone? But sometimes the autodidact decides, *Never again. Never should someone have to go through what I did just to figure out how to stand and be heard.* Sometimes, the autodidact becomes not just skillful as a teacher but obsessed: obsessed with collecting and codifying every fact and principle and making sure the discipline he discovered by accident will be revealed to the next generation with purpose and logic.

When Randy McCutcheon was growing up in Nebraska, his high school did not have a speech and debate team. He decided to start one. He got a few of his nerdy pals together and they went to Hastings to challenge a team there. They got clocked. They knew nothing. They started showing up at other tournaments, still knowing next to nothing. They lost constantly, but they wrote everything down: first, what the conventions and rules were in extemporaneous speech, oral interpretation, Lincoln-Douglas debate, parliamentary debate; then, what arguments and rhetorical devices the good teams and the good speakers employed and in what situations. The team that had invented itself taught itself, without coaches or adult supervision. Randy had fun.

He graduated from the University of Nebraska in 1971, where he'd studied speech and drama and worked at the campus radio station. After a few years as an advertising copywriter and radio announcer, he went to teach English at Lincoln East High School. He started coaching the speech team there. He had no prior experience as a formal coach. What he had was a book, not a very good one, and he would read a chapter before each practice and then teach it the next day. He taught his students to become fluent in the odd language of speech and debate the same way he had: by watching other teams, taking notes, discussing, coaching one another. His teams won the state championship nine out of the ten years he was at Lincoln. In 1985 he went to Milton Academy, near Boston, where his team won the national championship. He was named the Coach of the Year by the NFL (the National Forensics League, that is), then was recruited to Albuquerque Academy, where his teams won still more accolades. In his career, Randy has sent more than sixty individual debaters to NFL Nationals, and his teams have won twenty-three state and five national championships. He is one of the greats of his profession. Now, as an author of leading high school texts on communication, he literally is writing the book on speech and debate.

To get a sense of Randy, consider the title of an acclaimed volume he published called *Get Off My Brain: A Survival Guide for Lazy Students*. The playful book, a guide to developing better study skills, begins with a Mark Twain quote—"Education is not nearly as sudden as a massacre but in the long run it is more deadly"—and contains chapter titles like "You Can Have Your Cake and Edit, Too" and "Writer's Block but Seldom Tackle." Randy, as befits a Husker, is totally corny. It's not the corniness alone that makes him winning, but how unaffected the corniness is. He is authentic. He looks pretty much like who he is. He has a bushy, droopy mustache and wears his sandy hair just a little long in the back. His face is fleshy, pink, and unweathered. He has a laid-back demeanor and kindly voice, but if you spend any time with him you see he is fussy about details. He gives overly precise directions. He prefers blazers with elbow patches. He drives an immaculate Jaguar. He is big and tall, and seems to be stooping even when he is not. He has a very astute eye for talent.

The first time Randy saw Amaris Singer was in 1999, when she was running for freshman class president at Albuquerque Academy. He was in the auditorium to hear all the campaign speeches. She went to the podium, this petite blonde with a dancer's posture and apparent poise, and immediately revealed her inability to filter the stream of ideas burbling from mind to mouth. She was a real spaz. It was something everyone knew about her; it made her fun and sometimes irritating to be around. But he saw that this girl could think, and he saw that her eyes were alive. Randy walked up to her afterward and said, "Your speech was terrible but you could be scary." Before Amaris could decide whether that was a compliment, he added, "You're on the debate team. Come to practice tomorrow."

3

Extemporaneous is not to be confused with impromptu. In impromptu, it's just *bang* and you're off. In extemp, you are given the topic and time to prepare, albeit only minutes. Before you step onstage, you have to make a plan.

Randy's plan was not, strictly speaking, to create another national champion. His plan, in the first place, was to harness the frantic energy in this girl. Amaris had been too scared to say no when Randy had told her she was now on the team. But it wasn't fright or intimidation that brought her to practice the next day. It was the idea that someone had seen something in her—*what?*—and had been so certain of it. This was a hard thing to resist, another's faith, and yet a hard thing to trust. She didn't believe she had talent. All she knew she had, something she'd developed in dance, was a work ethic. So she worked.

The first thing was structure. In fact, everything was structure. Her natural ability to fly from tangent to tangent was a gift, but it was also a curse. She had to learn to convert a maelstrom into malleable material. Then she had to learn to shape it. Randy gave her a basic framework for effective extemp speech making:

- Start with a compelling insight. (*Did you know the average campaign sound bite in 1968 was forty-two seconds and now is seven?*)
- Justify why your topic matters. (*Oratory goes to the heart of how well we function as a society. If people today don't know how to speak clearly, pretty soon they won't know how to think clearly.*)
- State the question. (*Should oratory be required in schools?*)
- State the answer. (*Absolutely.*)
- Foreshadow the reasoning. (*The three reasons why are . . .*)
- Present the points and subpoints. (*The first reason has two elements . . .*)
- Transition to a conclusion. (*In the final analysis . . .*)
- Close with a zinger. (*Because a mouth is a terrible thing to waste.*)

That would be the outline for the next four years: of her speaking, thinking, being. Randy gave her old speeches, on paper and video, to study. He showed her the compass points of logic—deductive and inductive reasoning, parallel structure, syllogism, causality, analogy—and asked her to map and remap every speech she heard. He drilled her on the fluency of her memory: she would read an article in *The New York Times* and try to recite it to him. He conditioned her on intonation, to rid her of the girlish style of ending sentences with a rising pitch. They practiced gesture and body language. They spent days doing nothing but writing and delivering justifications ad nauseam and then they'd move on to transitions and then another speech chunk. When her sense of structure was strong enough, he let her unleash her natural improvisatory instincts a bit. He wasn't afraid anymore that she would run wild.

Amaris was as predicted: scary. Everything Randy threw at her she assimilated. Like a shark, Randy observed, always moving forward. She was intensely driven, and asked for ever more examples, more material, more trivia. She would stay at school working till nine, when Randy would finally drive her to her mother's house. She was easily trained in how to carry herself, how to walk from one side of the stage to the other when she was moving from one point to the next. There is something impressive—and either alluring or disturbing, it's hard for me to say which—about someone so young and unimposing having such complete command of self and subject. Impromptu types dazzled with wit and charm; Amaris was pure extemp: through superior preparation, she could come up with a speech in the time allotted on *anything*— terrorism, women in sports, the Russian economy, reality shows—and just nail it.

She went to tournaments and even when she was eliminated she would watch those who had advanced and do postgame analysis with Randy. Then she started winning tournaments. Small ones at first, but soon bigger ones, and before long Randy could see the possibilities. Within the high-achieving, overly serious, male-dominated realm of pre-cocious debate geeks, Amaris was becoming a star. *The Dork Celeb,* as she put it. *Queen of the Nerds.* By the time she was a junior, she was going to major events like Emory and Harvard and not just winning, but dominating multiple events. She was a gymnast who could win gold on the bars and the beam and the floor. She was a machine.

Amaris loved it. She loved the fit and click of a skill grooved perfectly to her temperament. Debate, for the serious ones, was not just something to do but something to be. She *was* debate now. She also liked the new identity that came along with it: the cute blonde who could stun with her smarts. She pulled the boys right through that pigeonhole, straining their stereotypes out. But Amaris was drawn even more to the idea that identity itself was something she could rewrite. Like a speech. She *was* the speech. And if she was dealt an unwieldy topic or an inattentive judge or too much noise in the hall, why did her delivery have to suffer? She was learning to transcend meager circumstance.

4

Sometimes she thought, *I ought to be medicated.* She was only half joking. It was so easy for her to convince herself that everything was going to turn out terribly—prom, midterms, college, whatever. Around every corner in the giant maze of high school, disaster seemed to lurk. She was under so much pressure. So sometimes she would just walk into Randy's office in the middle of the day and sit down. She might give a practice speech, to get her mind off things. Other days she would come in and be silent. He wouldn't say anything either. She'd sit there awhile, and pretty soon the tears would come. For no reason. For every reason. He would put on a CD and just let the music play. The school, the counselors, and other teachers worried about her, but Randy, himself the child of divorce, knew sometimes you just had to let the music play.

Speech was so public; the most public kind of activity. But it was always her private refuge. It was the thing that was most hers. She did not want her parents to listen to her. She did not want them to have access to this. Not that they were beating down the doors to come hear her. Her mother, with whom she lived most of the time, was just thankful that Randy was in her life. She was a customer service phone rep, struggling to make ends meet. She was smart but had never been pushed. She'd joined the navy out of high school and never went to college. "Randy was a manifestation of the escape she wanted for me," Amaris said. From this life. From this father. Amaris remembers Randy telling her father, early on, that she had the stuff to be a champion. She remembers her father saying later that the coach was just buttering him up. The envy was palpable—but did he envy more the coach or the daughter? Her father was an orthopedic surgeon but had stopped working when Amaris was in first grade. He collected vintage Jaguars. "He didn't believe in me until I started bringing trophies home," said Amaris. Then he wanted to own her accomplishments, bragging to others about her victories. He never offered to pick her up from practice or to pay for her trips to tournaments.

It was Randy who bore that responsibility for four years. It was Randy who first showed her the world outside New Mexico. It was Randy who introduced her to Thai food, when the team was on the road for a tournament. It was Randy who took her to Oklahoma City the day of the Timothy McVeigh execution, because they were in the state for a tournament and, well, how could you *not* take advantage of that teachable moment? It was Randy who watched movies with her, his headphones and hers plugged into a portable DVD player on the airplane, both of them laughing super-loud as they watched *Drop Dead Gorgeous.* It was Randy who would tease her for putting highlights in her hair. It was Randy who saw her future before she did. It was Randy who suggested that Harvard, this huge symbol of achievement that had mesmerized her and seemed to embody the righting of all the wrongs of her mother's life, wasn't the only option. And it was Randy whom her mother would cite as authority to clinch an argument, citing him as effectively as a veteran extemper might quote a famous expert: *Randy said it, so listen to him.* And Amaris usually would.

5

One autumn afternoon at Albuquerque Academy, I watched Randy at work with Amaris and another student named Anne. Amaris was a senior now, Anne a sophomore. Anne had just started in speech and debate that year. She gave a practice speech, on UN weapons inspections in Iraq. By any normal standard of what a sixteen-year-old should know and be able to say about this topic, Anne was quite an effective speaker. In this setting, she seemed a raw amateur. She was nervous and rushed her delivery. Her sentences were pockmarked with *um*s and small apologies for saying the wrong word, like *obviously* instead of the less presumptuous *clearly.* The road map of her argument was hard to follow. Her transitions were uncreative declarative sentences; she did not have the confidence to pose rhetorical questions. Her references seemed to be contrived, rather than flowing from her own reserves of knowledge. She went over the allotted seven minutes. Her stance was hunched slightly, her arms hung at her sides, and her feet were fixed. She sometimes forgot to breathe.

What was interesting about the session was that many of these comments came not from Randy but from Amaris. As she became a better student of speech, she also became more of a coach. But no; that makes it sound almost accidental. As Amaris became a better student, Randy saw that the best way to solidify her knowledge would be to let her teach. And so he did. He took no offense at her interjections during his critiques of other speakers. He encouraged her. He did not mind that where she once was a blank slate awaiting his inscriptions she now confidently saw herself as almost Randy's equal. "It happened seamlessly," she told me. "He's another mind now." He didn't bristle because he had a sense of what her progress would be, and this was part of it. What he also knew was that the more she coached others, the more she might perceive her own weaknesses.

What Amaris the coach revealed most about Amaris the student was that she still needed more humor and looseness in her language. That was one thing Anne had done well in her talk, throwing in some endearing jokes and being genuinely capable of laughter. Randy had seen it. The thing Amaris's presentations had often lacked was fun, especially earlier in her career, when she was getting good and starting to win. Her motions and thoughts had always been fluid, and yet something about the speeches gave the impression of stiffness. Joylessness. She was so overwrought about achieving. She had left no room for playfulness. The way to fix this, Randy had realized, was not to tweak the mechanics of her presentation. It was to address the root cause.

During her sophomore year, Amaris was in a round-robin competition with eleven other speakers. She was the youngest one there. One of the rounds was called "The Fun Round," and Randy told her this was her chance to take some chances. On the flight to the tournament, she'd gotten a goofy Southwest Airlines cap with wings sticking out of it. The topic she was assigned in this round was, by chance, airline safety. So when her turn came, she walked onstage wearing that ridiculous hat and she tried to crack a joke about it. She didn't pull it off. In fact, the joke fell flat. She was hot with embarrassment. But when she walked offstage, she had no regrets. It had been liberating to do something so stupid. The other kids thought she'd shown guts. But what she'd shown herself was that she could have fun. She could wing it, so to speak, and survive. For the rest of her high school career, if she screwed something up she now had a ready line for Randy: "At least I wasn't wearing an airplane hat."

The summer after I saw her working with Anne, Amaris taught for two weeks at an extemp camp in Minnesota. She realized as she was coaching these students that the voice she was speaking in was Randy's voice. They had the same way of explaining things, the same patterns of thought, the same responses to surprise. One of her students was a girl from Iowa who had no experience and no team. Amaris listened to this girl speak, to figure out what she would understand, and what needed work. She was like a doctor making a diagnosis, and even as the thought crossed her mind she could hear a typical Randy elaboration: *Will she need a Band-Aid, a crutch, an amputation, or a head transplant?* And as Amaris listened, to the girl before her and Randy all around her, it became clear: one thing this nervous newcomer needed to learn was how to insert some jokes and witty asides into her talks. How to keep loose.

6

When I saw them last, at a Starbucks across from the Academy, she was two weeks from heading to college. Yale. She was excited beyond words, and he was too, of course. He had gently nudged her in that direction, thinking that at Harvard she might focus more on the prizes of education than on the process. But the moment, as we stared through the window at the heat, was bittersweet. "I'm preparing her to leave the nest," Randy said. *I'm preparing her.* She smiled silently, granting him this claim of agency. Of guardianship.

Amaris did not win the NFL Nationals in Atlanta. She placed fourth, in fact. She had burned it up in the early rounds, moving relentlessly to the finals. But in the final speech of her career, she'd been given a vast and vaguely phrased topic: "A New New World Order?" It was a quagmire of a topic; Randy mockingly likened it to "Agriculture?" She fought like hell, though. Going in, Randy had mainly been concerned that the experience be a good memory for her. He wanted her to avoid disaster. She did far more. The feeling among many coaches was that she'd shown enough grit and resiliency to earn the win. As she was delivering it, Amaris could tell she was not quite conquering the moment. But she felt it was a strong speech. "It wasn't superficial or a sellout," she said. "I was taking myself seriously." In the end, she was proud, and he was proud that she was proud.

Now Amaris is at Yale, swimming with the swift. She tried parliamentary debate for the first few weeks, but it was too much of a social scene, and so now she has gotten into Model UN. "Debate here is kind of casual," she reports. "In Model UN, people think they're going to be senators in five years." Everywhere around her are people who know more than she does, have lived more than she has, and she likes that. It's not intimidating but exciting. "I like feeling I have nothing on my résumé right now," she says. "I feel like a baby again." But this is a special baby, blessed with knowledge of how she was born. On her Model UN team, there are kids from Australia, Croatia, California, and all points between. No one she has met so far came to college with what she had. No one else had a teacher who singled them out and believed in them completely. No one else had a teacher they knew so well that they could finish each other's thoughts.

She feels Randy's influence in the practical ways: when she took her first midterm, in international relations, she calmly structured her arguments instead of just spouting. She feels his presence on a deeper level as well. She feels it in her willingness to explore: she'd recently gone to hear Joan Didion speak at a Master's Tea, just because she could. She feels it in her ability to recall the airplane hat and laugh at herself: "In a serious institution like this, it's good to remember how lame I can be." She feels it in her fearlessness: shortly after arriving on campus she talked herself into a job as "coffee girl" for Ernesto Zedillo, the former president of Mexico who now runs a center on globalization at Yale. She feels it in her ability to remind herself, amidst the chaos and teeming bustle, that it's okay not to have it all figured out. "I want to consume things around me rather than be consumed by them," she says.

For all those years that Randy was training her and molding her and disciplining her, what he wanted more than anything else was that she learn to enjoy getting better at something, to genuinely revel in it, and to make choices on that basis first. For all the winning she did, Randy never actually emphasized winning. When she took top prizes for both oratory and extemp at Emory her junior year, he'd given her a wry smile and said, "Adequate." When she lost competitions (that is, failed to win them), he would talk about the arbitrariness of judgment, and that would steel her against self-doubt. Now she can see more clearly what he was up to. Now she can see farther in every direction.

She e-mails Randy a lot. E-mail is easier than writing a real letter. "It'd be too awkward. I couldn't possibly write what he really means to me if I'm writing something superficial about the leaves changing color or something. In e-mail I'm less committed to the words." She hasn't mentioned that on Elm Street, outside her Old Campus dorm, there are Thai food vendors who set up their pushcarts in between classes. They talk on the phone too, though sometimes it's hard to catch her because she often doesn't get back to her room till well after midnight. When they do connect, the enthusiasm in her voice is infectious. Her inner spaz is reemerging, in a good way. She sounds like a nineteen-year-old (Yalie). She threads her thoughts about Zedillo and Didion and the UN with "you know" and "cool" and other bits of teen babble once banished from her speech. As she reports on her new life, Randy hears in her disembodied voice his own sense of humor—"sarcasm with decency," as she once put it—and his sense of wonder.

Randy looks forward to those chats, but they also remind him how hard it is to let go of this child. He is back in Albuquerque, back inside his house. Every week he tunes in to *The Gilmore Girls,* a television drama in which the female lead is now a freshman at Yale. He still, out of habit, keeps mining newspapers and movies and sitcoms for material— lessons in structure, good lines, clever setups—that Amaris might use. He's retired from teaching but as it has always been, work is still his life. He's got a couple new education books in the publishing pipeline, and he is pushing them through with a certain urgency. "In my writing," he says, "I'm ten years behind where I should be, because no one ever helped me." He doesn't linger. "That's why I tried to show Amaris what she could be—so that she doesn't have to lose any time or miss an experience."

7

Through the glass door in the anteroom, she could see the other finalists. It was distracting to watch their mouths moving, to see them pacing and whispering to themselves. She could not hear them through the glass, and so finally she looked away. *Amaris?* It was time. She took a deep breath and walked out before the hundreds congregated in the church. Ebenezer Baptist. She looked through the rows of crowded pews, took measure of all the faces. She let the moment hang there. This was the perfect place for her to end, and to begin. She imagined the ghosts in this church and the stories they had to tell. She anticipated all the stories yet to be told that would now hold her voice as well, and before she formed even a single sentence for her audience, Amaris had decided that this, and nothing else, was victory.

A GURU'S GURU

FRAME

1

"I had been feeling just terribly inadequate," Ben told the group. "Anxious. Competitive. There was this voice in my head—and if you're asking yourself what voice, it's *that* voice,"—the chuckles grew as the joke sank in—"and the voice in my head was always saying to me, *It's not enough, it's not enough.* That voice cost me two marriages." Ben paused, and the room fell silent. "After my second marriage failed, I recalled a line from *The Importance of Being Earnest:* 'To lose one grandparent is unfortunate, but to lose two is careless.' " The crowd laughed now, and Ben beamed like a boy. "And I saw I had to change. Yes. I had to remind myself *I am a contribution!*"

As Benjamin Zander continued his talk, I kept tally of the buzz phrases. The forty MBA students visiting from South Africa were eating this up. Their faces were lit with surprise. Who would've thought that a skinny, eccentric sixty-five-year-old classical musician would have so much to tell them about the business of leadership? But not for nothing has überguru Tom Peters called Ben "the hottest property on the leadership guru circuit today." Ben had started out a little cranky today—he'd promised to do this presentation long ago, when he was last in Johannesburg—but once he walked into the Sheraton meeting room he was energized. Now he was playing the crowd like a familiar old instrument, reeling off paradigms and parables in his mellifluous English baritone. The taglines were familiar to me, so I counted as they came, but he folded them into his remarks so seamlessly that it seemed even to me that he was inventing them on the spot.

The night before, Ben had invited the students to hear a performance of the Boston Philharmonic, the orchestra that was created specially for him in 1979 and that he has conducted ever since. Mahler Four was the entirety of the program. It was enough: the symphony is staggeringly dense and textured. As is his custom, Ben had begun the performance with a lecture to the audience about the piece, previewing the motives and themes, giving the listeners a story to listen for. The students now reported what a difference that had made for them. Some of the South Africans had never been to the symphony, so the first question one of them asked was wonderful: How did Mahler write such music? Without even thinking, Ben said, "It's a total mystery." He went first to the highest meaning. Instead of getting into the mechanics of music-writing, he invoked the ineffable, elusive nature of inspiration. Such elusiveness, he said, is what makes a conductor's work so humbling and so fulfilling.

"The fundamental lesson," he told the students, "is that the conductor doesn't make a sound. The power comes from his ability to make other people powerful, to awaken possibility in other people. It's a wonderful metaphor for leadership." He told a story, possibly true, about the great conductor Toscanini, who was a domineering tyrant. One day a bassist played a wrong note in a rehearsal and was fired on the spot. As he stomped out, the bassist screamed, "You are a no-good son of a bitch!" To which Toscanini replied, "It is too late to apologize!" Again, the students loved it. Old-style, top-down leadership was out, Ben said. "The new model is to have a clear idea of what you want and then listen to what your players have to say." He described something he uses with his orchestra called "the white sheets." At the start of each rehearsal he leaves a blank paper on every player's music stand, and invites them to express themselves in writing. Ben quoted from one such white sheet—"Notice it's 'Dear Ben' and not 'Dear Maestro' "—in which a player had suggested a delay in the downbeat at measure such-and-such and a quicker tempo in the second movement. This he called *Leading from any chair*.

In brochures, he looks like a cross between Beethoven and Andrew Jackson: lean, severe, touched by fire. In person, or at least in performance, the severity gives way to a manic enthusiasm. Ben spoke like a preacher, though without notes or podium, moving with blithe confidence from one allegory to another. His gray and wiry hair would not stay on his head. It wandered up in staticky strands, filaments crackling with current. He talked about how every year he asks his students at the New England Conservatory to write him a letter, dated on the last day of class, explaining why they earned an A: how they'd grown and changed, what kind of musicians they had become. He asks them to write these on the *first* day of class. "And then I teach to the person they have described in that letter," he explained. This he called *Giving an A*. He talked about how crucial it was for conductors to cope with failure. *Rule Number Six*, he said, was "Don't take yourself so damn seriously. When you make a mistake, just say *'How fascinating!'*" He lifted up his arms, as if in triumph, and though no one mimicked him outright, many shoulders rose subtly, involuntarily. "Let's have more broken hearts and get on with it!" he said with a broad smile.

The leitmotif of Ben's sermon, doodled on easels behind him, was the juxtaposition of a downward spiral and a radiating sun. These were the two paths we could take, in our personal and professional lives. The downward spiral was the path of conflict and self-doubt and eviscerating judgment. The radiating sun was the path of possibility. Throughout his remarks he would return, physically, to these images, walking to the easels and re-squiggling the marker down in a spiral or relaunching the arrows that burst from his sun. Every story he told, every tagline, reinforced this basic theme: we have it in us to choose possibility, to reframe our perceptions and empower ourselves and others. "Possibility thinking is *not* positive thinking," he emphasized, "for that is just a reaction to negative thinking." Thoughtful scribblings by the students. He contrasted the profit-and-loss mind-set of business with an artist's vision-driven mind-set. "You can't say, 'Vision Accomplished,'" he said. "You cannot measure it, and yet you cannot succeed without it. Goals and measures of profit are good, but just remember: it's a game." The business students nodded.

In the notes he wrote to accompany one of his recordings of Mahler's Ninth Symphony, Ben wrote that words "are far less precise than music, and so the words one uses to describe a piece will always express the emotions conveyed by the piece less precisely than the piece itself." The same could be said of Ben's performance. Even though it consisted almost entirely of words—he played no piano, hummed no tunes; the easels were his only prop—mere words do not express his exuberance, the glee and playfulness of his manner, made all the more powerful by his erudition and pedigree: had he wanted to, with his grave features and deep voice, he could have played the acidly urbane professor, or the condescending high priest. We thrilled when he answered queries by saying, "Beautiful!" As if he couldn't have imagined a better question! His pleasure was infectious. We wanted it to be. We all seemed grateful, on an unconscious level, that he was giving us Ben and not some cold maestro.

I say "we." Minutes into his talk, I was as captivated as everyone else. I kept reminding myself to take notes, to keep an observer's distance. I recorded the contradictions and tensions—that for someone who espouses listening, he lectured nonstop; that the white sheets were *letters,* an oddly formal and distant way to express what could be said face to face; that for a leader to proclaim that everyone is a leader only underscores his power—it's the hierarchy of no hierarchy. But even as I jotted, I kept yielding. I kept thinking, *So* this *is what it feels like to be in the presence of a guru.* I'd been before charismatic politicians and ordained preachers but their speeches were never this personal and cleverly pedagogical. Ben left no doubt that he was talking about *me.* His ideas could change *my* life. How did he know so much about my soul? His intermingling of wit and fable and dictum and self-aggrandizing self-deprecation was intoxicating.

It would not be difficult to mock Ben. His ideas and devices are simple. He is a bit of a cartoon character when he gets going, his unruly hair and long arms and bushy eyebrows radiating outward like . . . well, like possibility itself. Ben's passion for emotional honesty and his disregard for what sophisticated grown-ups should say are reminders that the distance is small between the Guru and the Fool. So what was it about him that made me suspend mocking judgments? He is not a cynic. That's part of it. He is so nakedly uncynical that he forces you to lower your guard. He wants you to be a child with him. But I think what kept me there with him was not his earnestness. What kept me there with him was something he had said on the drive over to the Sheraton. He was telling me how, particularly with some of his more high-strung conservatory students, he often has to ham it up extra to invite them into relationship. "I have to show them by example," he said, "that it's fine to be made a fool of." In other words, there literally was method to his madness. The effect this disclosure would have on me was, as Ben might say, fascinating: the more he revealed the workings behind the curtain, the more I came to believe the performance.

2

The reason Ben started out cranky that day had something to do with me. I was late getting to his colonial Cambridge house that morning and so we had to rush down Storrow Drive in his dark green BMW to get to the hotel on time. But what really ticked him off was when he asked me how I had liked the previous night's concert, for which he had reserved me a ticket. I confessed that I had been unable to make it. He was silent, and if he *had* been a cartoon, you would have seen the dark cloud gathering over his head. His face became closed and tight. "You want to write about how I teach," he hissed, "and you don't even come to the concert? What's that all about?" The only sound in the car was his GPS directional console telling him when to turn. I braced for a chilly morning. But when I told him that I'd been to the same concert with the same program the last time I was visiting him, he loosened. "Oh! And the same program? Well, then. But it was so *wonderful* last night." He seemed more relieved than I that he didn't have to be angry anymore. When I told him later that the reason I'd missed this performance was a tough phone call I'd had with my mother, he loosened even more, and began to offer advice and to tell me about his father.

This was all in the course of a few minutes: from neutral to wounded to furious to charming to kind. Ben's wife, Rosamund Stone Zander, or Roz, as she is known in the operation, once described him to me as "emotionally wild," and this is what she meant. This was a glimpse of the downward-spiral Ben, the Ben who had carelessly lost two marriages. It was also Roz, a psychotherapist and landscape painter, who once told me that "Ben has always been a certain kind of student in life"—uniquely voracious, hungry for clarity and rigor, apt to put people on pedestals. These two aspects of the man seemed rather deeply related, as related as the concepts are of being childish and being childlike.

Ben was blessed from the start with great teachers. His father was a fervent and liberal Zionist, an inquisitive scholar and activist, someone for whom it was perfectly normal, while writing, to get up and go to Jerusalem for four days just to see what the Al Aksa Mosque truly meant to Arabs and Israelis. There was no phone or TV, not even a car—just music and ideas and a culture of exacting analysis and riveting story-telling. "Life's an inquiry, and then you die!" Ben likes to say. He was drawn to music early, composing his first pieces at age nine. At twelve he was apprenticed to the British composer Benjamin Britten and Imogen Holst, daughter of Gustav Holst. When he was fifteen he left England to study in Florence for five years under the Spanish cello virtuoso Gaspar Cassado. He went to London University, came to Harvard on a music fellowship, and from then on made his home in Boston. He conducted a small orchestra for several years before the Philharmonic was literally created and funded for him to direct. He's made it into an orchestra with an international reputation, especially for their exemplary interpretations of the Mahler symphonies.

For many years as a conductor, Ben bore more than a passing resemblance to the Toscanini he joked about. He was mercurial and oppressively unpredictable. He would crush people with sarcasm, then turn around and lavish praise. David St. George, a pianist and musicologist, has for two and a half decades been Ben's musical consigliere at the Philharmonic. In rehearsal, David sits five rows back and takes fastidious notes on all he hears. Every few minutes, Ben will turn around and ask, "Was that all right?" Offstage, they have unending discussions about the music—the history, the composer's intentions. David is one of the few who can speak totally bluntly to Ben about what he is doing wrong. "Ben gets flattered so much," David says. "He needs people who aren't part of the bandwagon." He adds, archly: "I met Ben pre-charisma. He didn't have the skills he has now of connecting with players. He would be autocratic. He would have rages and yell and shout, and as a result, the players just became *less* expressive and *more* frightened." What enabled Ben to grow into the conductor he is now? The short answer that Ben offers, nodding in the direction of David, is "I learned to surround myself with genius."

But perhaps the key part of that answer is not the last word but the first two: Ben learned. His saving grace has always been his capacity to learn and keep learning. That is a running theme in a highly popular management/self-help book he coauthored with Roz called *The Art of Possibility*. Most of the remarks Ben delivered to those MBA students came, in one fashion or another, from this book. *The Art of Possibility* is organized around several "practices," in both the Buddhist and musical senses, on how to give an A, how to lead from the eleventh chair, and so forth. Each one is illustrated by a variety of stories and commentaries. The book works on many levels. In music, the interior lines, between the melody and the bass, often hold the most musical riches: Bach and Vivaldi sound superficially similar, but it's the contrapuntal thickness of Bach's interior voices that makes him far more interesting. The interior line of *The Art of Possibility* is the story of Ben's own metamorphosis, from an insecure petty tyrant to a pastor of possibility. You realize as you read the book, then as you see him in person, that he embodies the very transformation he is exhorting upon you.

During his remarks at the Sheraton that day, as in almost any public speech he gives, Ben read passages from the book. The book is his bible. One anecdote involved Roz. He was in São Paulo, conducting a touring American youth orchestra. The first concert was a great success, and afterward the kids partied all night in the hotel, violating curfew and an alcohol ban. Clearly action was in order. As he often does in such situations, Ben called Roz. They asked a question they have trained themselves to ask: "What distinction shall we make here that will bring possibility to the situation?" As she queried him, Ben realized he'd never explicitly discussed the purpose, the vision, for being in Brazil. In the absence of a vision, why wouldn't teenagers default to the crudest kinds of enjoyment?

So when he addressed the kids the next day, he didn't give them the scolding they were expecting. He told them how grateful the audience had been for their performance. Then he asked what else they wanted to offer the Brazilian people. The kids spoke of friendship, cultural understanding, showing the best of America, and things in that spirit. When they'd offered enough, Ben said it was understandable how excited they'd been after the concert but that waking hotel guests obviously didn't epitomize the gifts they'd just described. "We got off track," he said. "You have to know where the track is to get back on, and you've all just expressed that beautifully." The kids then offered to write letters of apology and to make amends. That night's concert was another success.

There are several such stories in the book, where Ben turns to Roz in a moment of crisis and she helps him convert it into a moment of creation. And there are others not in the book. On one occasion, while conducting the London Royal Philharmonic, Ben mishandled and offended two of his players during rehearsal. When the letter of apology he wrote only made things worse, he called Roz urgently. "She made me see that my attention shouldn't have been on my justifications but on *their* experience." Another time, Ben was in Israel conducting. One of his violinists, seized by a fear of random violence, refused to leave her home. Ben called Roz for help. Roz told Ben, "Just tell her you are Merlin. Merlin lives his life backwards and has seen the future, so you know she will be safe." Roz knew Ben could pull off that line with just the fantastical touch that would make the violinist respond. He did, and she did.

As I heard such tales, I realized I'd found quite a character: a transformative public educator/performer, his gifts and flaws inseparable, surrounded offstage by wizardly aides like Roz and David who help regulate his moods, control his ego, provide reality checks, and generally keep him on track. To his credit, he let them work him over. "You cannot be a coach," Ben once said, "unless you are coachable." Roz, in particular, seemed to have a unique role: not only personal trainer, but personal therapist. How great would it be to have one of those? One day I asked Ben about Roz. "Oh, she's always coaching me," he said. "I actually think of Roz as the guru—not me." He seemed sincere, but I saw this simply as the ostentatious modesty of a practiced public figure. Ah, I thought, what a piece of work this Ben Zander is. It wasn't until later that I'd realize how much I hadn't seen.

REFRAME

1

In the grand piano room of Ben's old house in Cambridge hang two large canvases. They appear to be a set, and they depict afternoon in a shaded wood. The brushwork is extraordinary. It's an intensely dappled impressionism. The variations of green, the manipulations of light, make it difficult to distinguish a leaf from a patch of filtered sun. The images seem nearly photographic but the blurring of shape and shadow is just painterly enough; before you sense it, you have sensed a hand at work. Roz painted these many years ago in Maine, where she spends most summers and many weekends. Not all her work has this phenomenological closeness; other landscapes of hers are broad, clear vistas of sunset that evoke Bierstadt and the American West more than the French Impressionists. But regardless of the style she works in, what you notice is the way she has framed the image. She has an exquisite sense of composition. She creates balance from the subtlest asymmetries.

2

In her practice as a therapist Roz has created something called the accomplishment group. She gathers six to eight people and they work together over five or six months. Each person brings to the group a substantial creative project they want to accomplish—it could be finishing a novel, starting a magazine, launching a Web business, creating a sex therapy group, whatever. "My goal," Roz says, "is to reframe their thinking patterns." She starts the first session with a collection of about fifty buttons, each with a foible humorously printed on it (like "Cleverly Disguised as a Responsible Adult"). Then they play a game: pick a button representing the part of you most likely to get in the way of your project. "This is the calculating, downward-spiral self," Roz explains, "and now I've got it hooked to their lapels instead of inside of them." They learn to talk about their fears in a safely objectified way: "Remind me—what's your button?" Each week, Roz asks the members to do something in a nonlinear mode. What a great concept. And each week she asks them to take three steps toward their goals. "If they see they're not going to make it," she says, "we change the goalposts."

3

We will always be in relationship, she told him, but we just have to figure out the form. He was floored. What would this mean? She didn't have a clear idea, honestly, and she could sense his rising panic. She wanted to respond to it, so she said she had in mind that they might live together again. But she knew well that they were better off apart. They were both big people with lots of projects, she said, neither one subsuming easily under the other's life. The volume of Ben's voice and of his presence, the way his music absorbed all energy and crowded out all attention, was not good for the children, particularly Roz's two. "It was absurd to think he'd become more democratically oriented," she recalled. The only thing for them to do was to separate. Ben, at long last, relented.

There was one time a few years later when she thought she saw a change, enough to make her reconsider. She summoned the courage to invite him back. He was unsure. Early one morning they had what she described as their most intimate moment, walking among the paths and colonial headstones of old Mount Auburn Cemetery. As they talked it through, Ben realized at last that he could not give up the publicness of his life; the publicness *was* his life. He cried. He would not be coming back. But something stabilized that quiet dawn. They went on to talk about all the things they could still do together.

Ben and Roz have remained separated for nearly twenty years. They live in houses down the block from each other. They are on the phone often several times a day. They see each other nearly every day they are in the same city. They work far more closely together than most spouses and are far more emotionally "tuned up," as Roz puts it, than most business partners. And their relationship exists in an ambiguous zone between marriage and work. She keeps his name. In a social setting, she might call him her husband. It depends on the circumstances. And yet this is one of the marriages that Ben describes in public as failed: the second one, the one he lost so carelessly.

In any event, they rarely talk about the relationship per se. The familiar arguments—about his lack of attention to her, her criticisms of his calculating self—are past. They don't go there anymore. What they do now is *do*. For two decades they have tackled work problems. Ben calls her from all corners for counsel. "We don't even do small talk," he says cheerfully. They engage on projects together, like last summer in Maine when they wrote the extensive brochure for the Philharmonic's twenty-fifth anniversary season. "People tend to focus on the body and flesh as the identity," Roz said one day. "With Ben and me, the identity is in the in-between. We separated, reconstituted our ground as our own people, and came back into partnership to create." Ben said to me later, "The wonderful thing is, there is no hierarchy in our relationship."

4

"I listen for how the past is catching the person."

We are talking on the phone, so I cannot pick up any cues except what her voice offers. It offers a lot. Roz speaks haltingly. Tiny micropauses, half a second, randomly interrupt the stream of her words. It is not shyness, or at least not only shyness; she simply stops and thinks, even if she is mid-sentence. There is something birdlike about her, tentative and alert. For a moment it seems she has a faint English accent, but then it passes. Born and raised in Boston, she went to Swarthmore and then art school in New York, after which she got a degree in social work. She is telling me now about her therapy practice. "In my mind there is a line," she says. "All above the line is future creation. All below is history and a pool of assumptions. I am trying to help people get above that line. I see myself as a possibility coach."

It was Ben's suggestion that I contact Roz. My intention when I call is to ask her how she coaches Ben, how she has awakened him to his latent potential. Let me rephrase that: My intention when I call is to get some colorful details about Ben. She has interesting things to say. She speaks of the difference between performing and listening, how Ben's public lecturing requires him to tune in closely to the audience, to see whether they are with him, but does not require him to listen for individual lines. She observes that she is an abstract thinker where Ben is more concerned with everyday life. She tells me the Merlin story to illustrate how synchronized their thinking has become.

As she speaks, though, there is resistance in her voice, a slight chafe. "We see things now the same," she says. Mm-hmm, I respond. That's from being with Ben for so long? She goes into one of her pauses. I can practically hear the hard drive in her head whirring. "I create the paradigms," she resumes, "and Ben is an apt student." *Apt student,* I underline in my notes, intrigued by her word choice. So, I ask, you came up with the ideas in the book together? At last, the irritation must be too great; history is about to catch her again. "The ideas in the book are *mine,*" she replies. She tries hard not to sound prideful. "He is a *demonstration* of them." Now it's my turn for a micropause. "I wrote the whole book," she continues, "both his voice and mine." Now I'm rather glad we are on the phone and not in person. On the phone, I can recover and ask follow-up questions in a perfectly natural tone, as if to say *Of course I knew you wrote the whole book and that's just what I was going to ask about next.* In person, she would see the expressions cross my face one after the other: surprise, comprehension, then embarrassment at the limits of my sight.

Roz goes on to explain how she wrote the book. She knew his speaking style like her own, and could write in it freely. She knew his trove of stories as well, the memorable moments from his conducting career and the rhetorical set pieces he had started to use in his teaching. Rule Number Six ("Don't take yourself so damn seriously"), for example, came from a joke Ben had heard once. He and Roz had used it with each other in private, but it was Roz who made a paradigm and a practice out of it.

The giving of A's (and the letter from the future) Roz had suggested, as a way of encouraging Ben's students to be more expressive. And it was Roz who saw in that material the potential to spin a much more powerful metaphor. Of course, the core motif of "downward spiral versus radiating sun" was drawn from their relationship and the choice they made to end a marriage in order to save it. Even the idea of "practices" was something she conceptualized, and it didn't come until her fourth year of work on the book. She'd tried landscape forms, then musical ones, before finally landing on the form of practices.

Their interaction, as she describes it, is convective: Ben gives Roz raw content from his work; Roz converts that content into a language that orders not only Ben's presentations but his life. And as the creator, the teacher, she is free to add material from other sources she encounters as well: her own father, her clients. "Ben exists and invents within the paradigms I create," Roz says. She means this generously. For him to exist this way, to rein in his worst self, has required great force of will. For him to invent this way is something exceedingly rare. She could not take these ideas out into the world and perform them, improvise with them, the way he can. She would not, with Ben's bravado, tell *Fortune* 100 CEOs why they would be *lucky* to have a chance to underwrite Ben and his orchestra. She lacks his daring and buoyancy. His personal magnetism. She does not have his gift for building large-scale community either. With music as his tool, he can walk into a room in any country and create a spirit of mass fellowship. She sits quietly in a cabin and thinks; he goes out to proselytize.

"Ben thinks of me as his teacher, not vice versa," she says. But as Roz acknowledges, "this dynamic is led by Ben," and in his eagerness to learn he does set an example for Roz. His father, his first wife, David, Roz—all these are people Ben has sought out for intense learning. "He looks for teachers," she says, "and is without ego when that happens." Ben's father would see all sides of a situation, Roz says, and would enlarge the frame if people were upset about something. "Ben doesn't trust himself this way because he is so emotional and comes to conclusions at lightning speed." Ben echoes this, in a separate conversation. "In the emotional world of music and passion," he says, "often clarity is what is missing. Roz enables me to have clarity, so I don't go off track."

Those words are not all that different from things Ben has said to me in the past, about how masterful a teacher Roz is and how well she has trained him. Now I hear them anew. As Roz speaks of her creation, a new image forms in my mind. Imagine you are at the symphony. The conductor is the only individual you see. Everything else is collective: two dozen violins to the left, three dozen cellos and violas to the right, brass and wind instruments in between. But the conductor, who stands alone, stands apart. In him you invest everything: hope, attention, love. In him, in his smallest gestures, his expressive face and passionate dance, you see embodied the very spirit of music. It is so easy to forget, watching this great man perform, that he is here because someone else wrote the music.

INTERPRET

1

The class Ben teaches at the New England Conservatory is called "Interpretation." It is a famous class, and always fully enrolled. It is not about conducting or instrumental play. Nor is it a music history class. It is simply another setting for the gospel of possibility. Ben bounds into the large, high-ceilinged studio, an open grin on his face. The students, many foreign-born and many of those from Asia, titter.

He leads off with a white sheet from last week, reading the words of a student who says she is jealous of his energy. "It's not *my* energy," Ben insists, putting the paper down. "It is the energy of possibility and it is available to you. This is not about me; it is about a power." The students don't look convinced. Next he tries to open a conversation about the assignment he'd given them last week, which was to "Throw yourself into life like a pebble and watch the ripples." One of the students meekly offers that she convinced her in-laws, who knew little about music, to come to hear her play in recital. "Beautiful!" Ben exclaims. What kind of person, he asks the group, could get their in-laws to come to a concert? The students toss around various adjectives: *energetic, inspirational, persua-sive, influential, contagious.* "You've just described a great musician," Ben says. "Just add: *will stop at nothing.*"

The next few comments are from people who seem to want to make ripples but don't know how. One talks about how difficult it is to get pay-ing students. "Get yourself a student even if you have to pay *them*," Ben says, to giggles. "You *must* teach." To another who laments that she wants to perform but no one wants to hear her, Ben replies, still with his inno-cent smile, "You have a limited definition of 'performance.' Saying there are no audiences is like saying there are no people!" This leads him, sev-eral minutes later, to a riff on truth and story. "Nothing I say is true," he announces. "Do you understand that? I can tell stories, but don't expect to get the truth. One story is 'Classical music is dead.' Another is, 'You ain't seen nothin' yet.' Which one is true?" He tells them about a time he was snowed in at the Cleveland airport. There was nothing to do. So Ben, listening to a recording of the Philharmonic, started walking around the gate area, putting his headphones on any willing traveler. One of the peo-ple he accosted was an executive at Coca-Cola, who ended up being so enthralled with the music and Ben's missionary zeal that he later arranged corporate sponsorship for Ben's programs. "You cannot *not* create rip-ples!"

This was the entire first hour of class. The second hour is devoted to more explicitly musical work. A flautist, pianist, and cellist step up to the front of the class to play a Bach flute sonata. They play nicely and prettily, with few mistakes. As soon as they finish, Ben says to the class, "I want to introduce a new technical term to you: *boring.*" Turning to the players, he says, "You were trying to be expressive but weren't able to be." Now, to the class, "Let's hear the symptoms of this disease called *boring.* Who would like to be the doctor?" One student, looking at Ben, starts to say something but Ben cuts him off: "Speak to the patient." Another offers a hedging diagnosis, prompting Ben to advise, "If a doctor were to say, 'If you know what I mean' or 'You could sort of,' the patient would leave." Another student mumbles "Reduce the number of impulses." Ben asks her to be more precise and she says, "Play the phrases over four bars in-stead of one." The trio tries this. Not much effect. Try again. Another says, "All the focus is on the flute, maybe we should bring out the cello and piano." Nope, still boring. "A little faster." "Lean on the syncopation." "Start softly and build." The players try to respond to each suggestion, but to no avail.

At last, satisfied with the efforts of his interns, the attending physician reveals the true diagnosis: "The piece," he says, "begins with an ending. Which means the cello here is key." And indeed, unlike many pieces that start squarely on the downbeat, this sonata opens with the cello playing an upbeat from the end of an implied previous measure. Ben walks over and borrows the cello. He plays lightly, and a bit out of tune, but with enough fervor in his eyes and enough exaggerated breathing to impress upon them the difference between an inhale and an exhale. Try again. At first there isn't much difference, but Ben stands right in their midst, hovering over them, making eye contact—*conducting* them—and literally breathing life into their play. His excitement is infectious, and the players become more expansive, more dramatic in their crescendos and contrasts. His sharp intakes of breath, the sounds of spit being sucked in, come out in the rich oxygenated sound of their play. The flautist, a pretty girl with her hair tied back in a long ponytail, begins to rock her torso with the music. Ben notices and quickly walks behind her, letting her hair down as she plays. The liberty he has taken seems great but it is nothing more than the liberty he has given.

When the piece is done and everyone has come back down to earth, Ben adds a thought for emphasis. "Many pieces begin with an ending," he says. "It's called implied elision. I'll give you a dollar for every example you can find!" As a boy, to amuse myself, I would sometimes say, "Let's go pig" over and over again. After a few seconds of *letsgopigletsgopigletsgopig* it became hard to tell whether I was saying "Let's go pig" or "Go piglets" or "Pig let's go." It all depended on where I put the accent. "Once you see something as both an end and a beginning," Ben explains, "you can give the piece some direction." It's a game. "I call it, *What belongs to what?*"

2

Roz, on occasion, fills in for Ben at the conservatory. The thought of her teaching Interpretation makes me wonder. I wonder whether the students Ben touches in class retain the spirit he instills at that moment. Surely they remember the moment; it was indelible for me even as an observer. But do they preserve the feeling inside? Can they re-create it later? How does the feeling latch on to their inner selves? On what hook, what psychic hangnail, will the lesson catch? When Roz teaches this class, she says, "I listen for what their individual dream is." She asks what each of them wants. They begin with answers like, "I want to play the Sibelius concerto without mistakes." She pushes for bigger wants. She asks them what they would do if they could do *anything*. And pretty soon, they are talking about starting a restaurant. "I just ask them for a dream," she says.

Roz has been recognized for her paintings and her innovative therapy practice. But as Ben has become more famous, in good measure on the basis of their book and the ideas within, her relationship to renown has become more complex. There is an open space, she says, between the purely private and the purely public. That is the space she wants to occupy. Still, it's hard on her when people come up and tell her they love Ben's book. Her name is first on the hardcover. On the paperback, her name has even been enlarged. "Many people still don't see it. That can be maddening," she admits. "I don't have an ambition to be onstage, but I do like to be recognized for what I have done."

Ben takes pains to describe the book as her handiwork. "I'm a prominent character in it," he says, "but it is her book. *She* took the stories and fashioned them into something. *She* made the connections. It's her life-work." He reflects on the difficulty of overshadowing a teacher. "It's an ongoing conversation," he says. "She has had to come out from behind the shadows. She doesn't always like it when I push her out there." The unfortunate reality, he says, is that "people didn't want her book, they wanted my book. The world wants heroes to put on a pedestal, and that's a problem." When I compliment him on his ability to share credit, he admits, "I didn't always have this. I had to learn that partnership enhanced me; it didn't diminish me. The hero alone is less effective and has a less rich tapestry of gifts than one in partnership."

Roz tells me one day about her original concept for *The Art of Possibility*. We've been talking for a while, and her voice is enthusiastic. She describes the way she composed the book in three voices—Ben's, hers, and an omniscient—"because any transformation is about relationships. You can't do it in one voice." At that very moment, Ben bursts in. He'd been ringing her but wasn't getting through because Roz was on the line with me. So he walked down the block to her house. It's a crisis. One of his soloists has announced, without warning, that she will miss the concert. Ben gets on the line. "I'm terribly sorry, Eric," he says cheerfully. "I hope you'll understand!" I ask him to tell Roz I will e-mail her to arrange another call. "Wonderful, I will," he says, and he hangs up.

3

Ben no longer sees individual students. "Even if I am teaching one person," he says, "it's for everyone else in the room." I ask Roz about the difference between Ben's mass scale of teaching and her more intimate, one-on-one milieu. But she questions the premise. She thinks this idea of intimacy is complicated. "The psychoanalytic definition of long-term relationship is one thing," she says, "but intimacy might be instant too." Imagine if you are at a lecture and the speaker says, during Q&A, "I'm not sure I agree with you but let's meet for coffee afterward." Intimacy can be invented. "You can know each other and be in a mode of sharing and pick up the gate that is the border between us. As a therapist, I have to decide which gate to open to which emotion. I tell stories of myself, even dicey ones." Ben does this too, she says: he tells stories of himself that go to people's hearts. "That's why people feel intimate with him," she says. Even if it's not individually tailored, they still get to participate with him.

For his part, Ben knows "I can whisper to eighteen hundred people and they'll all say they felt like I was talking to them. But the dark side is I can't keep that presence up indefinitely." Also, it'll happen not infrequently that he will have no idea at the airport that he has just spoken to someone at one of his speeches and the person will leave offended. "The by-product of a completely public life," he says, "is that I'm a beginner at this." At intimacy. "I revere Roz's talent for it." She uses herself, he says, as an instrument for transformation. "If there is an obstacle, she asks what about her *self* is in the way, rather than just trying to help the student more and more. She is a full-blown adult, and I know very few. I'm on the way," Ben says. "But I'm still a student."

4

His father's life was nearing its end. He was ninety-four and could no longer see. Ben's brother advised him to spend just fifteen minutes in the room; the man was too weak now to talk more than that. Ben entered. He had just given a lecture, so his father asked, "What did you say?" It was one of Ben's typical performances, about conducting and music and fear and possibility. He spent an hour and a half telling his father about it. "How fascinating," his father said. He asked if Ben had a tape of the lecture. Ben did, and for another hour and a half they listened to it. At the end, his father said, "We didn't know anything else." The old authoritarian models, of how to lead and to teach, were all his generation had. *We didn't know.* At first Ben took it for apology, but then he understood it was regret, that another lifetime was not available to try the new way.

5

To write the book, Roz escaped to Maine. She had to get away from everyone. She lived in a tent for six weeks. She had a truck and she'd take her dog and go into a field to paint. She didn't think; she just painted for hours on end. Her eyes got very tuned up, and as they did, the light became more layered and delicious. "There was a conversation," she said, "between me and it." For a period, though, she fell into a funk and couldn't write. She was reading a book on evolution, and the whole of it—the idea that our instincts were made over eons, that it would take eons to unmake them—depressed her. "I couldn't see my way through," she said, "until I got above evolutionary principles. Then I saw that our *thoughts* can evolve more rapidly—way more rapidly—than we can." That was when the story finally came.

MIRROR, MIRROR, MIRROR

Sometimes, when my mother and I discover that we had the same reaction to a *Seinfeld* episode, or the same visceral response to a Chinese painting, or the same opinion about a political news item, she will say, "Well, of course; you're my son!" And I will say, "Well, of course; you're my mother!" I'll pronounce it *mah-ther,* extending the vowel so it mimics her accent. So it sounds like *mama.*

My mother was my first teacher. She still is. One of the many ways she has taught me is by simple precept. Over the years, like a professional politician, she's developed a few core messages that she repeats to me tirelessly. When we get on the phone, whatever we might start out discussing, the conversation will usually work its way back to one of her trusty statements: *Don't get cocky. Remember basic decency. Think from animal's point of view.*

Don't get cocky was something she started emphasizing when I was writing speeches for the president in my twenties and enjoying a burst of publicity as a whiz kid. She was proud, of course, and she knew I wasn't going to become a pompous monster. What she feared was that by degrees I might start to feel entitled to the attention; that I might mistake accolades for worth. *Remember basic decency* also grew out of my D.C. years, when she saw how easy it was for someone to become clever rather than wise. Today, she still scrutinizes all my public speeches and television commentaries. She will sit for hours at a stretch watching the video-tapes. When she's done, she'll tell me what she thought of my words and how I looked, but her real assessment will be whether I showed integrity—basic decency—or whether I gave off even the faintest vibe of being a cynic or a calculating tactician. *Think from animal's point of view* was the amusing finale of a litany she once recited after an argument we'd had. I needed to learn to see things from her point of view, she said. Or from Carroll's point of view, or from a friend's point of view, from an oppo-nent's, a tree's, and so on.

Another profound way she has shaped me has been by example. It's by her example, after all, that I put stock in simple precepts. It's by her example too that I've learned to have persistent faith in our own per-fectibility, in spite of all available evidence. My mother still believes that if our shortcomings are revealed to us in a candid and constructive way, we can fix them. It's by her example as well that I have learned how to ask a question. She is the most inquisitive nontoddler I know. Her curiosity is completely unaffected. Whether at a meeting or a cocktail party or a lec-ture or a dinner table, she has no inhibitions about asking one more *Why?*—and then one more after that. You're in the business of loading and off-loading barges? You are studying the science of sleep and dreams? You're going to help lead a citizens' initiative on school funding? You are a geriatrician? *How come? What does that mean? How does it work?* She never pretends to understand; she only does or does not.

Teaching by example is more indirect than teaching by precept. But the two approaches have in common the idea that lessons should be pack-ageable: an experience, like a maxim, may be used to represent a single lesson and then may be filed away. More elusive, more interesting, and perhaps more lasting is the third way my mother has taught me. And that is by letting me teach her.

In recent years I've become something of a workplace coach for my mother. She works for a big defense contractor that acquired the part of another company that had acquired the part of IBM that she came to work for when she first moved to Washington, D.C., thirteen years ago. She'd been living in upstate New York, an IBMer like my father and so many others in Poughkeepsie. Six months after his death she moved south to be nearer to me, and she stayed even after I left, putting down roots or something like them. Her work appeals to her puzzle-solving side. But in many ways, she's the last person you'd expect to find in a gigantic military-industrial concern. She has an artist's spirit, a painter's eye. She is full of wonder and is up for any new experience. When she discharges an adult responsibility, like bill-paying, she lets out a cheer and dances a silly dance that makes her look like a two-year-old. She has a novelist's ability to *feel;* to sense the meaning of stray details and the ambiguous, unresolvable nature of things. But she never has cultivated her ability to express any of this.

So there she is. There are things she wants to explore when retirement comes, as it will soon, but work does offer intellectual stimulation and a kind of community. The work itself is not easy. It requires her to make presentations to executives. She has to work with military men to organize multiteam projects, or communicate in her second language about things in a highly technical third language. Sometimes she needs advice. We talk things through. I have no context for the org charts and acronyms, so I try in a generic way to answer her questions. I coach her on how to be a better listener. How to reveal the right amount in a negotiation. How to make sure she has support in the team when she proposes something. How to be less *mán,* or impulsive. How to think ahead several moves, instead of following a philosophy of *zŏu yi bù, suàn yi bù:* walk a step, count a step.

This used to be work my father did. They used to sit at the table after supper, on nights when he didn't have to be on dialysis, and they'd smoke one or two cigarettes each and talk for hours about office politics, his and hers. She would describe tense situations and looming conflicts, some of which she was participating in and others just observing, and he would break them all down for her. He had all the answers. He had a way of cutting through problems, thorny tangles of bureaucracy and personality, and making them manageable. Just talking it through with Dad would make Mom feel better, even if it was too late to fix. When he died, there was no question she'd need me to be her sounding board, and no question I would be it. After nearly a decade and a half in this role, I am like a graft you no longer notice but whose underlying roughness remains.

Sometimes, when I'm doing this kind of work now, I get impatient with Mom. I can get frustrated with her mistakes; errors in judgment that are consequences of temperament and that give the lie to the faith we profess to have in human perfectibility. I might get annoyed that it takes her so long to explain the background of all the situations she's dealing with. I also have moments of self-pity, wishing Dad were here to help us both and wondering where *my* coach is to help with all *my* questions. On occasion I simply get angry at the way it seems fate has kept her from developing her truest talents. When I'm angry this way, I on occasion do an odd thing: I take it out on *her.* I get sarcastic, cut her off in mid-sentence. And when she bears it, I realize what a child I am still.

If I were more consistently aware, I might see more clearly what is happening. By asking for my help, by putting me in the role of coach, she is showing me a way to become the kind of teacher my father was. She is asking me to become as kind and patient and strategic and perceptive as he was. This is a chance for me to internalize what I teach; to practice self-improvement by preaching it. When I am urging her to stop procrastinating, I am underscoring my own need to do the same. When I am telling her that *zŏu yi bù* is not good enough, I am reminding myself of that. And when I say she needs to be less rash and more willing to step outside herself to analyze the situation, I reinforce that need in myself. In so many ways, my patterns mirror hers. We keep looking to each other, and to my father's memory, to triangulate our way to a clearing.

It's not literally true that my mother, with clinical intent to advance my education, "put" me in this position. Circumstance put us in this position. But it is true that in order for us to make the best of circumstance, she has had to yield. She has had to invite me into a new role, to set aside any pridefulness and be willing to depend upon my assistance. There are plenty of widowed parents who could not allow or acknowledge that. She has. She tells me how best to teach her. She gives feedback on whether my approach is helping and how I can improve it. How I should deliver a message so she will most readily receive it. How to assess her anxieties before I launch into a lesson. How to break things down and relate them to things she knows already. How to help her decode the many cultures she is trying to move in. She is teaching me how to teach. She is disabusing me, in the process, of the idea that I am the one helping her.

As I've grown conscious of this, I have begun to question my assumptions about what it means to be well cast or miscast in our lives. How many of us get to be perfectly cast, to have our aptitudes in complete alignment with our daily work? Yes, we should strive for perfect alignment. But my mother's example reminds me that the measure of what we are—today—is how well we learn to learn, no matter what role we find ourselves in. She's had the resiliency to keep narrowing the gap between the world she has now and the nirvana of fully realized potential. If it is trying for me to help her navigate the corporate maze, what must it be for her? And yet, she still discovers in her work many reasons to be passionate and creative. She keeps finding spores of inspiration.

Sometimes my mother leaves her office late at night, long after everyone else has returned to their homes, and as she crosses the nearly empty parking lot she glimpses a maple tree in full growth, the leaves catching the beam of a streetlamp and holding the light in soft green cradles. It doesn't matter how long a day it has been, how weary she might be at that moment. As she comes upon those leaves, lit that way, the branches swaying just so, she feels a sense of joy and wholeness and belonging. Of course, I paraphrase. I've tightened up the scene, put it all in one language, chosen apt words and proper grammar. I've said it correctly; she probably said it better. When my mother tells me things like this, when I try then to convey what it is she has said, I know what a student I am still. I've never seen that tree, but when she described the moment I knew exactly what she meant. Of course I did: I'm her son.

CHORALE 5

Switch Shoes

When we teach, we frequently get the advice that we should step into our students' shoes. And yes, we should: that is what it means to receive before transmitting. But when we are being truly transformative teachers, we enable students to step into *our* shoes. The best way to get someone to learn something is to invite her to teach it. By doing that, we give her a chance to see herself anew; to observe, out of body, her own patterns of performance; to imagine and articulate strategies for improvement. Like a coach. Those who look like great teachers are usually just great students, working overtime to learn.

What happens when teacher and learner switch shoes? What happens when we stand between two facing mirrors? We see ourselves in full. We find out who we are: what we've inherited, what surrounds us, what is ours alone. We mark the maturation of a relationship—and the birth of identity.

CODA

A parable. An old farmer, on his deathbed, tells his sons that there is treasure buried in the fields. After he dies, his sons dig and dig, turning the soil over in search of the treasure. They find nothing. But the next year, the harvest from those fields is the most bountiful ever.

What I like about that parable, which I got from Ben and Roz Zander and which they got from who knows who, is its indirection, and the cleverness of the old farmer. But the tale did leave me unsatisfied. What about all of us who don't have a farmer figure? I don't mean just a father. I mean a teacher. What about all of us who aren't ever prompted by somebody, even indirectly, to go out and make the discoveries that matter?

That's most of us, I think. Most of us go through life dimly aware that our trajectories could fill more of the sky, that our potential could be more fully realized, if someone were leading us through. But how do we find that guide? When I set out to write this book, I thought it would be only a matter of searching. So I searched awfully hard. I trod many winding paths. I logged thousands of miles, spent dozens of nights in airport motels, filled up sixteen notebooks and created hundreds of files with the stories of people who, in one form or another, were shepherds. It wasn't until long after I returned home that I realized I had found the meaning I was searching for. It had come not from any one of the shepherds, as remarkable as they were. It had come from the path. The trudging. The listening. The witnessing and the impulse for empathy.

At last, I was able to be an apprentice. I was apprenticed to the experience of searching for a master.

We forget so easily what we already know. We overlook so quickly what we already have inside us. Think about it. You know something already about how to receive before you transmit. How to unblock and unlock. How to zoom in and zoom out. How to use invisible hands. How to switch shoes. And you have it within you to get better at each one.

Revisit the notebooks of your own life, whether they are composed of paper or pixels or the chemical bath of dreams. Out of the stream, out of the record of all the teaching you have done—as a leader, as a tutor, as a healer, as a giver—an awareness will arise. A consciousness that speaks. And it will be saying to you: "Teacher, teach thyself."

Toward the end of my travels, I met a teacher of aerobatics, the beautiful and grueling sport of stunt flying. Sergei Boriak was once a star Soviet pilot and is now a legendary American coach. What surprised me about Sergei is that he doesn't leave the ground when he coaches. He sits in the airfield parking lot on a folding chair, his neck craned upward. As his students soar above, performing balletic aerial routines, he mutters into a small tape recorder: *More, more. Just the right foot. Not the best way. Better to make more distinct pitch. Exactly. When you start second roll, you have to pull the stick again enough to push forward. Perfect. Keep the nose down. Left foot, left foot, left foot. Good.*

As he speaks, his feet and hands twitch slightly, like the paws of a dreaming animal. He can feel the pedals and the levers. He can feel the rightness of the angles and the violence of the torque. Often he will pick up the radio and coach the pilot in real time. But much of the lesson comes via the recording. The student will land. She'll emerge from the plane, take the recording, go to the hangar and put on headphones. In her mind's eye, she'll re-create the routine and line up each of his comments with one of her moves. She'll stop the tape to jot some notes. Sometimes she'll stop the tape just to think, *How in the world did he know that?* Then she'll keep listening.

This is what teaching is all about: becoming the voice in someone's head. Whose voice do you carry with you? Who whispers to you like a conscience? I can say today, at the close of this journey, that fragments of Sergei Boriak's broken English are lodged in my head. Ivana Chubbuck's smoky voice, telling me how to live, insinuates itself into my internal monologues. I can hear Bryan Price after a bull pen session, and I can make out the rasp of Bob Abramson's one remaining vocal cord. David Boren is telling me something now, and though his Oklahoma lilt is different from Diane Dietz's Chicago flatness or Tom Brown's Anacostia cadence, they all are saying the same thing. Ellis Marsalis I hear distinctly, especially through Branford. There is Dick Monday, with astounding range. Judy Baca is recounting stories that fill my head with color. Danny Lehmann and Greg Boyle are speaking of new rites and flashlights, telling me of a spirit I think I now know better. I hear Alice Waters, cool and quiet, and then I hear Gunny Horton and the clockwork of close order drill, heels and rifles clicking. Randy McCutcheon is dispensing wisdom in humorous doses. And Ben Zander's instrument, layered in harmony with Roz Zander's, reverberates still. I hear my father. I do. I hear my mother, my wife, my daughter.

Now ask yourself: Who will carry *your* voice? With every pulse, every gesture, we send out signals like the satellites above. Years from now, who in the world will receive your signal? Who will hear the time-lapsed sound of your voice and respond as if you were right there? Whether we mean to or not, we all leave a legacy. And the legacy that matters most is measured not in steel or silver or bone or blood. It is measured in the voice we pass on, a voice, disembodied, that can turn anything—a cockpit, some headphones, the heavens themselves—into a classroom. Look around. Right now, this very day, you are sending someone aloft.

ACKNOWLEDGMENTS

During the two years I spent researching and writing this book, my wife, Carroll Haymon, often bore much of the load as parent and partner. Throughout, she shared stories from her work as a family doctor that shaped my way of thinking and listening. She is a healer and a teacher, giving and wise, and it is because of her that this book exists. I am grateful to her beyond words.

Rafe Sagalyn and Jon Karp, my literary agent and editor respectively, form an author's dream team. They understood this journey's potential well before I did. Rafe has been my coach, conspirator, and confessor for many years now, and yet each encounter still reveals something new about his subtle and humane spirit. He is a master. I am thankful every day to have a champion and guide at Random House as savvy and supportive as Jon. His editorial direction is like jujitsu: gracefully upending, perfectly realigning. He's shaped me in more ways than he knows.

I'm honored that Gina Centrello and so many talented people at Random House have believed in this book and brought it to life. Jonathan Jao deserves special thanks for all his assistance, as does Beth Pearson.

Many people read drafts of the manuscript and gave me encouragement and crucial advice. Among them are Po Bronson, David Greenberg, Davis Guggenheim, Ava Haymon, Leslie Koch, Mark Salzman, Ryan Sawyer, Karen Wickwire, and my wife, Carroll. Many others spent time to talk about ideas that have made their way into this book. Among the most generous were Jon Alter, Steve Badanes, Jenny Lyn Bader, Doug Becker, Roger Berkowitz, Michael Cendejas, Carole Cowan, Patricia Crosby, Chuck D, MJ Davidson, Bill Drayton, Joe Etter, Betsy Fader, Christine Goodheart, Alison Gopnik, Gloria Govrin, Stephen Heintz, Doug Hofstadter, Marcy Jackson, Rick Jackson, Michelle Kydd-Lee, Tod Machover, Robert McKee, David Milch, Ethelbert Miller, Richard Plepler, Jeremy Rosner, Steve Seidel, Rick Stengel, Pat Wasley, Jacob Weisberg, Jay Winsten, and Sue Wong.

The extraordinary teachers and learners in this book allowed me into their lives and their work, which was a great act of trust. I hope through these stories they will touch many other people. I interviewed and spent time with several hundred additional mentors and apprentices during my travels, and though they do not appear by name they do influence every page. I thank them as well.

Lena Barouh and Tara Williams were creative, inquisitive, dedicated research assistants, and I learned a great deal from them both. (Lena gets extra credit for suggesting the Bondurant School.)

I've done numerous workshops and talks on this book, and I'm grateful to the institutions that have supported these efforts, including the New America Foundation, Harvard Law School, the American Program Bureau, the University of Washington, the Seattle Public Schools, Arts Corps, and the National Association of Multicultural Educators.

Finally, I want to thank Julia Liu, my mother and most fundamental source of inspiration—and Olivia Liu, my daughter and unwitting teacher.

ABOUT THE AUTHOR

ERIC LIU is a fellow at the New America Foundation. The writer of *Slate*'s "Teachings" column, Liu is the author of *The Accidental Asian: Notes of a Native Speaker*, a *New York Times* Notable Book featured in the PBS documentary *Matters of Race*, and was editor of the Norton anthology *Next: Young American Writers on the New Generation*. Liu served as a speechwriter for President Bill Clinton and later as the president's deputy domestic policy adviser. After the White House, he worked as an executive at RealNetworks. A regular commentator on CNN and NPR, he is a frequent lecturer at campuses and conferences around the country, and he teaches at the Evans School of Public Affairs at the University of Washington. Liu is a graduate of Yale College and Harvard Law School and lives in Seattle with his wife and daughter.

To learn more about this book or Eric Liu, please visit www.guidinglightsnetwork.com or www.ericliu.com.

ABOUT THE TYPE

This book was set in Bulmer, a typeface designed in the late eighteenth century by the London type-cutter William Martin. The typeface was created especially for the Shakespeare Press, directed by William Bulmer; hence, the font's name. Bulmer is considered to be a transitional typeface, containing characteristics of old-style and modern designs. It is recognized for its elegantly proportioned letters, with their long ascenders and descenders.